FIXED INCOME ANALYSIS WORKBOOK

CFA Institute is the premier association for investment professionals around the world, with more than 150,000 CFA charterholders worldwide in 165+ countries and regions. Since 1963 the organization has developed and administered the renowned Chartered Financial Analyst® Program. With a rich history of leading the investment profession, CFA Institute has set the highest standards in ethics, education, and professional excellence within the global investment community and is the foremost authority on investment profession conduct and practice. Each book in the CFA Institute Investment Series is geared toward industry practitioners along with graduate-level finance students and covers the most important topics in the industry. The authors of these cutting-edge books are themselves industry professionals and academics and bring their wealth of knowledge and expertise to this series.

FIXED INCOME ANALYSIS WORKBOOK

Fifth Edition

James F. Adams, PhD, CFA

Donald J. Smith, PhD

WILEY

Cover image: Background © maxkrasnov/iStock.com
Cover design: Wiley

Published by John Wiley & Sons, Inc., Hoboken, New Jersey.
The First, Second, Third, and Fourth Editions of this book were published by Wiley in 2000, 2011, 2015, and 2019, respectively.
Published simultaneously in Canada.

For general information on our other products and services or for technical support, please contact our Customer Care Department within the United States at (800) 762-2974, outside the United States at (317) 572-3993, or fax (317) 572-4002.

Wiley publishes in a variety of print and electronic formats and by print-on-demand. Some material included with standard print versions of this book may not be included in e-books or in print-on-demand. If this book refers to media such as a CD or DVD that is not included in the version you purchased, you may download this material at http://booksupport.wiley.com. For more information about Wiley products, visit www.wiley.com.

ISBN 978-1-119-85299-5 (Paper)
ISBN 978-1-119-85300-8 (ePDF)
ISBN 978-1-119-85301-5 (ePub)

Printed in the United States of America.
SKY10094354_121924

CONTENTS

PART I

LEARNING OBJECTIVES, SUMMARY OVERVIEW, AND PROBLEMS

CHAPTER 1

FIXED-INCOME SECURITIES: DEFINING ELEMENTS

LEARNING OUTCOMES

The candidate should be able to:

- describe basic features of a fixed-income security;
- describe content of a bond indenture;
- compare affirmative and negative covenants and identify examples of each;
- describe how legal, regulatory, and tax considerations affect the issuance and trading of fixed-income securities;
- describe how cash flows of fixed-income securities are structured;
- describe contingency provisions affecting the timing and/or nature of cash flows of fixed-income securities and whether such provisions benefit the borrower or the lender.

SUMMARY OVERVIEW

This chapter introduces the salient features of fixed-income securities while noting how these features vary among different types of securities. Important points include the following:

- The three important elements that an investor needs to know when investing in a fixed-income security are: (1) the bond's features, which determine its scheduled cash flows and thus the bondholder's expected and actual return; (2) the legal, regulatory, and tax considerations that apply to the contractual agreement between the issuer and the bondholders; and (3) the contingency provisions that may affect the bond's scheduled cash flows.
- The basic features of a bond include the issuer, maturity, par value (or principal), coupon rate and frequency, and currency denomination.
- Issuers of bonds include supranational organizations, sovereign governments, non-sovereign governments, quasi-government entities, and corporate issuers.
- Bondholders are exposed to credit risk and may use bond credit ratings to assess the credit quality of a bond.

- A bond's principal is the amount the issuer agrees to pay the bondholder when the bond matures.
- The coupon rate is the interest rate that the issuer agrees to pay to the bondholder each year. The coupon rate can be a fixed rate or a floating rate. Bonds may offer annual, semi-annual, quarterly, or monthly coupon payments depending on the type of bond and where the bond is issued.
- Bonds can be issued in any currency. Such bonds as dual-currency bonds and currency option bonds are connected to two currencies.
- The yield-to-maturity is the discount rate that equates the present value of the bond's future cash flows until maturity to its price. Yield-to-maturity can be considered an estimate of the market's expectation for the bond's return.
- A plain vanilla bond has a known cash flow pattern. It has a fixed maturity date and pays a fixed rate of interest over the bond's life.
- The bond indenture or trust deed is the legal contract that describes the form of the bond, the issuer's obligations, and the investor's rights. The indenture is usually held by a financial institution called a trustee, which performs various duties specified in the indenture.
- The issuer is identified in the indenture by its legal name and is obligated to make timely payments of interest and repayment of principal.
- For asset-backed securities, the legal obligation to repay bondholders often lies with a separate legal entity—that is, a bankruptcy-remote vehicle that uses the assets as guarantees to back a bond issue.
- How the issuer intends to service the debt and repay the principal should be described in the indenture. The source of repayment proceeds varies depending on the type of bond.
- Collateral backing is a way to alleviate credit risk. Secured bonds are backed by assets or financial guarantees pledged to ensure debt payment. Examples of collateral-backed bonds include collateral trust bonds, equipment trust certificates, mortgage-backed securities, and covered bonds.
- Credit enhancement can be internal or external. Examples of internal credit enhancement include subordination, overcollateralization, and reserve accounts. A bank guarantee, a surety bond, a letter of credit, and a cash collateral account are examples of external credit enhancement.
- Bond covenants are legally enforceable rules that borrowers and lenders agree on at the time of a new bond issue. Affirmative covenants enumerate what issuers are required to do, whereas negative covenants enumerate what issuers are prohibited from doing.
- An important consideration for investors is where the bonds are issued and traded, because it affects the laws, regulation, and tax status that apply. Bonds issued in a country in local currency are domestic bonds if they are issued by entities incorporated in the country and foreign bonds if they are issued by entities incorporated in another country. Eurobonds are issued internationally, outside the jurisdiction of any single country and are subject to a lower level of listing, disclosure, and regulatory requirements than domestic or foreign bonds. Global bonds are issued in the Eurobond market and at least one domestic market at the same time.
- Although some bonds may offer special tax advantages, as a general rule, interest is taxed at the ordinary income tax rate. Some countries also implement a capital gains tax. There may be specific tax provisions for bonds issued at a discount or bought at a premium.
- An amortizing bond is a bond whose payment schedule requires periodic payment of interest and repayment of principal. This differs from a bullet bond, whose entire payment of principal occurs at maturity. The amortizing bond's outstanding principal amount is reduced to

zero by the maturity date for a fully amortized bond, but a balloon payment is required at maturity to retire the bond's outstanding principal amount for a partially amortized bond.

- Sinking fund agreements provide another approach to the periodic retirement of principal, in which an amount of the bond's principal outstanding amount is usually repaid each year throughout the bond's life or after a specified date.

- A floating-rate note, or floater, is a bond whose coupon is set based on a market reference rate (MRR) plus a spread. FRNs can be floored, capped, or collared. An inverse FRN is a bond whose coupon has an inverse relationship to the reference rate.

- Other coupon payment structures include bonds with step-up coupons, which pay coupons that increase by specified amounts on specified dates; bonds with credit-linked coupons, which change when the issuer's credit rating changes; bonds with payment-in-kind coupons, which allow the issuer to pay coupons with additional amounts of the bond issue rather than in cash; and bonds with deferred coupons, which pay no coupons in the early years following the issue but higher coupons thereafter.

- The payment structures for index-linked bonds vary considerably among countries. A common index-linked bond is an inflation-linked bond, or linker, whose coupon payments and/or principal repayments are linked to a price index. Index-linked payment structures include zero-coupon-indexed bonds, interest-indexed bonds, capital-indexed bonds, and indexed-annuity bonds.

- Common types of bonds with embedded options include callable bonds, putable bonds, and convertible bonds. These options are "embedded" in the sense that there are provisions provided in the indenture that grant either the issuer or the bondholder certain rights affecting the disposal or redemption of the bond. They are not separately traded securities.

- Callable bonds give the issuer the right to buy bonds back prior to maturity, thereby raising the reinvestment risk for the bondholder. For this reason, callable bonds have to offer a higher yield and sell at a lower price than otherwise similar non-callable bonds to compensate the bondholders for the value of the call option to the issuer.

- Putable bonds give the bondholder the right to sell bonds back to the issuer prior to maturity. Putable bonds offer a lower yield and sell at a higher price than otherwise similar non-putable bonds to compensate the issuer for the value of the put option to the bondholders.

- A convertible bond gives the bondholder the right to convert the bond into common shares of the issuing company. Because this option favors the bondholder, convertible bonds offer a lower yield and sell at a higher price than otherwise similar non-convertible bonds.

PROBLEMS

1. A 10-year bond was issued four years ago. The bond is denominated in US dollars, offers a coupon rate of 10% with interest paid semi-annually, and is currently priced at 102% of par. The bond's:
   A. tenor is six years.
   B. nominal rate is 5%.
   C. redemption value is 102% of the par value.

2. A sovereign bond has a maturity of 15 years. The bond is *best* described as a:
   A. perpetual bond.
   B. pure discount bond.
   C. capital market security.

3. A company has issued a floating-rate note with a coupon rate equal to the three-month MRR + 65 bps. Interest payments are made quarterly on 31 March, 30 June, 30 September, and 31 December. On 31 March and 30 June, the three-month MRR is 1.55% and 1.35%, respectively. The coupon rate for the interest payment made on 30 June is:
   A. 2.00%.
   B. 2.10%.
   C. 2.20%.

4. The legal contract that describes the form of the bond, the obligations of the issuer, and the rights of the bondholders can be *best* described as a bond's:
   A. covenant.
   B. indenture.
   C. debenture.

5. Which of the following is a type of external credit enhancement?
   A. Covenants
   B. A surety bond
   C. Overcollateralization

6. An affirmative covenant is *most likely* to stipulate:
   A. limits on the issuer's leverage ratio.
   B. how the proceeds of the bond issue will be used.
   C. the maximum percentage of the issuer's gross assets that can be sold.

7. Which of the following *best* describes a negative bond covenant? The issuer is:
   A. required to pay taxes as they come due.
   B. prohibited from investing in risky projects.
   C. required to maintain its current lines of business.

8. A South African company issues bonds denominated in pound sterling that are sold to investors in the United Kingdom. These bonds can be *best* described as:
   A. Eurobonds.
   B. global bonds.
   C. foreign bonds.

9. Relative to domestic and foreign bonds, Eurobonds are *most likely* to be:
   A. bearer bonds.
   B. registered bonds.
   C. subject to greater regulation.

10. An investor in a country with an original issue discount tax provision purchases a 20-year zero-coupon bond at a deep discount to par value. The investor plans to hold the bond until the maturity date. The investor will *most likely* report:
    A. a capital gain at maturity.
    B. a tax deduction in the year the bond is purchased.
    C. taxable income from the bond every year until maturity.

11. A bond that is characterized by a fixed periodic payment schedule that reduces the bond's outstanding principal amount to zero by the maturity date is *best* described as a:
    A. bullet bond.
    B. plain vanilla bond.
    C. fully amortized bond.

12. If interest rates are expected to increase, the coupon payment structure *most likely* to benefit the issuer is a:
    A. step-up coupon.
    B. inflation-linked coupon.
    C. cap in a floating-rate note.

13. Investors who believe that interest rates will rise *most likely* prefer to invest in:
    A. inverse floaters.
    B. fixed-rate bonds.
    C. floating-rate notes.

14. A 10-year, capital-indexed bond linked to the Consumer Price Index (CPI) is issued with a coupon rate of 6% and a par value of 1,000. The bond pays interest semi-annually. During the first six months after the bond's issuance, the CPI increases by 2%. On the first coupon payment date, the bond's:
    A. coupon rate increases to 8%.
    B. coupon payment is equal to 40.
    C. principal amount increases to 1,020.

15. The provision that provides bondholders the right to sell the bond back to the issuer at a predetermined price prior to the bond's maturity date is referred to as:
    A. a put provision.
    B. a make-whole call provision.
    C. an original issue discount provision.

16. Which of the following provisions is a benefit to the issuer?
    A. Put provision
    B. Call provision
    C. Conversion provision

17. Relative to an otherwise similar option-free bond, a:
    A. putable bond will trade at a higher price.
    B. callable bond will trade at a higher price.
    C. convertible bond will trade at a lower price.

18. Which type of bond *most likely* earns interest on an implied basis?
    A. Floater
    B. Conventional bond
    C. Pure discount bond

19. Clauses that specify the rights of the bondholders and any actions that the issuer is obligated to perform or is prohibited from performing are:
    A. covenants.
    B. collaterals.
    C. credit enhancements.

20. Which of the following type of debt obligation *most likely* protects bondholders when the assets serving as collateral are non-performing?
    A. Covered bonds
    B. Collateral trust bonds
    C. Mortgage-backed securities

21. Which of the following *best* describes a negative bond covenant? The requirement to:
    A. insure and maintain assets.
    B. comply with all laws and regulations.
    C. maintain a minimum interest coverage ratio.

22. Contrary to positive bond covenants, negative covenants are *most likely*:
    A. costlier.
    B. legally enforceable.
    C. enacted at time of issue.

23. A five-year bond has the following cash flows:

£230.97   £230.97   £230.97   £230.97   £230.97

£1,000

The bond can *best* be described as a:
- A. bullet bond.
- B. fully amortized bond.
- C. partially amortized bond.

24. Investors seeking some general protection against a poor economy are *most likely* to select a:
- A. deferred coupon bond.
- B. credit-linked coupon bond.
- C. payment-in-kind coupon bond.

25. The benefit to the issuer of a deferred coupon bond is *most likely* related to:
- A. tax management.
- B. cash flow management.
- C. original issue discount price.

26. Which of the following bond types provides the *most* benefit to a bondholder when bond prices are declining?
- A. Callable
- B. Plain vanilla
- C. Multiple put

27. Which type of call bond option offers the *greatest* flexibility as to when the issuer can exercise the option?
- A. Bermuda call
- B. European call
- C. American call

28. Which of the following *best* describes a convertible bond's conversion premium?
- A. Bond price minus conversion value
- B. Par value divided by conversion price
- C. Current share price multiplied by conversion ratio

CHAPTER 2

FIXED-INCOME MARKETS: ISSUANCE, TRADING, AND FUNDING

LEARNING OUTCOMES

The candidate should be able to:

- describe classifications of global fixed-income markets;
- describe the use of interbank offered rates as reference rates in floating-rate debt;
- describe mechanisms available for issuing bonds in primary markets;
- describe secondary markets for bonds;
- describe securities issued by sovereign governments;
- describe securities issued by non-sovereign governments, quasi-government entities, and supranational agencies;
- describe types of debt issued by corporations;
- describe structured financial instruments;
- describe short-term funding alternatives available to banks;
- describe repurchase agreements (repos) and the risks associated with them.

SUMMARY OVERVIEW

Debt financing is an important source of funds for households, governments, government-related entities, financial institutions, and non-financial companies. Well-functioning fixed-income markets help ensure that capital is allocated efficiently to its highest and best use globally. Important points include the following:

- The most widely used ways of classifying fixed-income markets include the type of issuer; the bonds' credit quality, maturity, currency denomination, and type of coupon; and where the bonds are issued and traded.

- Based on the type of issuer, the four major bond market sectors are the household, non-financial corporate, government, and financial institution sectors.
- Investors distinguish between investment-grade and high-yield bond markets based on the issuer's credit quality.
- Money markets are where securities with original maturities ranging from overnight to one year are issued and traded, whereas capital markets are where securities with original maturities longer than one year are issued and traded.
- The majority of bonds are denominated in either euros or US dollars.
- Investors distinguish between bonds that pay a fixed rate versus a floating rate of interest. The coupon rate of floating-rate bonds is often expressed as a reference rate plus a spread. Interbank offered rates, such as Libor, historically have been the most commonly used reference rates for floating-rate debt and other financial instruments but are being phased out to be replaced by alternative reference rates.
- Based on where the bonds are issued and traded, investors distinguish between domestic and international bond markets. The latter includes the Eurobond market, which falls outside the jurisdiction of any single country and is characterized by less reporting, regulatory, and tax constraints. Investors also distinguish between developed and emerging bond markets.
- Investors and investment managers use fixed-income indexes to describe bond markets or sectors and to evaluate performance of investments and investment managers.
- The largest investors in bonds include central banks; institutional investors, such as pension funds, hedge funds, charitable foundations and endowments, insurance companies, mutual funds and ETFs, and banks; and retail investors, typically by means of indirect investments.
- Primary markets are markets in which issuers first sell bonds to investors to raise capital. Secondary markets are markets in which existing bonds are subsequently traded among investors.
- There are two mechanisms for issuing a bond in primary markets: a public offering, in which any member of the public may buy the bonds, or a private placement, in which only an investor or small group of investors may buy the bonds either directly from the issuer or through an investment bank.
- Public bond issuing mechanisms include underwritten offerings, best-efforts offerings, shelf registrations, and auctions.
- When an investment bank underwrites a bond issue, it buys the entire issue and takes the risk of reselling it to investors or dealers. In contrast, in a best-efforts offering, the investment bank serves only as a broker and sells the bond issue only if it is able to do so. Underwritten and best-efforts offerings are frequently used in the issuance of corporate bonds.
- The underwriting process typically includes six phases: the determination of the funding needs, the selection of the underwriter, the structuring and announcement of the bond offering, pricing, issuance, and closing.
- A shelf registration is a method for issuing securities in which the issuer files a single document with regulators that describes and allows for a range of future issuances.
- An auction is a public offering method that involves bidding and is helpful both in providing price discovery and in allocating securities. Auctions are frequently used in the issuance of sovereign bonds.
- Most bonds are traded in OTC markets, and institutional investors are the major buyers and sellers of bonds in secondary markets.
- Sovereign bonds are issued by national governments primarily for fiscal reasons. These bonds take different names and forms depending on where they are issued, their maturities, and

their coupon types. Most sovereign bonds are fixed-rate bonds, although some national governments also issue floating-rate bonds and inflation-linked bonds.

- Local governments, quasi-government entities, and supranational agencies issue bonds, which are named non-sovereign, quasi-government, and supranational bonds, respectively.
- Companies raise debt in the form of bilateral loans, syndicated loans, commercial paper, notes, and bonds.
- Commercial paper is a short-term unsecured security that companies use as a source of short-term and bridge financing. Investors in commercial paper are exposed to credit risk, although defaults are rare. Many issuers roll over their commercial paper on a regular basis.
- Corporate bonds and notes take different forms depending on the maturities, coupon payment, and principal repayment structures. Important considerations also include collateral backing and contingency provisions.
- Medium-term notes are securities that are offered continuously to investors by an agent of the issuer. They can have short-term or long-term maturities.
- The structured finance sector includes asset-backed securities, collateralized debt obligations, and other structured financial instruments. All of these seemingly disparate financial instruments share the common attribute of repackaging risks.
- Many structured financial instruments are customized instruments that often combine a bond and at least one derivative. The redemption and often the coupons of these structured financial instruments are linked via a formula to the performance of the underlying asset(s). Thus, the bond's payment features are replaced with non-traditional payoffs derived not from the issuer's cash flows but from the performance of the underlying asset(s). Capital protected, yield enhancement, participation and leveraged instruments are typical examples of structured financial instruments.
- Financial institutions have access to additional sources of funds, such as retail deposits, central bank funds, interbank funds, large-denomination negotiable certificates of deposit, and repurchase agreements.
- A repurchase agreement is similar to a collateralized loan. It involves the sale of a security (the collateral) with a simultaneous agreement by the seller (the borrower) to buy back the same security from the purchaser (the lender) at an agreed-on price in the future. Repurchase agreements are a common source of funding for dealer firms and are also used to borrow securities to implement short positions.

PROBLEMS

1. The distinction between investment-grade debt and non-investment-grade debt is *best* described by differences in:
   A. tax status.
   B. credit quality.
   C. maturity dates.
2. A bond issued internationally, outside the jurisdiction of the country in whose currency the bond is denominated, is *best* described as a:
   A. Eurobond.
   B. foreign bond.
   C. municipal bond.

3. When classified by type of issuer, asset-backed securities are part of the:
   A. corporate sector.
   B. structured finance sector.
   C. government and government-related sector.
4. Compared with developed market bonds, emerging market bonds *most likely*:
   A. offer lower yields.
   B. exhibit higher risk.
   C. benefit from lower growth prospects.
5. With respect to floating-rate bonds, a reference rate (such as MRR) is *most likely* used to determine the bond's:
   A. spread.
   B. coupon rate.
   C. frequency of coupon payments.
6. The variability of the coupon rate on a Libor-based floating-rate bond is *most likely* caused by:
   A. periodic resets of the reference rate.
   B. market-based reassessments of the issuer's creditworthiness.
   C. changing estimates by the Libor administrator of borrowing capacity.
7. Which of the following statements is *most accurate*? An interbank offered rate:
   A. is a single reference rate.
   B. applies to borrowing periods of up to 10 years.
   C. is used as a reference rate for interest rate swaps.
8. An investment bank that underwrites a bond issue *most likely*:
   A. buys and resells the newly issued bonds to investors or dealers.
   B. acts as a broker and receives a commission for selling the bonds to investors.
   C. incurs less risk associated with selling the bonds than in a best-efforts offering.
9. In major developed bond markets, newly issued sovereign bonds are *most* often sold to the public via a(n):
   A. auction.
   B. private placement.
   C. best-efforts offering.
10. Which of the following describes privately placed bonds?
    A. They are non-underwritten and unregistered.
    B. They usually have active secondary markets.
    C. They are less customized than publicly offered bonds.
11. A mechanism by which an issuer may be able to offer additional bonds to the general public without preparing a new and separate offering circular *best* describes:
    A. the grey market.
    B. a shelf registration.
    C. a private placement.
12. Which of the following statements related to secondary bond markets is *most accurate*?
    A. Newly issued corporate bonds are issued in secondary bond markets.
    B. Secondary bond markets are where bonds are traded between investors.
    C. The major participants in secondary bond markets globally are retail investors.
13. A bond market in which a communications network matches buy and sell orders initiated from various locations is *best* described as an:
    A. organized exchange.
    B. open market operation.
    C. over-the-counter market.

14. A liquid secondary bond market allows an investor to sell a bond at:
    A. the desired price.
    B. a price at least equal to the purchase price.
    C. a price close to the bond's fair market value.
15. Corporate bond secondary market trading *most often* occurs:
    A. on a book-entry basis.
    B. on organized exchanges.
    C. prior to settlement at $T + 1$.
16. Sovereign bonds are *best* described as:
    A. bonds issued by local governments.
    B. secured obligations of a national government.
    C. bonds backed by the taxing authority of a national government.
17. Which factor is associated with a more favorable quality sovereign bond credit rating?
    A. Issued in local currency, only
    B. Strong domestic savings base, only
    C. Issued in local currency of country with strong domestic savings base
18. Which type of sovereign bond has the lowest interest rate risk for an investor?
    A. Floaters
    B. Coupon bonds
    C. Discount bonds
19. Agency bonds are issued by:
    A. local governments.
    B. national governments.
    C. quasi-government entities.
20. The type of bond issued by a multilateral agency such as the International Monetary Fund (IMF) is *best* described as a:
    A. sovereign bond.
    B. supranational bond.
    C. quasi-government bond.
21. A bond issued by a local government authority, typically without an explicit funding commitment from the national government, is *most likely* classified as a:
    A. sovereign bond.
    B. quasi-government bond
    C. non-sovereign government bond.
22. Which of the following statements relating to commercial paper is *most accurate*?
    A. There is no secondary market for trading commercial paper.
    B. Only the strongest, highly rated companies issue commercial paper.
    C. Commercial paper is a source of interim financing for long-term projects.
23. Eurocommercial paper is *most likely*:
    A. negotiable.
    B. denominated in euros.
    C. issued on a discount basis.
24. For the issuer, a sinking fund arrangement is *most similar* to a:
    A. term maturity structure.
    B. serial maturity structure.
    C. bondholder put provision.

25. When issuing debt, a company may use a sinking fund arrangement as a means of reducing:
    A. credit risk.
    B. inflation risk.
    C. interest rate risk.

26. Which of the following is a source of wholesale funds for banks?
    A. Demand deposits
    B. Money market accounts
    C. Negotiable certificates of deposit

27. A characteristic of negotiable certificates of deposit is:
    A. they are mostly available in small denominations.
    B. they can be sold in the open market prior to maturity.
    C. a penalty is imposed if the depositor withdraws funds prior to maturity.

28. A repurchase agreement is *most* comparable to a(n):
    A. interbank deposit.
    B. collateralized loan.
    C. negotiable certificate of deposit.

29. The repo margin is:
    A. negotiated between counterparties.
    B. established independently of market-related conditions.
    C. structured on an agreement assuming equal credit risks to all counterparties.

30. The repo margin on a repurchase agreement is *most likely* to be lower when:
    A. the underlying collateral is in short supply.
    B. the maturity of the repurchase agreement is long.
    C. the credit risk associated with the underlying collateral is high.

CHAPTER 3

INTRODUCTION TO FIXED-INCOME VALUATION

LEARNING OUTCOMES

The candidate should be able to:

- calculate a bond's price given a market discount rate;
- identify the relationships among a bond's price, coupon rate, maturity, and market discount rate (yield-to-maturity);
- define spot rates and calculate the price of a bond using spot rates;
- describe and calculate the flat price, accrued interest, and the full price of a bond;
- describe matrix pricing;
- calculate annual yield on a bond for varying compounding periods in a year;
- calculate and interpret yield measures for fixed-rate bonds and floating-rate notes;
- calculate and interpret yield measures for money market instruments;
- define and compare the spot curve, yield curve on coupon bonds, par curve, and forward curve;
- define forward rates and calculate spot rates from forward rates, forward rates from spot rates, and the price of a bond using forward rates;
- compare, calculate, and interpret yield spread measures.

SUMMARY OVERVIEW

We have covered the principles and techniques that are used in the valuation of fixed-rate bonds, as well as floating-rate notes and money market instruments. These building blocks are used extensively in fixed-income analysis. The following are the main points made:

- The market discount rate is the rate of return required by investors given the risk of the investment in the bond.
- A bond is priced at a premium above par value when the coupon rate is greater than the market discount rate.

- A bond is priced at a discount below par value when the coupon rate is less than the market discount rate.
- The amount of any premium or discount is the present value of the "excess" or "deficiency" in the coupon payments relative to the yield-to-maturity.
- The yield-to-maturity, the internal rate of return on the cash flows, is the implied market discount rate given the price of the bond.
- A bond price moves inversely with its market discount rate.
- The relationship between a bond price and its market discount rate is convex.
- The price of a lower-coupon bond is more volatile than the price of a higher-coupon bond, other things being equal.
- Generally, the price of a longer-term bond is more volatile than the price of a shorter-term bond, other things being equal. An exception to this phenomenon can occur on low-coupon (but not zero-coupon) bonds that are priced at a discount to par value.
- Assuming no default, premium and discount bond prices are "pulled to par" as maturity nears.
- A spot rate is the yield-to-maturity on a zero-coupon bond.
- A yield-to-maturity can be approximated as a weighted average of the underlying spot rates.
- Between coupon dates, the full (or invoice, or "dirty") price of a bond is split between the flat (or quoted, or "clean") price and the accrued interest.
- Flat prices are quoted to not misrepresent the daily increase in the full price as a result of interest accruals.
- Accrued interest is calculated as a proportional share of the next coupon payment using either the actual/actual or 30/360 methods to count days.
- Matrix pricing is used to value illiquid bonds by using prices and yields on comparable securities having the same or similar credit risk, coupon rate, and maturity.
- The periodicity of an annual interest rate is the number of periods in the year.
- A yield quoted on a semiannual bond basis is an annual rate for a periodicity of two. It is the yield per semiannual period times two.
- The general rule for periodicity conversions is that compounding more frequently at a lower annual rate corresponds to compounding less frequently at a higher annual rate.
- Street convention yields assume payments are made on scheduled dates, neglecting weekends and holidays.
- The current yield is the annual coupon payment divided by the flat price, thereby neglecting as a measure of the investor's rate of return the time value of money, any accrued interest, and the gain from buying at a discount or the loss from buying at a premium.
- The simple yield is like the current yield but includes the straight-line amortization of the discount or premium.
- The yield-to-worst on a callable bond is the lowest of the yield-to-first-call, yield-to-second-call, and so on, calculated using the call price for the future value and the call date for the number of periods.
- The option-adjusted yield on a callable bond is the yield-to-maturity after adding the theoretical value of the call option to the price.
- A floating-rate note (floater, or FRN) maintains a more stable price than a fixed-rate note because interest payments adjust for changes in market interest rates.
- The quoted margin on a floater is typically the specified yield spread over or under the reference rate, which we refer to as the Market Reference Rate.

- The discount margin on a floater is the spread required by investors, and to which the quoted margin must be set, for the FRN to trade at par value on a rate reset date.
- Money market instruments, having one year or less time-to-maturity, are quoted on a discount rate or add-on rate basis.
- Money market discount rates understate the investor's rate of return (and the borrower's cost of funds) because the interest income is divided by the face value or the total amount redeemed at maturity, and not by the amount of the investment.
- Money market instruments need to be converted to a common basis for analysis.
- A money market bond equivalent yield is an add-on rate for a 365-day year.
- The periodicity of a money market instrument is the number of days in the year divided by the number of days to maturity. Therefore, money market instruments with different times-to-maturity have annual rates for different periodicities.
- In theory, the maturity structure, or term structure, of interest rates is the relationship between yields-to-maturity and times-to-maturity on bonds having the same currency, credit risk, liquidity, tax status, and periodicity.
- A spot curve is a series of yields-to-maturity on zero-coupon bonds.
- A frequently used yield curve is a series of yields-to-maturity on coupon bonds.
- A par curve is a series of yields-to-maturity assuming the bonds are priced at par value.
- In a cash market, the delivery of the security and cash payment is made on a settlement date within a customary time period after the trade date—for example, "$T + 3$."
- In a forward market, the delivery of the security and cash payment are made on a predetermined future date.
- A forward rate is the interest rate on a bond or money market instrument traded in a forward market.
- An implied forward rate (or forward yield) is the breakeven reinvestment rate linking the return on an investment in a shorter-term zero-coupon bond to the return on an investment in a longer-term zero-coupon bond.
- An implied forward curve can be calculated from the spot curve.
- Implied spot rates can be calculated as geometric averages of forward rates.
- A fixed-income bond can be valued using a market discount rate, a series of spot rates, or a series of forward rates.
- A bond yield-to-maturity can be separated into a benchmark and a spread.
- Changes in benchmark rates capture macroeconomic factors that affect all bonds in the market—inflation, economic growth, foreign exchange rates, and monetary and fiscal policy.
- Changes in spreads typically capture microeconomic factors that affect the particular bond—credit risk, liquidity, and tax effects.
- Benchmark rates are usually yields-to-maturity on government bonds or fixed rates on interest rate swaps.
- A G-spread is the spread over or under a government bond rate, and an I-spread is the spread over or under an interest rate swap rate.
- A G-spread or an I-spread can be based on a specific benchmark rate or on a rate interpolated from the benchmark yield curve.
- A Z-spread (zero-volatility spread) is based on the entire benchmark spot curve. It is the constant spread that is added to each spot rate such that the present value of the cash flows matches the price of the bond.
- An option-adjusted spread (OAS) on a callable bond is the Z-spread minus the theoretical value of the embedded call option.

PROBLEMS

1. A portfolio manager is considering the purchase of a bond with a 5.5% coupon rate that pays interest annually and matures in three years. If the required rate of return on the bond is 5%, the price of the bond per 100 of par value is *closest* to:
   A. 98.65.
   B. 101.36.
   C. 106.43.

2. A bond with two years remaining until maturity offers a 3% coupon rate with interest paid annually. At a market discount rate of 4%, the price of this bond per 100 of par value is *closest* to:
   A. 95.34.
   B. 98.00.
   C. 98.11.

3. An investor who owns a bond with a 9% coupon rate that pays interest semiannually and matures in three years is considering its sale. If the required rate of return on the bond is 11%, the price of the bond per 100 of par value is *closest* to:
   A. 95.00.
   B. 95.11.
   C. 105.15.

4. A bond offers an annual coupon rate of 4%, with interest paid semiannually. The bond matures in two years. At a market discount rate of 6%, the price of this bond per 100 of par value is *closest* to:
   A. 93.07.
   B. 96.28.
   C. 96.33.

5. A bond offers an annual coupon rate of 5%, with interest paid semiannually. The bond matures in seven years. At a market discount rate of 3%, the price of this bond per 100 of par value is *closest* to:
   A. 106.60.
   B. 112.54.
   C. 143.90.

6. A zero-coupon bond matures in 15 years. At a market discount rate of 4.5% per year and assuming annual compounding, the price of the bond per 100 of par value is *closest* to:
   A. 51.30.
   B. 51.67.
   C. 71.62.

7. Consider the following two bonds that pay interest annually:

Bond	Coupon Rate	Time-to-Maturity
A	5%	2 years
B	3%	2 years

At a market discount rate of 4%, the price difference between Bond A and Bond B per 100 of par value is *closest* to:
   A. 3.70.
   B. 3.77.
   C. 4.00.

The following information relates to Questions 8 and 9

Bond	Price	Coupon Rate	Time-to-Maturity
A	101.886	5%	2 years
B	100.000	6%	2 years
C	97.327	5%	3 years

8. Which bond offers the lowest yield-to-maturity?
   A. Bond A
   B. Bond B
   C. Bond C
9. Which bond will *most likely* experience the smallest percent change in price if the market discount rates for all three bonds increase by 100 bps?
   A. Bond A
   B. Bond B
   C. Bond C

---

10. Suppose a bond's price is expected to increase by 5% if its market discount rate decreases by 100 bps. If the bond's market discount rate increases by 100 bps, the bond price is *most likely* to change by:
    A. 5%.
    B. less than 5%.
    C. more than 5%.

The following information relates to Questions 11 and 12

Bond	Coupon Rate	Maturity (years)
A	6%	10
B	6%	5
C	8%	5

All three bonds are currently trading at par value.

11. Relative to Bond C, for a 200 bp decrease in the required rate of return, Bond B will *most likely* exhibit a(n):
    A. equal percentage price change.
    B. greater percentage price change.
    C. smaller percentage price change.
12. Which bond will *most likely* experience the greatest percentage change in price if the market discount rates for all three bonds increase by 100 bps?
    A. Bond A
    B. Bond B
    C. Bond C

---

13. An investor considers the purchase of a two-year bond with a 5% coupon rate, with interest paid annually. Assuming the sequence of spot rates shown below, the price of the bond is *closest* to:

Time-to-Maturity	Spot Rates
1 year	3%
2 years	4%

A. 101.93.
B. 102.85.
C. 105.81.

14. A three-year bond offers a 10% coupon rate with interest paid annually. Assuming the following sequence of spot rates, the price of the bond is *closest* to:

Time-to-Maturity	Spot Rates
1 year	8.0%
2 years	9.0%
3 years	9.5%

A. 96.98.
B. 101.46.
C. 102.95.

The following information relates to Questions 15–17

Bond	Coupon Rate	Time-to-Maturity	Time-to-Maturity	Spot Rates
X	8%	3 years	1 year	8%
Y	7%	3 years	2 years	9%
Z	6%	3 years	3 years	10%

All three bonds pay interest annually.

15. Based on the given sequence of spot rates, the price of Bond X is *closest* to:
    A. 95.02.
    B. 95.28.
    C. 97.63.
16. Based on the given sequence of spot rates, the price of Bond Y is *closest* to:
    A. 87.50.
    B. 92.54.
    C. 92.76.
17. Based on the given sequence of spot rates, the yield-to-maturity of Bond Z is *closest* to:
    A. 9.00%.
    B. 9.92%.
    C. 11.93%.

---

18. Bond dealers *most* often quote the:
    A. flat price.
    B. full price.
    C. full price plus accrued interest.

The following information relates to Questions 19–21

Bond G, described in the exhibit below, is sold for settlement on 16 June 2020.

Annual Coupon	5%
Coupon Payment Frequency	Semiannual
Interest Payment Dates	10 April and 10 October
Maturity Date	10 October 2022
Day-Count Convention	30/360
Annual Yield-to-Maturity	4%

19. The full price that Bond G settles at on 16 June 2020 is *closest* to:
    A. 102.36.
    B. 103.10.
    C. 103.65.

20. The accrued interest per 100 of par value for Bond G on the settlement date of 16 June 2020 is *closest* to:
    A. 0.46.
    B. 0.73.
    C. 0.92.

21. The flat price for Bond G on the settlement date of 16 June 2020 is *closest* to:
    A. 102.18.
    B. 103.10.
    C. 104.02.

---

22. Matrix pricing allows investors to estimate market discount rates and prices for bonds:
    A. with different coupon rates.
    B. that are not actively traded.
    C. with different credit quality.

23. When underwriting new corporate bonds, matrix pricing is used to get an estimate of the:
    A. required yield spread over the benchmark rate.
    B. market discount rate of other comparable corporate bonds.
    C. yield-to-maturity on a government bond having a similar time-to-maturity.

24. A bond with 20 years remaining until maturity is currently trading for 111 per 100 of par value. The bond offers a 5% coupon rate with interest paid semiannually. The bond's annual yield-to-maturity is *closest* to:
    A. 2.09%.
    B. 4.18%.
    C. 4.50%.

25. The annual yield-to-maturity, stated for with a periodicity of 12, for a four-year, zero-coupon bond priced at 75 per 100 of par value is *closest* to:
    A. 6.25%.
    B. 7.21%.
    C. 7.46%.

26. A five-year, 5% semiannual coupon payment corporate bond is priced at 104.967 per 100 of par value. The bond's yield-to-maturity, quoted on a semiannual bond basis, is 3.897%. An analyst has been asked to convert to a monthly periodicity. Under this conversion, the yield-to-maturity is *closest to*:
    A. 3.87%.
    B. 4.95%.
    C. 7.67%.

The following information relates to Questions 27–30

A bond with five years remaining until maturity is currently trading for 101 per 100 of par value. The bond offers a 6% coupon rate with interest paid semiannually. The bond is first callable in three years and is callable after that date on coupon dates according to the following schedule:

End of Year	Call Price
3	102
4	101
5	100

27. The bond's annual yield-to-maturity is *closest* to:
    A. 2.88%.
    B. 5.77%.
    C. 5.94%.
28. The bond's annual yield-to-first-call is *closest* to:
    A. 3.12%.
    B. 6.11%.
    C. 6.25%.
29. The bond's annual yield-to-second-call is *closest* to:
    A. 2.97%.
    B. 5.72%.
    C. 5.94%.
30. The bond's yield-to-worst is *closest* to:
    A. 2.88%.
    B. 5.77%.
    C. 6.25%.

31. A two-year floating-rate note pays six-month Libor plus 80 bps. The floater is priced at 97 per 100 of par value. The current six-month MRR is 1.00%. Assume a 30/360 day-count convention and evenly spaced periods. The discount margin for the floater in basis points is *closest* to:
    A. 180 bps.
    B. 236 bps.
    C. 420 bps.
32. An analyst evaluates the following information relating to floating-rate notes (FRNs) issued at par value that have three-month MRR as a reference rate:

Floating-Rate Note	Quoted Margin	Discount Margin
X	0.40%	0.32%
Y	0.45%	0.45%
Z	0.55%	0.72%

Based only on the information provided, the FRN that will be priced at a premium on the next reset date is:
    A. FRN X.
    B. FRN Y.
    C. FRN Z.

33. A 365-day year bank certificate of deposit has an initial principal amount of USD96.5 million and a redemption amount due at maturity of USD100 million. The number of days between settlement and maturity is 350. The bond equivalent yield is *closest* to:
    A. 3.48%.
    B. 3.65%.
    C. 3.78%.

34. The bond equivalent yield of a 180-day banker's acceptance quoted at a discount rate of 4.25% for a 360-day year is *closest* to:
    A. 4.31%.
    B. 4.34%.
    C. 4.40%.

35. Which of the following statements describing a par curve is *incorrect*?
    A. A par curve is obtained from a spot curve.
    B. All bonds on a par curve are assumed to have different credit risk.
    C. A par curve is a sequence of yields-to-maturity such that each bond is priced at par value.

36. A yield curve constructed from a sequence of yields-to-maturity on zero-coupon bonds is the:
    A. par curve.
    B. spot curve.
    C. forward curve.

37. The rate interpreted to be the incremental return for extending the time-to-maturity of an investment for an additional time period is the:
    A. add-on rate.
    B. forward rate.
    C. yield-to-maturity.

The following information relates to Questions 38 and 39

Time Period	Forward Rate
"0y1y"	0.80%
"1y1y"	1.12%
"2y1y"	3.94%
"3y1y"	3.28%
"4y1y"	3.14%

All rates are annual rates stated for a periodicity of one (effective annual rates).

38. The three-year implied spot rate is *closest* to:
    A. 1.18%.
    B. 1.94%.
    C. 2.28%.

39. The value per 100 of par value of a two-year, 3.5% coupon bond with interest payments paid annually is *closest* to:
    A. 101.58.
    B. 105.01.
    C. 105.82.

40. The spread component of a specific bond's yield-to-maturity is *least likely* impacted by changes in:
    A. its tax status.
    B. its quality rating.
    C. inflation in its currency of denomination.
41. The yield spread of a specific bond over the standard swap rate in that currency of the same tenor is *best* described as the:
    A. I-spread.
    B. Z-spread.
    C. G-spread.

The following information relates to Question 42

Bond	Coupon Rate	Time-to-Maturity	Price
UK Government Benchmark Bond	2%	3 years	100.25
UK Corporate Bond	5%	3 years	100.65

Both bonds pay interest annually. The current three-year EUR interest rate swap benchmark is 2.12%.

42. The G-spread in basis points on the UK corporate bond is *closest* to:
    A. 264 bps.
    B. 285 bps.
    C. 300 bps.

___

43. A corporate bond offers a 5% coupon rate and has exactly three years remaining to maturity. Interest is paid annually. The following rates are from the benchmark spot curve:

Time-to-Maturity	Spot Rate
1 year	4.86%
2 years	4.95%
3 years	5.65%

The bond is currently trading at a Z-spread of 234 bps. The value of the bond is *closest to*:
    A. 92.38.
    B. 98.35.
    C. 106.56.
44. An option-adjusted spread (OAS) on a callable bond is the Z-spread:
    A. over the benchmark spot curve.
    B. minus the standard swap rate in that currency of the same tenor.
    C. minus the value of the embedded call option expressed in basis points per year.

CHAPTER 4

INTRODUCTION TO ASSET-BACKED SECURITIES

LEARNING OUTCOMES

The candidate should be able to:

- explain benefits of securitization for economies and financial markets;
- describe securitization, including the parties involved in the process and the roles they play;
- describe typical structures of securitizations, including credit tranching and time tranching;
- describe types and characteristics of residential mortgage loans that are typically securitized;
- describe types and characteristics of residential mortgage-backed securities, including mortgage pass-through securities and collateralized mortgage obligations, and explain the cash flows and risks for each type;
- define prepayment risk and describe the prepayment risk of mortgage-backed securities;
- describe characteristics and risks of commercial mortgage-backed securities;
- describe types and characteristics of non-mortgage asset-backed securities, including the cash flows and risks of each type;
- describe collateralized debt obligations, including their cash flows and risks;
- describe characteristics and risks of covered bonds and how they differ from other asset-backed securities.

SUMMARY OVERVIEW

- Securitization involves pooling debt obligations, such as loans or receivables, and creating securities backed by the pool of debt obligations called asset-backed securities (ABS). The cash flows of the debt obligations are used to make interest payments and principal repayments to the holders of the ABS.
- Securitization has several benefits. It allows investors direct access to liquid investments and payment streams that would be unattainable if all the financing were performed through banks. It enables banks to increase loan originations at economic scales greater than if they used only their own in-house loan portfolios. Thus, securitization contributes to lower costs

of borrowing for entities raising funds, higher risk-adjusted returns to investors, and greater efficiency and profitability for the banking sector.

- The parties to a securitization include the seller of the collateral (pool of loans), the servicer of the loans, and the special purpose entity (SPE). The SPE is bankruptcy remote, which plays a pivotal role in the securitization.

- A common structure in a securitization is subordination, which leads to the creation of more than one bond class or tranche. Bond classes differ as to how they will share any losses resulting from defaults of the borrowers whose loans are in the collateral. The credit ratings assigned to the various bond classes depend on how the credit-rating agencies evaluate the credit risks of the collateral and any credit enhancements.

- The motivation for the creation of different types of structures is to redistribute prepayment risk and credit risk efficiently among different bond classes in the securitization. Prepayment risk is the uncertainty that the actual cash flows will be different from the scheduled cash flows as set forth in the loan agreements because borrowers may choose to repay the principal early to take advantage of interest rate movements.

- Because of the SPE, the securitization of a company's assets may include some bond classes that have better credit ratings than the company itself or its corporate bonds. Thus, the company's funding cost is often lower when raising funds through securitization than when issuing corporate bonds.

- A mortgage is a loan secured by the collateral of some specified real estate property that obliges the borrower to make a predetermined series of payments to the lender. The cash flow of a mortgage includes (1) interest, (2) scheduled principal payments, and (3) prepayments (any principal repaid in excess of the scheduled principal payment).

- The various mortgage designs throughout the world specify (1) the maturity of the loan; (2) how the interest rate is determined (i.e., fixed rate versus adjustable or variable rate); (3) how the principal is repaid (i.e., whether the loan is amortizing and if it is, whether it is fully amortizing or partially amortizing with a balloon payment); (4) whether the borrower has the option to prepay and if so, whether any prepayment penalties might be imposed; and (5) the rights of the lender in a foreclosure (i.e., whether the loan is a recourse or non-recourse loan).

- In the United States, there are three sectors for securities backed by residential mortgages: (1) those guaranteed by a federal agency (Ginnie Mae) whose securities are backed by the full faith and credit of the US government, (2) those guaranteed by a GSE (e.g., Fannie Mae and Freddie Mac) but not by the US government, and (3) those issued by private entities that are not guaranteed by a federal agency or a GSE. The first two sectors are referred to as agency residential mortgage-backed securities (RMBS), and the third sector, as non-agency RMBS.

- A mortgage pass-through security is created when one or more holders of mortgages form a pool of mortgages and sell shares or participation certificates in the pool. The cash flow of a mortgage pass-through security depends on the cash flow of the underlying pool of mortgages and consists of monthly mortgage payments representing interest, the scheduled repayment of principal, and any prepayments, net of servicing and other administrative fees.

- Market participants measure the prepayment rate using two measures: the single monthly mortality rate (SMM) and its corresponding annualized rate—namely, the conditional prepayment rate (CPR). For MBS, a measure widely used by market participants to assess effective duration is the weighted average life or simply the average life of the MBS.

- Market participants use the Public Securities Association (PSA) prepayment benchmark to describe prepayment rates. A PSA assumption greater than 100 PSA means that prepayments are assumed to occur faster than the benchmark, whereas a PSA assumption lower than 100 PSA means that prepayments are assumed to occur slower than the benchmark.

- Prepayment risk includes two components: contraction risk and extension risk. The former is the risk that when interest rates decline, the security will have a shorter maturity than was anticipated at the time of purchase because homeowners will refinance at the new, lower interest rates. The latter is the risk that when interest rates rise, fewer prepayments will occur than what was anticipated at the time of purchase because homeowners are reluctant to give up the benefits of a contractual interest rate that now looks low.

- The creation of a collateralized mortgage obligation (CMO) can help manage prepayment risk by distributing the various forms of prepayment risk among different classes of bond-holders. The CMO's major financial innovation is that the securities created more closely satisfy the asset/liability needs of institutional investors, thereby broadening the appeal of mortgage-backed products.

- The most common types of CMO tranche are sequential-pay tranches, planned amortization class (PAC) tranches, support tranches, and floating-rate tranches.

- Non-agency RMBS share many features and structuring techniques with agency CMOs. However, they typically include two complementary mechanisms. First, the cash flows are distributed by rules that dictate the allocation of interest payments and principal repayments to tranches with various degrees of priority/seniority. Second, there are rules for the allocation of realized losses that specify that subordinated bond classes have lower payment priority than senior classes.

- In order to obtain favorable credit ratings, non-agency RMBS and non-mortgage ABS often require one or more credit enhancements. The most common forms of internal credit enhancement are senior/subordinated structures, reserve funds, and overcollateralization. In external credit enhancement, credit support in the case of defaults resulting in losses in the pool of loans is provided in the form of a financial guarantee by a third party to the transaction.

- Commercial mortgage-backed securities (CMBS) are securities backed by a pool of commercial mortgages on income-producing property.

- Two key indicators of the potential credit performance of CMBS are the debt-service-coverage (DSC) ratio and the loan-to-value ratio (LTV). The DSC ratio is the property's annual net operating income divided by the debt service.

- CMBS have considerable call protection, which allows CMBS to trade in the market more like corporate bonds than like RMBS. This call protection comes in two forms: at the structure level and at the loan level. The creation of sequential-pay tranches is an example of call protection at the structure level. At the loan level, four mechanisms offer investors call protection: prepayment lockouts, prepayment penalty points, yield maintenance charges, and defeasance.

- ABS are backed by a wide range of asset types. The most popular non-mortgage ABS are auto loan ABS and credit card receivable ABS. The collateral is amortizing for auto loan ABS and non-amortizing for credit card receivable ABS. As with non-agency RMBS, these ABS must offer credit enhancement to be appealing to investors.

- A collateralized debt obligation (CDO) is a generic term used to describe a security backed by a diversified pool of one or more debt obligations (e.g., corporate and emerging market bonds, leveraged bank loans, ABS, RMBS, and CMBS).

- A CDO involves the creation of an SPE. The funds necessary to pay the bond classes come from a pool of loans that must be serviced. A CDO requires a collateral manager to buy and sell debt obligations for and from the CDO's portfolio of assets to generate sufficient cash

flows to meet the obligations of the CDO bondholders and to generate a fair return for the equityholders.
- The structure of a CDO includes senior, mezzanine, and subordinated/equity bond classes.
- Covered bonds are similar to ABS, but they differ because of their dual recourse nature, strict eligibility criteria, dynamic cover pool, and redemption regimes in the event of sponsor default.

PROBLEMS

1. Securitization is beneficial for banks because it:
   A. repackages bank loans into simpler structures.
   B. increases the funds available for banks to lend.
   C. allows banks to maintain ownership of their securitized assets.
2. Securitization benefits financial markets by:
   A. increasing the role of intermediaries.
   B. establishing a barrier between investors and originating borrowers.
   C. allowing investors to tailor credit risk and interest rate risk exposures to meet their individual needs.
3. A benefit of securitization is the:
   A. reduction in disintermediation.
   B. simplification of debt obligations.
   C. creation of tradable securities with greater liquidity than the original loans.
4. Securitization benefits investors by:
   A. providing more direct access to a wider range of assets.
   B. reducing the inherent credit risk of pools of loans and receivables.
   C. eliminating cash flow timing risks of an ABS, such as contraction and extension risks.
5. In a securitization, the special purpose entity (SPE) is responsible for the:
   A. issuance of the asset-backed securities.
   B. collection of payments from the borrowers.
   C. recovery of underlying assets from delinquent borrowers.
6. In a securitization, the collateral is initially sold by the:
   A. issuer.
   B. depositor.
   C. underwriter.
7. A special purpose entity issues asset-backed securities in the following structure.

Bond Class	Par Value (€ millions)
A (senior)	200
B (subordinated)	20
C (subordinated)	5

At which of the following amounts of default in par value would Bond Class A experience a loss?
   A. €20 million
   B. €25 million
   C. €26 million

8. In a securitization, time tranching provides investors with the ability to choose between:
   A. extension and contraction risks.
   B. senior and subordinated bond classes.
   C. fully amortizing and partially amortizing loans.
9. The creation of bond classes with a waterfall structure for sharing losses is referred to as:
   A. time tranching.
   B. credit tranching.
   C. overcollateralization.
10. Which of the following statements related to securitization is correct?
    A. Time tranching addresses the uncertainty of a decline in interest rates.
    B. Securitizations are rarely structured to include both credit tranching and time tranching.
    C. Junior and senior bond classes differ in that junior classes can be paid off only at the bond's set maturity.
11. A goal of securitization is to:
    A. separate the seller's collateral from its credit ratings.
    B. uphold the absolute priority rule in bankruptcy reorganizations.
    C. account for collateral's primary influence on corporate bond credit spreads.
12. The last payment in a partially amortizing residential mortgage loan is *best* referred to as a:
    A. waterfall.
    B. principal repayment.
    C. balloon payment.
13. If a mortgage borrower makes prepayments without penalty to take advantage of falling interest rates, the lender will *most likely* experience:
    A. extension risk.
    B. contraction risk.
    C. yield maintenance.
14. Which of the following characteristics of a residential mortgage loan would *best* protect the lender from a strategic default by the borrower?
    A. Recourse
    B. A prepayment option
    C. Interest-only payments
15. William Marolf obtains a EUR5 million mortgage loan from Bank Nederlandse. A year later, the principal on the loan is EUR4 million and Marolf defaults on the loan. Bank Nederlandse forecloses, sells the property for EUR2.5 million, and is entitled to collect the EUR1.5 million shortfall from Marolf. Marolf *most likely* had a:
    A. bullet loan.
    B. recourse loan.
    C. non-recourse loan.
16. Fran Martin obtains a non-recourse mortgage loan for $500,000. One year later, when the outstanding balance of the mortgage is $490,000, Martin cannot make his mortgage payments and defaults on the loan. The lender forecloses on the loan and sells the house for $315,000. What amount is the lender entitled to claim from Martin?
    A. $0.
    B. $175,000.
    C. $185,000.

17. A balloon payment equal to a mortgage's original loan amount is a characteristic of a:
    A. bullet mortgage.
    B. fully amortizing mortgage.
    C. partially amortizing mortgage.

18. Which of the following statements is correct concerning mortgage loan defaults?
    A. A non-recourse jurisdiction poses higher default risks for lenders.
    B. In a non-recourse jurisdiction, strategic default will not affect the defaulting borrower's future access to credit.
    C. When a recourse loan defaults, the mortgaged property is the lender's sole source for recovery of the outstanding mortgage balance.

19. Which of the following describes a typical feature of a non-agency residential mortgage-backed security (RMBS)?
    A. Senior/subordinated structure
    B. A pool of conforming mortgages as collateral
    C. A guarantee by a government-sponsored enterprise

20. If interest rates increase, an investor who owns a mortgage pass-through security is *most likely* affected by:
    A. credit risk.
    B. extension risk.
    C. contraction risk.

21. Which of the following is *most likely* an advantage of collateralized mortgage obligations (CMOs)? CMOs can
    A. eliminate prepayment risk.
    B. be created directly from a pool of mortgage loans.
    C. meet the asset/liability requirements of institutional investors.

22. The longest-term tranche of a sequential-pay CMO is *most likely* to have the lowest:
    A. average life.
    B. extension risk.
    C. contraction risk.

23. The tranches in a collateralized mortgage obligation that are *most likely* to provide protection for investors against both extension and contraction risk are:
    A. planned amortization class (PAC) tranches.
    B. support tranches.
    C. sequential-pay tranches.

24. Support tranches are *most* appropriate for investors who are:
    A. concerned about their exposure to extension risk.
    B. concerned about their exposure to concentration risk.
    C. willing to accept prepayment risk in exchange for higher returns.

25. In the context of mortgage-backed securities, a conditional prepayment rate (CPR) of 8% means that approximately 8% of the outstanding mortgage pool balance at the beginning of the year is expected to be prepaid:
    A. in the current month.
    B. by the end of the year.
    C. over the life of the mortgages.

26. For a mortgage pass-through security, which of the following risks *most likely* increases as interest rates decline?
    A. Balloon
    B. Extension
    C. Contraction

27. Compared with the weighted average coupon rate of its underlying pool of mortgages, the pass-through rate on a mortgage pass-through security is:
    A. lower.
    B. the same.
    C. higher.
28. The single monthly mortality rate (SMM) *most likely:*
    A. increases as extension risk rises.
    B. decreases as contraction risk falls.
    C. stays fixed over time when the standard prepayment model remains at 100 PSA.
29. Credit risk is an important consideration for commercial mortgage-backed securities (CMBS) if the CMBS are backed by mortgage loans that:
    A. are non-recourse.
    B. have call protection.
    C. have prepayment penalty points.
30. Which commercial mortgage-backed security characteristic causes a CMBS to trade more like a corporate bond than a residential mortgage-backed security?
    A. Call protection
    B. Internal credit enhancement
    C. Debt-service-coverage ratio level
31. A commercial mortgage-backed security does not meet the debt-to-service coverage at the loan level necessary to achieve a desired credit rating. Which of the following features would *most likely* improve the credit rating of the CMBS?
    A. Subordination
    B. Call protection
    C. Balloon payments
32. If a default occurs in a non-recourse commercial mortgage-backed security, the lender will *most likely*:
    A. recover prepayment penalty points paid by the borrower to offset losses.
    B. use only the proceeds received from the sale of the property to recover losses.
    C. initiate a claim against the borrower for any shortfall resulting from the sale of the property.
33. Which of the following investments is least subject to prepayment risk?
    A. Auto loan receivable–backed securities
    B. Commercial mortgage-backed securities
    C. Non-agency residential mortgage-backed securities
34. An excess spread account incorporated into a securitization is designed to limit:
    A. credit risk.
    B. extension risk.
    C. contraction risk.
35. Which of the following *best* describes the cash flow that owners of credit card receivable asset-backed securities receive during the lockout period?
    A. No cash flow
    B. Only principal payments collected
    C. Only finance charges collected and fees
36. Which type of asset-backed security is not affected by prepayment risk?
    A. Auto loan ABS
    B. Residential MBS
    C. Credit card receivable ABS

37. In auto loan ABS, the form of credit enhancement that *most likely* serves as the first line of loss protection is the:
    A. excess spread account.
    B. sequential-pay structure.
    C. proceeds from repossession sales.

38. In credit card receivable ABS, principal cash flows can be altered only when the:
    A. lockout period expires.
    B. excess spread account is depleted.
    C. early amortization provision is triggered.

39. The CDO tranche with a credit-rating status between senior and subordinated bond classes is called the:
    A. equity tranche.
    B. residual tranche.
    C. mezzanine tranche.

40. The key to a CDO's viability is the creation of a structure with a competitive return for the:
    A. senior tranche.
    B. mezzanine tranche.
    C. subordinated tranche.

41. When the collateral manager fails pre-specified risk tests, a CDO is:
    A. deleveraged by reducing the senior bond class.
    B. restructured to reduce its most expensive funding source.
    C. liquidated by paying off the bond classes in order of seniority.

42. Collateralized mortgage obligations are designed to:
    A. eliminate contraction risk in support tranches.
    B. distribute prepayment risk to various tranches.
    C. eliminate extension risk in planned amortization tranches.

43. Which statement about covered bonds is *least* accurate?
    A. Covered bonds provide investors with dual recourse, to the cover pool and also to the issuer.
    B. Covered bonds usually carry higher credit risks and offer higher yields than otherwise similar ABS.
    C. Covered bonds have a dynamic cover pool, meaning sponsors must replace any pre-paid or non-performing assets.

CHAPTER 5

UNDERSTANDING FIXED-INCOME RISK AND RETURN

LEARNING OUTCOMES

The candidate should be able to:

- calculate and interpret the sources of return from investing in a fixed-rate bond;
- define, calculate, and interpret Macaulay, modified, and effective durations;
- explain why effective duration is the most appropriate measure of interest rate risk for bonds with embedded options;
- define key rate duration and describe the use of key rate durations in measuring the sensitivity of bonds to changes in the shape of the benchmark yield curve;
- explain how a bond's maturity, coupon, and yield level affect its interest rate risk;
- calculate the duration of a portfolio and explain the limitations of portfolio duration;
- calculate and interpret the money duration of a bond and price value of a basis point (PVBP);
- calculate and interpret approximate convexity and compare approximate and effective convexity;
- calculate the percentage price change of a bond for a specified change in yield, given the bond's approximate duration and convexity;
- describe how the term structure of yield volatility affects the interest rate risk of a bond;
- describe the relationships among a bond's holding period return, its duration, and the investment horizon;
- explain how changes in credit spread and liquidity affect yield-to-maturity of a bond and how duration and convexity can be used to estimate the price effect of the changes.
- describe the difference between empirical duration and analytical duration.

SUMMARY OVERVIEW

This chapter covers the risk and return characteristics of fixed-rate bonds. The focus is on the widely used measures of interest rate risk—duration and convexity. These statistics are used extensively in fixed-income analysis. The following are the main points made in the chapter:

- The three sources of return on a fixed-rate bond purchased at par value are: (1) receipt of the promised coupon and principal payments on the scheduled dates, (2) reinvestment of coupon payments, and (3) potential capital gains, as well as losses, on the sale of the bond prior to maturity.
- For a bond purchased at a discount or premium, the rate of return also includes the effect of the price being "pulled to par" as maturity nears, assuming no default.
- The total return is the future value of reinvested coupon interest payments and the sale price (or redemption of principal if the bond is held to maturity).
- The horizon yield (or holding period rate of return) is the internal rate of return between the total return and purchase price of the bond.
- Coupon reinvestment risk increases with a higher coupon rate and a longer reinvestment time period.
- Capital gains and losses are measured from the carrying value of the bond and not from the purchase price. The carrying value includes the amortization of the discount or premium if the bond is purchased at a price below or above par value. The carrying value is any point on the constant-yield price trajectory.
- Interest income on a bond is the return associated with the passage of time. Capital gains and losses are the returns associated with a change in the value of a bond as indicated by a change in the yield-to-maturity.
- The two types of interest rate risk on a fixed-rate bond are coupon reinvestment risk and market price risk. These risks offset each other to a certain extent. An investor gains from higher rates on reinvested coupons but loses if the bond is sold at a capital loss because the price is below the constant-yield price trajectory. An investor loses from lower rates on reinvested coupon but gains if the bond is sold at a capital gain because the price is above the constant-yield price trajectory.
- Market price risk dominates coupon reinvestment risk when the investor has a short-term horizon (relative to the time-to-maturity on the bond).
- Coupon reinvestment risk dominates market price risk when the investor has a long-term horizon (relative to the time-to-maturity)—for instance, a buy-and-hold investor.
- Bond duration, in general, measures the sensitivity of the full price (including accrued interest) to a change in interest rates.
- Yield duration statistics measuring the sensitivity of a bond's full price to the bond's own yield-to-maturity include the Macaulay duration, modified duration, money duration, and price value of a basis point.
- Curve duration statistics measuring the sensitivity of a bond's full price to the benchmark yield curve are usually called "effective durations."
- Macaulay duration is the weighted average of the time to receipt of coupon interest and principal payments, in which the weights are the shares of the full price corresponding to each payment. This statistic is annualized by dividing by the periodicity (number of coupon payments or compounding periods in a year).
- Modified duration provides a linear estimate of the percentage price change for a bond given a change in its yield-to-maturity.

- Approximate modified duration approaches modified duration as the change in the yield-to-maturity approaches zero.
- Effective duration is very similar to approximate modified duration. The difference is that approximate modified duration is a yield duration statistic that measures interest rate risk in terms of a change in the bond's own yield-to-maturity, whereas effective duration is a curve duration statistic that measures interest rate risk assuming a parallel shift in the benchmark yield curve.
- Key rate duration is a measure of a bond's sensitivity to a change in the benchmark yield curve at specific maturity segments. Key rate durations can be used to measure a bond's sensitivity to changes in the shape of the yield curve.
- Bonds with an embedded option do not have a meaningful internal rate of return because future cash flows are contingent on interest rates. Therefore, effective duration is the appropriate interest rate risk measure, not modified duration.
- The effective duration of a traditional (option-free) fixed-rate bond is its sensitivity to the benchmark yield curve, which can differ from its sensitivity to its own yield-to-maturity. Therefore, modified duration and effective duration on a traditional (option-free) fixed-rate bond are not necessarily equal.
- During a coupon period, Macaulay and modified durations decline smoothly in a "sawtooth" pattern, assuming the yield-to-maturity is constant. When the coupon payment is made, the durations jump upward.
- Macaulay and modified durations are inversely related to the coupon rate and the yield-to-maturity.
- Time-to-maturity and Macaulay and modified durations are *usually* positively related. They are *always* positively related on bonds priced at par or at a premium above par value. They are *usually* positively related on bonds priced at a discount below par value. The exception is on long-term, low-coupon bonds, on which it is possible to have a lower duration than on an otherwise comparable shorter-term bond.
- The presence of an embedded call option reduces a bond's effective duration compared with that of an otherwise comparable non-callable bond. The reduction in the effective duration is greater when interest rates are low and the issuer is more likely to exercise the call option.
- The presence of an embedded put option reduces a bond's effective duration compared with that of an otherwise comparable non-putable bond. The reduction in the effective duration is greater when interest rates are high and the investor is more likely to exercise the put option.
- The duration of a bond portfolio can be calculated in two ways: (1) the weighted average of the time to receipt of *aggregate* cash flows and (2) the weighted average of the durations of individual bonds that compose the portfolio.
- The first method to calculate portfolio duration is based on the cash flow yield, which is the internal rate of return on the aggregate cash flows. It cannot be used for bonds with embedded options or for floating-rate notes.
- The second method is simpler to use and quite accurate when the yield curve is relatively flat. Its main limitation is that it assumes a parallel shift in the yield curve in that the yields on all bonds in the portfolio change by the same amount.
- Money duration is a measure of the price change in terms of units of the currency in which the bond is denominated.
- The price value of a basis point (PVBP) is an estimate of the change in the full price of a bond given a 1 bp change in the yield-to-maturity.

- Modified duration is the primary, or first-order, effect on a bond's percentage price change given a change in the yield-to-maturity. Convexity is the secondary, or second-order, effect. It indicates the change in the modified duration as the yield-to-maturity changes.
- Money convexity is convexity times the full price of the bond. Combined with money duration, money convexity estimates the change in the full price of a bond in units of currency given a change in the yield-to-maturity.
- Convexity is a positive attribute for a bond. Other things being equal, a more convex bond appreciates in price more than a less convex bond when yields fall and depreciates less when yields rise.
- Effective convexity is the second-order effect on a bond price given a change in the benchmark yield curve. It is similar to approximate convexity. The difference is that approximate convexity is based on a yield-to-maturity change and effective convexity is based on a benchmark yield curve change.
- Callable bonds have negative effective convexity when interest rates are low. The increase in price when the benchmark yield is reduced is less in absolute value than the decrease in price when the benchmark yield is raised.
- The change in a bond price is the product of: (1) the impact per basis-point change in the yield-to-maturity and (2) the number of basis points in the yield change. The first factor is estimated by duration and convexity. The second factor depends on yield volatility.
- The investment horizon is essential in measuring the interest rate risk on a fixed-rate bond.
- For a particular assumption about yield volatility, the Macaulay duration indicates the investment horizon for which coupon reinvestment risk and market price risk offset each other. The assumption is a one-time parallel shift to the yield curve in which the yield-to-maturity and coupon reinvestment rates change by the same amount in the same direction.
- When the investment horizon is greater than the Macaulay duration of the bond, coupon reinvestment risk dominates price risk. The investor's risk is to lower interest rates. The duration gap is negative.
- When the investment horizon is equal to the Macaulay duration of the bond, coupon reinvestment risk offsets price risk. The duration gap is zero.
- When the investment horizon is less than the Macaulay duration of the bond, price risk dominates coupon reinvestment risk. The investor's risk is to higher interest rates. The duration gap is positive.
- Credit risk involves the probability of default and degree of recovery if default occurs, whereas liquidity risk refers to the transaction costs associated with selling a bond.
- For a traditional (option-free) fixed-rate bond, the same duration and convexity statistics apply if a change occurs in the benchmark yield or a change occurs in the spread. The change in the spread can result from a change in credit risk or liquidity risk.
- In practice, there often is interaction between changes in benchmark yields and in the spread over the benchmark.
- Empirical duration uses statistical methods and historical bond prices to derive the price–yield relationship for specific bonds or bond portfolios.

PROBLEMS

1. A "buy-and-hold" investor purchases a fixed-rate bond at a discount and holds the security until it matures. Which of the following sources of return is *least likely* to contribute to the investor's total return over the investment horizon, assuming all payments are made as scheduled?

A. Capital gain
B. Principal payment
C. Reinvestment of coupon payments

2. Which of the following sources of return is *most likely* exposed to interest rate risk for an investor of a fixed-rate bond who holds the bond until maturity?
   A. Capital gain or loss
   B. Redemption of principal
   C. Reinvestment of coupon payments

3. An investor purchases a bond at a price above par value. Two years later, the investor sells the bond. The resulting capital gain or loss is measured by comparing the price at which the bond is sold to the:
   A. carrying value.
   B. original purchase price.
   C. original purchase price value plus the amortized amount of the premium.

The following information relates to Questions 4–6

An investor purchases a nine-year, 7% annual coupon payment bond at a price equal to par value. After the bond is purchased and before the first coupon is received, interest rates increase to 8%. The investor sells the bond after five years. Assume that interest rates remain unchanged at 8% over the five-year holding period.

4. Per 100 of par value, the future value of the reinvested coupon payments at the end of the holding period is *closest* to:
   A. 35.00.
   B. 40.26.
   C. 41.07.

5. The capital gain/loss per 100 of par value resulting from the sale of the bond at the end of the five-year holding period is *closest* to a:
   A. loss of 8.45.
   B. loss of 3.31.
   C. gain of 2.75.

6. Assuming that all coupons are reinvested over the holding period, the investor's five-year horizon yield is *closest* to:
   A. 5.66%.
   B. 6.62%.
   C. 7.12%.

7. An investor buys a three-year bond with a 5% coupon rate paid annually. The bond, with a yield-to-maturity of 3%, is purchased at a price of 105.657223 per 100 of par value. Assuming a 5-basis point change in yield-to-maturity, the bond's approximate modified duration is *closest* to:
   A. 2.78.
   B. 2.86.
   C. 5.56.

8. Which of the following statements about duration is correct? A bond's:
   A. effective duration is a measure of yield duration.
   B. modified duration is a measure of curve duration.
   C. modified duration cannot be larger than its Macaulay duration (assuming a positive yield-to-maturity).

9. An investor buys a 6% annual payment bond with three years to maturity. The bond has a yield-to-maturity of 8% and is currently priced at 94.845806 per 100 of par. The bond's Macaulay duration is *closest* to:
   A. 2.62.
   B. 2.78.
   C. 2.83.

10. The interest rate risk of a fixed-rate bond with an embedded call option is *best* measured by:
    A. effective duration.
    B. modified duration.
    C. Macaulay duration.

11. Which of the following is *most* appropriate for measuring a bond's sensitivity to shaping risk?
    A. Key rate duration
    B. Effective duration
    C. Modified duration

12. A Canadian pension fund manager seeks to measure the sensitivity of her pension liabilities to market interest rate changes. The manager determines the present value of the liabilities under three interest rate scenarios: a base rate of 7%, a 100 basis point increase in rates up to 8%, and a 100 basis point drop in rates down to 6%. The results of the manager's analysis are presented below:

Interest Rate Assumption	Present Value of Liabilities
6%	CAD510.1 million
7%	CAD455.4 million
8%	CAD373.6 million

The effective duration of the pension fund's liabilities is *closest* to:
    A. 1.49.
    B. 14.99.
    C. 29.97.

13. Which of the following statements about Macaulay duration is correct?
    A. A bond's coupon rate and Macaulay duration are positively related.
    B. A bond's Macaulay duration is inversely related to its yield-to-maturity.
    C. The Macaulay duration of a zero-coupon bond is less than its time-to-maturity.

14. Assuming no change in the credit risk of a bond, the presence of an embedded put option:
    A. reduces the effective duration of the bond.
    B. increases the effective duration of the bond.
    C. does not change the effective duration of the bond.

15. A bond portfolio consists of the following three fixed-rate bonds. Assume annual coupon payments and no accrued interest on the bonds. Prices are per 100 of par value.

Bond	Maturity	Market Value	Price	Coupon	Yield-to-Maturity	Modified Duration
A	6 years	170,000	85.0000	2.00%	4.95%	5.42
B	10 years	120,000	80.0000	2.40%	4.99%	8.44
C	15 years	100,000	100.0000	5.00%	5.00%	10.38

The bond portfolio's modified duration is *closest* to:

A. 7.62.

B. 8.08.

C. 8.20.

16. A limitation of calculating a bond portfolio's duration as the weighted average of the yield durations of the individual bonds that compose the portfolio is that it:

A. assumes a parallel shift to the yield curve.

B. is less accurate when the yield curve is less steeply sloped.

C. is not applicable to portfolios that have bonds with embedded options.

17. Using the information below, which bond has the *greatest* money duration per 100 of par value assuming annual coupon payments and no accrued interest?

Bond	Time-to-Maturity	Price Per 100 of Par Value	Coupon Rate	Yield-to-Maturity	Modified Duration
A	6 years	85.00	2.00%	4.95%	5.42
B	10 years	80.00	2.40%	4.99%	8.44
C	9 years	85.78	3.00%	5.00%	7.54

A. Bond A

B. Bond B

C. Bond C

18. A bond with exactly nine years remaining until maturity offers a 3% coupon rate with annual coupons. The bond, with a yield-to-maturity of 5%, is priced at 85.784357 per 100 of par value. The estimated price value of a basis point for the bond is *closest* to:

A. 0.0086.

B. 0.0648.

C. 0.1295.

19. The "second-order" effect on a bond's percentage price change given a change in yield-to-maturity can be *best* described as:

A. duration.

B. convexity.

C. yield volatility.

20. A bond is currently trading for 98.722 per 100 of par value. If the bond's yield-to-maturity (YTM) rises by 10 basis points, the bond's full price is expected to fall to 98.669. If the bond's YTM decreases by 10 basis points, the bond's full price is expected to increase to 98.782. The bond's approximate convexity is *closest* to:

A. 0.071.

B. 70.906.

C. 1,144.628.

21. A bond has an annual modified duration of 7.020 and annual convexity of 65.180. If the bond's yield-to-maturity decreases by 25 basis points, the expected percentage price change is *closest* to:

A. 1.73%.

B. 1.76%.

C. 1.78%.

22. A bond has an annual modified duration of 7.140 and annual convexity of 66.200. The bond's yield-to-maturity is expected to increase by 50 basis points. The expected percentage price change is *closest* to:
    A. −3.40%.
    B. −3.49%.
    C. −3.57%.

23. Which of the following statements relating to yield volatility is *most* accurate? If the term structure of yield volatility is downward sloping, then:
    A. short-term rates are higher than long-term rates.
    B. long-term yields are more stable than short-term yields.
    C. short-term bonds will always experience greater price fluctuation than long-term bonds.

24. The holding period for a bond at which the coupon reinvestment risk offsets the market price risk is *best* approximated by:
    A. duration gap.
    B. modified duration.
    C. Macaulay duration.

25. When the investor's investment horizon is less than the Macaulay duration of the bond she owns:
    A. the investor is hedged against interest rate risk.
    B. reinvestment risk dominates, and the investor is at risk of lower rates.
    C. market price risk dominates, and the investor is at risk of higher rates.

26. An investor purchases an annual coupon bond with a 6% coupon rate and exactly 20 years remaining until maturity at a price equal to par value. The investor's investment horizon is eight years. The approximate modified duration of the bond is 11.470 years. The duration gap at the time of purchase is *closest* to:
    A. −7.842.
    B. 3.470.
    C. 4.158.

27. A manufacturing company receives a ratings upgrade and the price increases on its fixed-rate bond. The price increase was *most likely* caused by a(n):
    A. decrease in the bond's credit spread.
    B. increase in the bond's liquidity spread.
    C. increase of the bond's underlying benchmark rate.

28. Empirical duration is likely the best measure of the impact of yield changes on portfolio value, especially under stressed market conditions, for a portfolio consisting of:
    A. 100% sovereign bonds of several AAA rated euro area issuers.
    B. 100% covered bonds of several AAA rated euro area corporate issuers.
    C. 25% AAA rated sovereign bonds, 25% AAA rated corporate bonds, and 50% high-yield (i.e., speculative-grade) corporate bonds, all from various euro area sovereign and corporate issuers.

CHAPTER 6

FUNDAMENTALS OF CREDIT ANALYSIS

LEARNING OUTCOMES

The candidate should be able to:

- describe credit risk and credit-related risks affecting corporate bonds;
- describe default probability and loss severity as components of credit risk;
- describe seniority rankings of corporate debt and explain the potential violation of the priority of claims in a bankruptcy proceeding;
- compare and contrast corporate issuer credit ratings and issue credit ratings and describe the rating agency practice of "notching";
- explain risks in relying on ratings from credit rating agencies;
- explain the four Cs (Capacity, Collateral, Covenants, and Character) of traditional credit analysis;
- calculate and interpret financial ratios used in credit analysis;
- evaluate the credit quality of a corporate bond issuer and a bond of that issuer, given key financial ratios of the issuer and the industry;
- describe macroeconomic, market, and issuer-specific factors that influence the level and volatility of yield spreads;
- explain special considerations when evaluating the credit of high-yield, sovereign, and non-sovereign government debt issuers and issues.

SUMMARY OVERVIEW

We introduced basic principles of credit analysis. We described the importance of the credit markets and credit and credit-related risks. We discussed the role and importance of credit ratings and the methodology associated with assigning ratings, as well as the risks of relying on credit ratings. We covered the key components of credit analysis and the financial measure used to help assess creditworthiness.

We also discussed risk versus return when investing in credit and how spread changes affect holding period returns. In addition, we addressed the special considerations to take into account when doing credit analysis of high-yield companies, sovereign borrowers, and non-sovereign government bonds.

- Credit risk is the risk of loss resulting from the borrower failing to make full and timely payments of interest and/or principal.
- The key components of credit risk are risk of default and loss severity in the event of default. The product of the two is expected loss. Investors in higher-quality bonds tend not to focus on loss severity because default risk for those securities is low.
- Loss severity equals (1 − Recovery rate).
- Credit-related risks include downgrade risk (also called credit migration risk) and market liquidity risk. Either of these can cause yield spreads—yield premiums—to rise and bond prices to fall.
- Downgrade risk refers to a decline in an issuer's creditworthiness. Downgrades will cause its bonds to trade with wider yield spreads and thus lower prices.
- Market liquidity risk refers to a widening of the bid–ask spread on an issuer's bonds. Lower-quality bonds tend to have greater market liquidity risk than higher-quality bonds, and during times of market or financial stress, market liquidity risk rises.
- The composition of an issuer's debt and equity is referred to as its "capital structure." Debt ranks ahead of all types of equity with respect to priority of payment, and within the debt component of the capital structure, there can be varying levels of seniority.
- With respect to priority of claims, secured debt ranks ahead of unsecured debt, and within unsecured debt, senior debt ranks ahead of subordinated debt. In the typical case, all of an issuer's bonds have the same probability of default due to cross-default provisions in most indentures. Higher priority of claim implies higher recovery rate—lower loss severity—in the event of default.
- For issuers with more complex corporate structures—for example, a parent holding company that has operating subsidiaries—debt at the holding company is structurally subordinated to the subsidiary debt, although the possibility of more diverse assets and earnings streams from other sources could still result in the parent having higher effective credit quality than a particular subsidiary.
- Recovery rates can vary greatly by issuer and industry. They are influenced by the composition of an issuer's capital structure, where in the economic and credit cycle the default occurred, and what the market's view of the future prospects are for the issuer and its industry.
- The priority of claims in bankruptcy is not always absolute. It can be influenced by several factors, including some leeway accorded to bankruptcy judges, government involvement, or a desire on the part of the more senior creditors to settle with the more junior creditors and allow the issuer to emerge from bankruptcy as a going concern, rather than risking smaller and delayed recovery in the event of a liquidation of the borrower.
- Credit rating agencies, such as Moody's, Standard & Poor's, and Fitch, play a central role in the credit markets. Nearly every bond issued in the broad debt markets carries credit ratings, which are opinions about a bond issue's creditworthiness. Credit ratings enable investors to compare the credit risk of debt issues and issuers within a given industry, across industries, and across geographic markets.
- Bonds rated Aaa to Baa3 by Moody's and AAA to BBB– by Standard & Poor's (S&P) and/or Fitch (higher to lower) are referred to as "investment grade." Bonds rated lower than that—Ba1 or lower by Moody's and BB+ or lower by S&P and/or Fitch—are referred to as "below investment grade" or "speculative grade." Below-investment-grade bonds are also called "high-yield" or "junk" bonds.

- The rating agencies rate both issuers and issues. Issuer ratings are meant to address an issuer's overall creditworthiness—its risk of default. Ratings for issues incorporate such factors as their rankings in the capital structure.
- The rating agencies will notch issue ratings up or down to account for such factors as capital structure ranking for secured or subordinated bonds, reflecting different recovery rates in the event of default. Ratings may also be notched due to structural subordination.
- Rating agencies incorporate ESG factors into their ratings of firms. Some have launched a set of ratings that aim to measure a company's attitudes, practices, and advances related to ESG. They identify and track leaders and laggards in the space. Companies are evaluated according to their exposure to ESG risks and how well they manage those risks relative to peers.
- There are risks in relying too much on credit agency ratings. Creditworthiness may change over time, and initial/current ratings do not necessarily reflect the creditworthiness of an issuer or bond over an investor's holding period. Valuations often adjust before ratings change, and the notching process may not adequately reflect the price decline of a bond that is lower ranked in the capital structure. Because ratings primarily reflect the probability of default but not necessarily the severity of loss given default, bonds with the same rating may have significantly different expected losses (default probability times loss severity). And like analysts, credit rating agencies may have difficulty forecasting certain credit-negative outcomes, such as adverse litigation and leveraging corporate transactions, and such low probability/high severity events as earthquakes and hurricanes.
- The role of corporate credit analysis is to assess the company's ability to make timely payments of interest and to repay principal at maturity.
- Credit analysis is similar to equity analysis. It is important to understand, however, that bonds are contracts and that management's duty to bondholders and other creditors is limited to the terms of the contract. In contrast, management's duty to shareholders is to act in their best interest by trying to maximize the value of the company—perhaps even at the expense of bondholders at times.
- Credit analysts tend to focus more on the downside risk given the asymmetry of risk/return, whereas equity analysts focus more on upside opportunity from earnings growth, and so on.
- The "4 Cs" of credit—capacity, collateral, covenants, and character—provide a useful framework for evaluating credit risk.
- Credit analysis focuses on an issuer's ability to generate cash flow. The analysis starts with an industry assessment—structure and fundamentals—and continues with an analysis of an issuer's competitive position, management strategy, and track record.
- Credit measures are used to calculate an issuer's creditworthiness, as well as to compare its credit quality with peer companies. Key credit ratios focus on leverage and interest coverage and use such measures as EBITDA, free cash flow, funds from operations, interest expense, and balance sheet debt.
- An issuer's ability to access liquidity is also an important consideration in credit analysis.
- The higher the credit risk, the greater the offered/required yield and potential return demanded by investors. Over time, bonds with more credit risk offer higher returns but with greater volatility of return than bonds with lower credit risk.
- The yield on a credit-risky bond comprises the yield on a default risk–free bond with a comparable maturity plus a yield premium, or "spread," that comprises a credit spread and a liquidity premium. That spread is intended to compensate investors for credit risk—risk of default and loss severity in the event of default—and the credit-related risks that can cause

spreads to widen and prices to decline—downgrade or credit migration risk and market liquidity risk.

$$\text{Yield spread} = \text{Liquidity premium} + \text{Credit spread}$$

- In times of financial market stress, the liquidity premium can increase sharply, causing spreads to widen on all credit-risky bonds, with lower-quality issuers most affected. In times of credit improvement or stability, however, credit spreads can narrow sharply as well, providing attractive investment returns.
- The impact of spread changes on holding period returns for credit-risky bonds is a product of two primary factors: the basis point spread change and the sensitivity of price to yield as reflected by (end-of-period) modified duration and convexity. Spread narrowing enhances holding period returns, whereas spread widening has a negative impact on holding period returns. Longer-duration bonds have greater price and return sensitivity to changes in spread than shorter-duration bonds.

$$\text{Price impact} \approx -(\text{AnnModDur} \times \Delta\text{Spread}) + \tfrac{1}{2}\text{AnnConvexity} \times (\Delta\text{Spread})^2$$

- For high-yield bonds, with their greater risk of default, more emphasis should be placed on an issuer's sources of liquidity and its debt structure and corporate structure. Credit risk can vary greatly across an issuer's debt structure depending on the seniority ranking. Many high-yield companies have complex capital structures, resulting in different levels of credit risk depending on where the debt resides.
- Covenant analysis is especially important for high-yield bonds. Key covenants include payment restrictions, limitation on liens, change of control, coverage maintenance tests (often limited to bank loans), and any guarantees from restricted subsidiaries. Covenant language can be very technical and legalistic, so it may help to seek legal or expert assistance.
- An equity-like approach to high-yield analysis can be helpful. Calculating and comparing enterprise value with EBITDA and debt/EBITDA can show a level of equity "cushion" or support beneath an issuer's debt.
- Sovereign credit analysis includes assessing both an issuer's ability and willingness to pay its debt obligations. Willingness to pay is important because, due to sovereign immunity, a sovereign government cannot be forced to pay its debts.
- In assessing sovereign credit risk, a helpful framework is to focus on five broad areas: (1) institutional effectiveness and political risks, (2) economic structure and growth prospects, (3) external liquidity and international investment position, (4) fiscal performance, flexibility, and debt burden, and (5) monetary flexibility.
- Among the characteristics of a high-quality sovereign credit are the absence of corruption and/or challenges to political framework; governmental checks and balances; respect for rule of law and property rights; commitment to honor debts; high per capita income with stable, broad-based growth prospects; control of a reserve or actively traded currency; currency flexibility; low foreign debt and foreign financing needs relative to receipts in foreign currencies; stable or declining ratio of debt to GDP; low debt service as a percentage of revenue; low ratio of net debt to GDP; operationally independent central bank; track record of low and stable inflation; and a well-developed banking system and active money market.
- Non-sovereign or local government bonds, including municipal bonds, are typically either general obligation bonds or revenue bonds.

- General obligation (GO) bonds are backed by the taxing authority of the issuing non-sovereign government. The credit analysis of GO bonds has some similarities to sovereign analysis—debt burden per capita versus income per capita, tax burden, demographics, and economic diversity. Underfunded and "off-balance-sheet" liabilities, such as pensions for public employees and retirees, are debt-like in nature.
- Revenue-backed bonds support specific projects, such as toll roads, bridges, airports, and other infrastructure. The creditworthiness comes from the revenues generated by usage fees and tolls levied.

PROBLEMS

1. The risk that a bond's creditworthiness declines is *best* described by:
   A. credit migration risk.
   B. market liquidity risk.
   C. spread widening risk.
2. Stedsmart Ltd and Fignermo Ltd are alike with respect to financial and operating characteristics, except that Stedsmart Ltd has less publicly traded debt outstanding than Fignermo Ltd. Stedsmart Ltd is *most likely* to have:
   A. no market liquidity risk.
   B. lower market liquidity risk.
   C. higher market liquidity risk.
3. In the event of default, the recovery rate of which of the following bonds would *most likely* be the highest?
   A. First mortgage debt
   B. Senior unsecured debt
   C. Junior subordinate debt
4. During bankruptcy proceedings of a firm, the priority of claims was not strictly adhered to. Which of the following is the *least likely* explanation for this outcome?
   A. Senior creditors compromised.
   B. The value of secured assets was less than the amount of the claims.
   C. A judge's order resulted in actual claims not adhering to strict priority of claims.
5. A fixed-income analyst is *least likely* to conduct an independent analysis of credit risk because credit rating agencies:
   A. may at times mis-rate issues.
   B. often lag the market in pricing credit risk.
   C. cannot foresee future debt-financed acquisitions.
6. If goodwill makes up a large percentage of a company's total assets, this *most likely* indicates that:
   A. the company has low free cash flow before dividends.
   B. there is a low likelihood that the market price of the company's common stock is below book value.
   C. a large percentage of the company's assets are not of high quality.
7. In order to analyze the **collateral** of a company, a credit analyst should assess the:
   A. cash flows of the company.
   B. soundness of management's strategy.
   C. value of the company's assets in relation to the level of debt.

8. In order to determine the **capacity** of a company, it would be *most* appropriate to analyze the:
   A. company's strategy.
   B. growth prospects of the industry.
   C. aggressiveness of the company's accounting policies.
9. A credit analyst is evaluating the credit worthiness of three companies: a construction company, a travel and tourism company, and a beverage company. Both the construction and travel and tourism companies are cyclical, whereas the beverage company is non-cyclical. The construction company has the highest debt level of the three companies. The highest credit risk is *most likely* exhibited by the:
   A. construction company.
   B. beverage company.
   C. travel and tourism company.
10. Based on the information provided in Exhibit 1, the EBITDA interest coverage ratio of Adidas AG is *closest* to:
    A. 16.02x.
    B. 23.34x.
    C. 37.98x.

EXHIBIT 1   Adidas AG Excerpt from Consolidated Income Statement in a given year (€ in millions)

Gross profit	12,293
Royalty and commission income	154
Other operating income	56
Other operating expenses	9,843
Operating profit	2,660
Interest income	64
Interest expense	166
Income before taxes	2,558
Income taxes	640
Net income	1,918

Additional information:
Depreciation and amortization: €1,214 million

Source: Adidas AG Annual Financial Statements, December 2019.

11. The following information is from the annual report of Adidas AG for December 2019:
    - Depreciation and amortization: €1,214 million
    - Total assets: €20,640 million
    - Total debt: €4,364 million
    - Shareholders' equity: €7,058 million

    The debt/capital of Adidas AG is *closest* to:
    A. 21.14%.
    B. 38.21%.
    C. 61.83%.

12. Funds from operations (FFO) of Pay Handle Ltd (a fictitious company) increased in 20X1. In 20X1, the total debt of the company remained unchanged while additional common shares were issued. Pay Handle Ltd's ability to service its debt in 20X1, as compared to 20X0, *most likely*:
    A. improved.
    B. worsened.
    C. remained the same.

13. Based on the information in Exhibit 2, GZ Group's (a hypothetical company) credit risk is *most likely*:
    A. lower than the industry.
    B. higher than the industry.
    C. the same as the industry.

EXHIBIT 2   European Food, Beverage, and Tobacco Industry and GZ Group Selected Financial Ratios for 20X0

	Total Debt/Total Capital (%)	FFO/Total Debt (%)	Return on Capital (%)	Total Debt/ EBITDA (x)	EBITDA Interest Coverage (x)
GZ Group	47.1	77.5	19.6	1.2	17.7
Industry median	**42.4**	**23.6**	**6.55**	**2.85**	**6.45**

14. Based on the information in Exhibit 3, the credit rating of DCM Group (a hypothetical company in the European food & beverage sector) is *most likely*:
    A. lower than AB plc.
    B. higher than AB plc.
    C. the same as AB plc.

EXHIBIT 3   DCM Group and AB plc Selected Financial Ratios for 20X0

Company	Total Debt/Total Capital (%)	FFO/Total Debt (%)	Return on Capital (%)	Total Debt/ EBITDA (x)	EBITDA Interest Coverage (x)
AB plc	0.2	84.3	0.1	1.0	13.9
DCM Group	42.9	22.9	8.2	3.2	3.2
European Food, Beverage, and Tobacco median	**42.4**	**23.6**	**6.55**	**2.85**	**6.45**

15. Holding all other factors constant, the *most likely* effect of low demand and heavy new issue supply on bond yield spreads is that yield spreads will:
    A. widen.
    B. tighten.
    C. not be affected.

16. Credit risk of a corporate bond is *best* described as the:
    A. risk that an issuer's creditworthiness deteriorates.
    B. probability that the issuer fails to make full and timely payments.
    C. risk of loss resulting from the issuer failing to make full and timely payments.

17. The risk that the price at which investors can actually transact differs from the quoted price in the market is called:
    A. spread risk.
    B. credit migration risk.
    C. market liquidity risk.
18. Loss severity is *best* described as the:
    A. default probability multiplied by the loss given default.
    B. portion of a bond's value recovered by bondholders in the event of default.
    C. portion of a bond's value, including unpaid interest, an investor loses in the event of default.
19. The two components of credit risk are default probability and:
    A. spread risk.
    B. loss severity.
    C. market liquidity risk.
20. For a high-quality debt issuer with a large amount of publicly traded debt, bond investors tend to devote *most* effort to assessing the issuer's:
    A. default risk.
    B. loss severity.
    C. market liquidity risk.
21. The expected loss for a given debt instrument is estimated as the product of default probability and:
    A. (1 + Recovery rate).
    B. (1 − Recovery rate).
    C. 1/(1 + Recovery rate).
22. The priority of claims for senior subordinated debt is:
    A. lower than for senior unsecured debt.
    B. the same as for senior unsecured debt.
    C. higher than for senior unsecured debt.
23. A senior unsecured credit instrument holds a higher priority of claims than one ranked as:
    A. mortgage debt.
    B. second lien loan.
    C. senior subordinated.
24. In a bankruptcy proceeding, when the absolute priority of claims is enforced:
    A. senior subordinated creditors rank above second lien holders.
    B. preferred equity shareholders rank above unsecured creditors.
    C. creditors with a secured claim have the first right to the value of that specific property.
25. In the event of default, which of the following is *most likely* to have the highest recovery rate?
    A. Second lien
    B. Senior unsecured
    C. Senior subordinated
26. The process of moving credit ratings of different issues up or down from the issuer rating in response to different payment priorities is *best* described as:
    A. notching.
    B. structural subordination.
    C. cross-default provisions.
27. The factor considered by rating agencies when a corporation has debt at both its parent holding company and operating subsidiaries is *best* referred to as:
    A. credit migration risk.
    B. corporate family rating.
    C. structural subordination.

28. Which type of security is *most likely* to have the same rating as the issuer?
    A. Preferred stock
    B. Senior secured bond
    C. Senior unsecured bond
29. Which of the following corporate debt instruments has the highest seniority ranking?
    A. Second lien
    B. Senior unsecured
    C. Senior subordinated
30. An issuer credit rating usually applies to a company's:
    A. secured debt.
    B. subordinated debt.
    C. senior unsecured debt.
31. The rating agency process whereby the credit ratings on issues are moved up or down from the issuer rating *best* describes:
    A. notching.
    B. pari passu ranking.
    C. cross-default provisions.
32. The notching adjustment for corporate bonds rated Aa2/AA is *most likely*:
    A. larger than the notching adjustment for corporate bonds rated B2/B.
    B. the same as the notching adjustment for corporate bonds rated B2/B.
    C. smaller than the notching adjustment for corporate bonds rated B2/B.
33. Which of the following statements about credit ratings is *most accurate*?
    A. Credit ratings can migrate over time.
    B. Changes in bond credit ratings precede changes in bond prices.
    C. Credit ratings are focused on expected loss rather than risk of default.
34. Which industry characteristic *most likely* has a positive effect on a company's ability to service debt?
    A. Low barriers to entry in the industry
    B. High number of suppliers to the industry
    C. Broadly dispersed market share among large number of companies in the industry
35. When determining the capacity of a borrower to service debt, a credit analyst should begin with an examination of:
    A. industry structure.
    B. industry fundamentals.
    C. company fundamentals.
36. Which of the following accounting issues should *mostly likely* be considered a character warning flag in credit analysis?
    A. Expensing items immediately
    B. Changing auditors infrequently
    C. Significant off-balance-sheet financing
37. In credit analysis, capacity is *best* described as the:
    A. quality of management.
    B. ability of the borrower to make its debt payments on time.
    C. quality and value of the assets supporting an issuer's indebtedness.
38. Among the four Cs of credit analysis, the recognition of revenue prematurely *most likely* reflects a company's:
    A. character.
    B. covenants.
    C. collateral.

The following information relates to Questions 39 and 40

EXHIBIT 4   Industrial Comparative Ratio Analysis, Year 20XX

	EBITDA Margin (%)	Return on Capital (%)	EBIT/Interest Expense (×)	EBITDA/ Interest Expense (×)	Debt/ EBITDA (×)	Debt/Capital (%)
Company A	25.1	25.0	15.9	19.6	1.6	35.2
Company B	29.6	36.3	58.2	62.4	0.5	15.9
Company C	21.8	16.6	8.9	12.4	2.5	46.3

39. Based on only the leverage ratios in Exhibit 4, the company with the *highest* credit risk is:
    A. Company A.
    B. Company B.
    C. Company C.
40. Based on only the coverage ratios in Exhibit 4, the company with the *highest* credit quality is:
    A. Company A.
    B. Company B.
    C. Company C.

The following information relates to Questions 41 and 42

EXHIBIT 5   Consolidated Income Statement (£ millions)

	Company X	Company Y
Net revenues	50.7	83.7
Operating expenses	49.6	70.4
Operating income	1.1	13.3
Interest income	0.0	0.0
Interest expense	0.6	0.8
Income before income taxes	0.5	12.5
Provision for income taxes	−0.2	−3.5
Net income	0.3	9.0

EXHIBIT 6   Consolidated Balance Sheets (£ millions)

	Company X	Company Y
ASSETS		
Current assets	10.3	21.9
Property, plant, and equipment, net	3.5	20.1

	Company X	Company Y
Goodwill	8.3	85.0
Other assets	0.9	5.1
Total assets	23.0	132.1

LIABILITIES AND SHAREHOLDERS' EQUITY

Current liabilities		
Accounts payable and accrued expenses	8.4	16.2
Short-term debt	0.5	8.7
Total current liabilities	8.9	24.9
Long-term debt	11.7	21.1
Other non-current liabilities	1.1	22.1
Total liabilities	21.7	68.1
Total shareholders' equity	1.3	64.0
Total liabilities and shareholders' equity	23.0	132.1

EXHIBIT 7   Consolidated Statements of Cash Flow (£ millions)

	Company X	Company Y
CASH FLOWS FROM OPERATING ACTIVITIES		
Net income	0.3	9.0
Depreciation	1.0	3.8
Goodwill impairment	2.0	1.6
Changes in working capital	0.0	−0.4
Net cash provided by operating activities	3.3	14.0
CASH FLOWS FROM INVESTING ACTIVITIES		
Additions to property and equipment	−1.0	−4.0
Additions to marketable securities	−0.1	0.0
Proceeds from sale of property and equipment	0.2	2.9
Proceeds from sale of marketable securities	0.3	0.0
Net cash used in investing activities	−0.6	−1.1
CASH FLOWS FROM FINANCING ACTIVITIES		
Repurchase of common stock	−1.5	−4.0
Dividends to shareholders	−0.3	−6.1
Change in short-term debt	0.0	−3.4

(continued)

EXHIBIT 7   (Continued)

	Company X	Company Y
Additions to long-term debt	3.9	3.9
Reductions in long-term debt	−3.4	−2.5
Net cash–financing activities	−1.3	−12.1
NET INCREASE IN CASH AND CASH EQUIVALENTS	1.4	0.8

41. Based on Exhibits 5–7, in comparison to Company X, Company Y has a higher:
    A. debt/capital.
    B. debt/EBITDA.
    C. free cash flow after dividends/debt.

42. Based on Exhibits 5–7, in comparison to Company Y, Company X has greater:
    A. leverage.
    B. interest coverage.
    C. operating profit margin.

43. Credit yield spreads *most likely* widen in response to:
    A. high demand for bonds.
    B. weak performance of equities.
    C. strengthening economic conditions.

44. The factor that *most likely* results in corporate credit spreads widening is:
    A. an improving credit cycle.
    B. weakening economic conditions.
    C. a period of high demand for bonds.

45. Credit spreads are *most likely* to widen:
    A. in a strengthening economy.
    B. as the credit cycle improves.
    C. in periods of heavy new issue supply and low borrower demand.

46. Which of the following factors in credit analysis is more important for general obligation non-sovereign government debt than for sovereign debt?
    A. Per capita income
    B. Power to levy and collect taxes
    C. Requirement to balance an operating budget

47. In contrast to high-yield credit analysis, investment-grade analysis is *more likely* to rely on:
    A. spread risk.
    B. an assessment of bank credit facilities.
    C. matching of liquidity sources to upcoming debt maturities.

48. Which of the following factors would *best* justify a decision to avoid investing in a country's sovereign debt?
    A. Freely floating currency
    B. A population that is not growing
    C. Suitable checks and balances in policymaking

CHAPTER 7

THE TERM STRUCTURE AND INTEREST RATE DYNAMICS

LEARNING OUTCOMES

The candidate should be able to:

- describe relationships among spot rates, forward rates, yield to maturity, expected and realized returns on bonds, and the shape of the yield curve;
- describe how zero-coupon rates (spot rates) may be obtained from the par curve by bootstrapping;
- describe the assumptions concerning the evolution of spot rates in relation to forward rates implicit in active bond portfolio management;
- describe the strategy of rolling down the yield curve;
- explain the swap rate curve and why and how market participants use it in valuation;
- calculate and interpret the swap spread for a given maturity;
- describe short-term interest rate spreads used to gauge economy-wide credit risk and liquidity risk;
- explain traditional theories of the term structure of interest rates and describe the implications of each theory for forward rates and the shape of the yield curve;
- explain how a bond's exposure to each of the factors driving the yield curve can be measured and how these exposures can be used to manage yield curve risks;
- explain the maturity structure of yield volatilities and their effect on price volatility;
- explain how key economic factors are used to establish a view on benchmark rates, spreads, and yield curve changes.

SUMMARY OVERVIEW

- The spot rate for a given maturity can be expressed as a geometric average of the short-term rate and a series of forward rates.
- Forward rates are above (below) spot rates when the spot curve is upward (downward) sloping, whereas forward rates are equal to spot rates when the spot curve is flat.

- If forward rates are realized, then all bonds, regardless of maturity, will have the same one-period realized return, which is the first-period spot rate.
- If the spot rate curve is upward sloping and is unchanged, then each bond "rolls down" the curve and earns the forward rate that rolls out of its pricing (i.e., an N-period zero-coupon bond earns the N-period forward rate as it rolls down to be an $N-1$ period security). This dynamic implies an expected return in excess of short-maturity bonds (i.e., a **term premium**) for longer-maturity bonds if the yield curve is upward sloping.
- Active bond portfolio management is consistent with the expectation that today's forward curve does not accurately reflect future spot rates.
- The swap curve provides another measure of the time value of money.
- Swaps are an essential tool frequently used by investors to hedge, take a position in, or otherwise modify interest rate risk.
- Bond quote conventions often use measures of spreads. Those quoted spreads can be used to determine a bond's price.
- Swap curves and Treasury curves can differ because of differences in their credit exposures, liquidity, and other supply/demand factors.
- Market participants often use interest rate spreads between short-term government and risky rates as a barometer to evaluate relative credit and liquidity risk.
- The local expectations theory, liquidity preference theory, segmented markets theory, and preferred habitat theory provide traditional explanations for the shape of the yield curve.
- Historical yield curve movements suggest that they can be explained by a linear combination of three principal movements: level, steepness, and curvature.
- The volatility term structure can be measured using historical data and depicts yield curve risk.
- The sensitivity of a bond value to yield curve changes may make use of effective duration, key rate durations, or sensitivities to parallel, steepness, and curvature movements. Using key rate durations or sensitivities to parallel, steepness, and curvature movements allows one to measure and manage shaping risk.
- The term bond risk premium refers to the expected excess return of a default-free long-term bond less that of an equivalent short-term bond or the one-period risk-free rate
- Several macroeconomic factors influence bond pricing and required returns such as inflation, economic growth, and monetary policy, among others.
- During highly uncertain market periods, investors flock to government bonds in a flight to quality that is often associated with bullish flattening, in which long-term rates fall by more than short-term rates.
- Investors expecting rates to fall will generally extend (shorten) portfolio duration to take advantage of expected bond price increases (decreases)
- When investors expect a steeper (flatter) curve under which long-term rates rise (fall) relative to short-term rates, they will sell (buy) long-term bonds and purchase (sell) short-term bonds.

PROBLEMS

1. Given spot rates for one-, two-, and three-year zero coupon bonds, how many forward rates can be calculated?
2. Give two interpretations for the following forward rate: The two-year forward rate one year from now is 2%.
3. Describe the relationship between forward rates and spot rates if the yield curve is flat.

4. A. Define the yield-to-maturity for a coupon bond.

   B. Is it possible for a coupon bond to earn less than the yield-to-maturity if held to maturity?

5. If a bond trader believes that current forward rates overstate future spot rates, how might she profit from that conclusion?

6. Explain the strategy of rolling down the yield curve.

7. What are the advantages of using the swap curve as a benchmark of interest rates relative to a government bond yield curve?

8. What is the TED spread, and what type of risk does it measure?

9. What is the SOFR rate, and which market conditions does it reflect?

10. According to the local expectations theory, what would be the difference in the one-month total return if an investor purchased a five-year zero-coupon bond versus a two-year zero-coupon bond?

11. Compare the segmented market and the preferred habitat term structure theories.

12. A. List the three factors that have empirically been observed to affect Treasury security returns and explain how each of these factors affects returns on Treasury securities.

   B. What has been observed to be the most important factor in affecting Treasury returns?

   C. Which measures of yield curve risk can measure shaping risk?

13. Which forward rate cannot be computed from the one-, two-, three-, and four-year spot rates? The rate for a:

   A. one-year loan beginning in two years

   B. two-year loan beginning in two years

   C. three-year loan beginning in two years

14. Consider spot rates for three zero-coupon bonds: $z(1) = 3\%$, $z(2) = 4\%$, and $z(3) = 5\%$. Which statement is correct? The forward rate for a one-year loan beginning in one year will be:

   A. less than the forward rate for a one-year loan beginning in two years.

   B. greater than the forward rate for a two-year loan beginning in one year.

   C. greater than the forward rate for a one-year loan beginning in two years.

15. If one-period forward rates are decreasing with maturity, the yield curve is *most likely*:

   A. flat.

   B. upward sloping.

   C. downward sloping.

The following information relates to Questions 16–19

A one-year zero-coupon bond yields 4.0%. The two- and three-year zero-coupon bonds yield 5.0% and 6.0%, respectively.

16. The rate for a one-year loan beginning in one year is *closest* to:

   A. 4.5%.

   B. 5.0%.

   C. 6.0%.

17. The forward rate for a two-year loan beginning in one year is *closest* to:

   A. 5.0%.

   B. 6.0%.

   C. 7.0%.

18. The forward rate for a one-year loan beginning in two years is *closest* to:

   A. 6.0%.

   B. 7.0%.

   C. 8.0%.

19. The five-year spot rate is not provided here; however, the forward price for a two-year zero-coupon bond beginning in three years is known to be 0.8479. The price today of a five-year zero-coupon bond is *closest* to:
    A. 0.7119.
    B. 0.7835.
    C. 0.9524.

---

20. The one-year spot rate z_1 is 4%, the forward rate for a one-year loan beginning in one year is 6%, and the forward rate for a one-year loan beginning in two years is 8%. Which of the following rates is *closest* to the three-year spot rate?
    A. 4.0%
    B. 6.0%
    C. 8.0%
21. The one-year spot rate z_1 is 5%, and the forward price for a one-year zero-coupon bond beginning in one year is 0.9346. The spot price of a two-year zero-coupon bond is *closest* to:
    A. 0.87.
    B. 0.89.
    C. 0.93.
22. In a typical interest rate swap contract, the swap rate is *best* described as the interest rate for the:
    A. fixed-rate leg of the swap.
    B. floating-rate leg of the swap.
    C. difference between the fixed and floating legs of the swap.
23. A two-year fixed-for-floating MRR swap is 1.00%, and the two-year US Treasury bond is yielding 0.63%. The swap spread is *closest* to:
    A. 37 bps.
    B. 100 bps.
    C. 163 bps.
24. The swap spread is quoted as 50 bps. If the five-year US Treasury bond is yielding 2%, the rate paid by the fixed payer in a five-year interest rate swap is *closest* to:
    A. 0.50%.
    B. 1.50%.
    C. 2.50%.
25. If the three-month T-bill rate drops and Libor remains the same, the relevant TED spread:
    A. increases.
    B. decreases.
    C. does not change.
26. Given the yield curve for US Treasury zero-coupon bonds, which spread is *most* helpful pricing a corporate bond? The:
    A. Z-spread.
    B. TED spread.
    C. Libor–OIS spread.

The following information relates to Questions 27–33

Jane Nguyen is a senior bond trader for an investment bank, and Chris Alexander is a junior bond trader at the bank. Nguyen is responsible for her own trading activities and also for providing assignments to Alexander that will develop his skills and create profitable trade ideas. Exhibit 1 presents the current par and spot rates.

EXHIBIT 1   Current Par and Spot Rates

Maturity	Par Rate	Spot Rate
One year	2.50%	2.50%
Two years	2.99%	3.00%
Three years	3.48%	3.50%
Four years	3.95%	4.00%
Five years	4.37%	

Note: Par and spot rates are based on annual-coupon sovereign bonds.

Nguyen gives Alexander two assignments that involve researching various questions:

Assignment 1:   What is the yield-to-maturity of the option-free, default-risk-free bond presented in Exhibit 2? Assume that the bond is held to maturity, and use the rates shown in Exhibit 1.

EXHIBIT 2   Selected Data for $1,000 Par Bond

Bond Name	Maturity (*T*)	Coupon
Bond Z	Three years	6.00%

Note: Terms are today for a *T*-year loan.

Assignment 2:   Assuming that the projected spot curve two years from today will be below the current forward curve, is Bond Z fairly valued, undervalued, or overvalued?

After completing his assignments, Alexander asks about Nguyen's current trading activities. Nguyen states that she has a two-year investment horizon and will purchase Bond Z as part of a strategy to ride the yield curve. Exhibit 1 shows Nguyen's yield curve assumptions implied by the spot rates.

27. Based on Exhibit 1, the five-year spot rate is *closest* to:
    A. 4.40%.
    B. 4.45%.
    C. 4.50%.
28. Based on Exhibit 1, the market is *most likely* expecting:
    A. deflation.
    B. inflation.
    C. no risk premiums.
29. Based on Exhibit 1, the forward rate of a one-year loan beginning in three years is *closest* to:
    A. 4.17%.
    B. 4.50%.
    C. 5.51%.
30. Based on Exhibit 1, which of the following forward rates can be computed?
    A. A one-year loan beginning in five years
    B. A three-year loan beginning in three years
    C. A four-year loan beginning in one year

31. For Assignment 1, the yield-to-maturity for Bond Z is *closest* to the:
    A. one-year spot rate.
    B. two-year spot rate.
    C. three-year spot rate.

32. For Assignment 2, Alexander should conclude that Bond Z is currently:
    A. undervalued.
    B. fairly valued.
    C. overvalued.

33. By choosing to buy Bond Z, Nguyen is *most likely* making which of the following assumptions?
    A. Bond Z will be held to maturity.
    B. The three-year forward curve is above the spot curve.
    C. Future spot rates do not accurately reflect future inflation.

The following information relates to Questions 34–38

Laura Mathews recently hired Robert Smith, an investment adviser at Shire Gate Advisers, to assist her in investing. Mathews states that her investment time horizon is short, approximately two years or less. Smith gathers information on spot rates for on-the-run annual-coupon government securities and swap spreads, as presented in Exhibit 1. Shire Gate Advisers recently published a report for its clients stating its belief that, based on the weakness in the financial markets, interest rates will remain stable, the yield curve will not change its level or shape for the next two years, and swap spreads will also remain unchanged.

EXHIBIT 1   Government Spot Rates and Swap Spreads

	Maturity (years)			
	1	2	3	4
Government spot rate	2.25%	2.70%	3.30%	4.05%
Swap spread	0.25%	0.30%	0.45%	0.70%

Smith decides to examine the following three investment options for Mathews:

Investment 1:   Buy a government security that would have an annualized return that is nearly risk free. Smith is considering two possible implementations: a two-year investment or a combination of two one-year investments.

Investment 2:   Buy a four-year, zero-coupon corporate bond and then sell it after two years. Smith illustrates the returns from this strategy using the swap rate as a proxy for corporate yields.

Investment 3:   Buy a lower-quality, two-year corporate bond with a coupon rate of 4.15% and a Z-spread of 65 bps.

When Smith meets with Mathews to present these choices, Mathews tells him that she is somewhat confused by the various spread measures. She is curious to know whether there is one spread measure that could be used as a good indicator of the risk and liquidity of money market securities during the recent past.

34. In his presentation of Investment 1, Smith could show that under the no-arbitrage principle, the forward price of a one-year government bond to be issued in one year is *closest* to:
   A. 0.9662.
   B. 0.9694.
   C. 0.9780.
35. In presenting Investment 1, using Shire Gate Advisers' interest rate outlook, Smith could show that riding the yield curve provides a total return that is *most likely*:
   A. lower than the return on a maturity-matching strategy.
   B. equal to the return on a maturity-matching strategy.
   C. higher than the return on a maturity-matching strategy.
36. In presenting Investment 2, Smith should show an annual return *closest* to:
   A. 4.31%.
   B. 5.42%.
   C. 6.53%.
37. The bond in Investment 3 is *most likely* trading at a price of:
   A. 100.97.
   B. 101.54.
   C. 104.09.
38. The *most* appropriate response to Mathews' question regarding a spread measure is the:
   A. Z-spread.
   B. TED spread.
   C. Libor–OIS spread.

The following information relates to Questions 39–42

Rowan Madison is a junior analyst at Cardinal Capital. Sage Winter, a senior portfolio manager and Madison's supervisor, meets with Madison to discuss interest rates and review two bond positions in the firm's fixed-income portfolio.

Winter begins the meeting by asking Madison to state her views on the term structure of interest rates. Madison responds:

> "Yields are a reflection of expected spot rates and risk premiums. Investors demand risk premiums for holding long-term bonds, and these risk premiums increase with maturity."

Winter tells Madison that, based on recent changes in spreads, she is concerned about a perceived increase in counterparty risk in the economy and its effect on the portfolio. Madison asks Winter:

> "Which spread measure should we use to assess changes in counterparty risk in the economy?"

Winter is also worried about the effect of yield volatility on the portfolio. She asks Madison to identify the economic factors that affect short-term and long-term rate volatility. Madison responds:

> "Short-term rate volatility is mostly linked to uncertainty regarding monetary policy, whereas long-term rate volatility is mostly linked to uncertainty regarding the real economy and inflation."

Finally, Winter asks Madison to analyze the interest rate risk portfolio positions in a 5-year and a 20-year bond. Winter requests that the analysis be based on level, slope, and curvature as term structure factors. Madison presents her analysis in Exhibit 1.

EXHIBIT 1   Three-Factor Model of Term Structure

	Time to Maturity (years)	
Factor	5	20
Level	−0.4352%	−0.5128%
Steepness	−0.0515%	−0.3015%
Curvature	0.3963%	0.5227%

Note: Entries indicate how yields would change for a one standard deviation increase in a factor.

Winter asks Madison to perform two analyses:

Analysis 1:   Calculate the expected change in yield on the 20-year bond resulting from a two-standard-deviation increase in the steepness factor.

Analysis 2:   Calculate the expected change in yield on the five-year bond resulting from a one-standard-deviation decrease in the level factor and a one-standard-deviation decrease in the curvature factor.

39. Madison's views on the term structure of interest rates are *most* consistent with the:
   A. local expectations theory.
   B. segmented markets theory.
   C. liquidity preference theory.
40. Is Madison's response regarding the factors that affect short-term and long-term rate volatility correct?
   A. Yes
   B. No, she is incorrect regarding factors linked to long-term rate volatility
   C. No, she is incorrect regarding factors linked to short-term rate volatility
41. Based on Exhibit 1, the results of Analysis 1 should show the yield on the 20-year bond decreasing by:
   A. 0.3015%.
   B. 0.6030%.
   C. 0.8946%.
42. Based on Exhibit 1, the results of Analysis 2 should show the yield on the five-year bond:
   A. decreasing by 0.8315%.
   B. decreasing by 0.0389%.
   C. increasing by 0.0389%.

The following information relates to Questions 43–50

Liz Tyo is a fund manager for an actively managed global fixed-income fund that buys bonds issued in Countries A, B, and C. She and her assistant are preparing the quarterly markets update. Tyo begins the meeting by distributing the daily rates sheet, which includes the current government spot rates for Countries A, B, and C as shown in Exhibit 1.

EXHIBIT 1   Today's Government Spot Rates

Maturity	Country A	Country B	Country C
One year	0.40%	−0.22%	14.00%
Two years	0.70	−0.20	12.40
Three years	1.00	−0.12	11.80
Four years	1.30	−0.02	11.00
Five years	1.50	0.13	10.70

Tyo asks her assistant how these spot rates were obtained. The assistant replies, "Spot rates are determined through the process of bootstrapping. It entails backward substitution using par yields to solve for zero-coupon rates one by one, in order from latest to earliest maturities."

Tyo then provides a review of the fund's performance during the last year and comments, "The choice of an appropriate benchmark depends on the country's characteristics. For example, although Countries A and B have both an active government bond market and a swap market, Country C's private sector is much bigger than its public sector, and its government bond market lacks liquidity."

Tyo further points out, "The fund's results were mixed; returns did not benefit from taking on additional risk. We are especially monitoring the riskiness of the corporate bond holdings. For example, our largest holdings consist of three four-year corporate bonds (Bonds 1, 2, and 3) with identical maturities, coupon rates, and other contract terms. These bonds have Z-spreads of 0.55%, 1.52%, and 1.76%, respectively."

Tyo continues, "We also look at risk in terms of the swap spread. We considered historical three-year swap spreads for Country B, which reflect that market's credit and liquidity risks, at three different points in time." Tyo provides the information in Exhibit 2.

EXHIBIT 2   Selected Historical Three-Year Rates for Country B

Period	Government Bond Yield (%)	Fixed-for-Floating Libor Swap (%)
1 month ago	−0.10	0.16
6 months ago	−0.08	0.01
12 months ago	−0.07	0.71

Tyo then suggests that the firm was able to add return by riding the yield curve. The fund plans to continue to use this strategy but only in markets with an attractive yield curve for this strategy.

She moves on to present her market views on the respective yield curves for a five-year investment horizon.

Country A: "The government yield curve has changed little in terms of its level and shape during the last few years, and I expect this trend to continue. We assume that future spot rates reflect the current forward curve for all maturities."

Country B: "Because of recent economic trends, I expect a reversal in the slope of the current yield curve. We assume that future spot rates will be higher than current forward rates for all maturities."

Country C: "To improve liquidity, Country C's central bank is expected to intervene, leading to a reversal in the slope of the existing yield curve. We assume that future spot rates will be lower than today's forward rates for all maturities."

Tyo's assistant asks, "Assuming investors require liquidity premiums, how can a yield curve slope downward? What does this imply about forward rates?"

Tyo answers, "Even if investors require compensation for holding longer-term bonds, the yield curve can slope downward—for example, if there is an expectation of severe deflation. Regarding forward rates, it can be helpful to understand yield curve dynamics by calculating implied forward rates. To see what I mean, we can use Exhibit 1 to calculate the forward rate for a two-year Country C loan beginning in three years."

43. Did Tyo's assistant accurately describe the process of bootstrapping?
   A. Yes
   B. No, with respect to par yields
   C. No, with respect to backward substitution
44. The swap curve is a better benchmark than the government spot curve for:
   A. Country A.
   B. Country B.
   C. Country C.
45. Based on Exhibit 2, the implied credit and liquidity risks as indicated by the historical three-year swap spreads for Country B were the lowest:
   A. 1 month ago.
   B. 6 months ago.
   C. 12 months ago.
46. Based on Exhibit 1 and Tyo's expectations, which country's term structure is currently best for traders seeking to ride the yield curve?
   A. Country A
   B. Country B
   C. Country C
47. Based on Exhibit 1 and assuming Tyo's market views on yield curve changes are realized, the forward curve of which country will lie below its spot curve?
   A. Country A
   B. Country B
   C. Country C
48. Based on Exhibit 1 and Tyo's expectations for the yield curves, Tyo *most likely* perceives the bonds of which country to be fairly valued?
   A. Country A
   B. Country B
   C. Country C
49. With respect to their discussion of yield curves, Tyo and her assistant are *most likely* discussing which term structure theory?
   A. Pure expectations theory
   B. Local expectations theory
   C. Liquidity preference theory
50. Tyo's assistant should calculate a forward rate *closest* to:
   A. 9.07%.
   B. 9.58%.
   C. 9.97%.

51. During economic expansions, monetary authorities raise benchmark rates to help control inflation. This action is *most often* consistent with:
    A. bearish flattening.
    B. bullish steepening.
    C. bearish steepening.
52. When government budget deficits fall, fiscal supply-side effects are *most likely* to result in:
    A. higher bond yields.
    B. a steeper yield curve.
    C. lower bond yields.
53. A flight to quality is *most often* associated with:
    A. a general rise in the level of interest rates.
    B. bullish flattening.
    C. bearish flattening.

CHAPTER 8

THE ARBITRAGE-FREE VALUATION FRAMEWORK

LEARNING OUTCOMES

The candidate should be able to:

- explain what is meant by arbitrage-free valuation of a fixed-income instrument;
- calculate the arbitrage-free value of an option-free, fixed-rate coupon bond;
- describe a binomial interest rate tree framework;
- describe the process of calibrating a binomial interest rate tree to match a specific term structure;
- describe the backward induction valuation methodology and calculate the value of a fixed-income instrument given its cash flow at each node;
- compare pricing using the zero-coupon yield curve with pricing using an arbitrage-free binomial lattice;
- describe pathwise valuation in a binomial interest rate framework and calculate the value of a fixed-income instrument given its cash flows along each path;
- describe a Monte Carlo forward-rate simulation and its application;
- describe term structure models and how they are used.

SUMMARY OVERVIEW

This chapter presents the principles and tools for arbitrage valuation of fixed-income securities. Much of the discussion centers on the binomial interest rate tree, which can be used extensively to value both option-free bonds and bonds with embedded options. The following are the main points made in the chapter:

- A fundamental principle of valuation is that the value of any financial asset is equal to the present value of its expected future cash flows.

- A fixed-income security is a portfolio of zero-coupon bonds, each with its own discount rate that depends on the shape of the yield curve and when the cash flow is delivered in time.
- In well-functioning markets, prices adjust until there are no opportunities for arbitrage, or a transaction that involves no cash outlay yet results in a riskless profit.
- Using the arbitrage-free approach, viewing a security as a package of zero-coupon bonds means that two bonds with the same maturity and different coupon rates are viewed as different packages of zero-coupon bonds and valued accordingly.
- For bonds that are option-free, an arbitrage-free value is simply the present value of expected future values using the benchmark spot rates.
- A binomial interest rate tree permits the short interest rate to take on one of two possible values consistent with the volatility assumption and an interest rate model based on a log-normal random walk.
- An interest rate tree is a visual representation of the possible values of interest rates (forward rates) based on an interest rate model and an assumption about interest rate volatility.
- The possible interest rates for any following period are consistent with the following three assumptions: (1) an interest rate model that governs the random process of interest rates, (2) the assumed level of interest rate volatility, and (3) the current benchmark yield curve.
- From the lognormal distribution, adjacent interest rates on the tree are multiples of e raised to the 2σ power, with the absolute change in interest rates becoming smaller and smaller as rates approach zero.
- We use the backward induction valuation methodology that involves starting at maturity, filling in those values, and working back from right to left to find the bond's value at the desired node.
- The interest rate tree is fit to the current yield curve by choosing interest rates that result in the benchmark bond value. By doing this, the bond value is arbitrage free.
- An option-free bond that is valued by using the binomial interest rate tree should have the same value as when discounting by the spot rates.
- Pathwise valuation calculates the present value of a bond for each possible interest rate path and takes the average of these values across paths.
- The Monte Carlo method is an alternative method for simulating a sufficiently large number of potential interest rate paths in an effort to discover how the value of a security is affected, and it involves randomly selecting paths in an effort to approximate the results of a complete pathwise valuation.
- Term structure models seek to explain the yield curve shape and are used to value bonds (including those with embedded options) and bond-related derivatives. General equilibrium and arbitrage-free models are the two major types of such models.
- Arbitrage-free models are frequently used to value bonds with embedded options. Unlike equilibrium models, arbitrage-free models begin with the observed market prices of a reference set of financial instruments, and the underlying assumption is that the reference set is correctly priced.

PROBLEMS

The following information relates to Questions 1–6

Katrina Black, a portfolio manager at Coral Bond Management, Ltd., is conducting a training session with Alex Sun, a junior analyst in the fixed-income department. Black wants to explain to Sun the arbitrage-free valuation framework used by the firm. Black presents Sun with Exhibit 1, showing a fictitious bond being traded on three exchanges, and asks Sun to identify the arbitrage opportunity of the bond. Sun agrees to ignore transaction costs in his analysis.

EXHIBIT 1   Three-Year, €100 par, 3.00% Coupon, Annual Pay Option-Free Bond

	Eurex	NYSE Euronext	Frankfurt
Price	€103.7956	€103.7815	€103.7565

Black shows Sun some exhibits that were part of a recent presentation. Exhibit 3 presents most of the data of a binomial lognormal interest rate tree fit to the yield curve shown in Exhibit 2. Exhibit 4 presents most of the data of the implied values for a four-year, option-free, annual pay bond with a 2.5% coupon based on the information in Exhibit 3.

EXHIBIT 2   Yield-to-Maturity Par Rates for One-, Two-, and Three-Year Annual Pay Option-Free Bonds

One-year	Two-year	Three-year
1.25%	1.50%	1.70%

EXHIBIT 3   Binomial Interest Rate Tree Fit to the Yield Curve (Volatility = 10%)

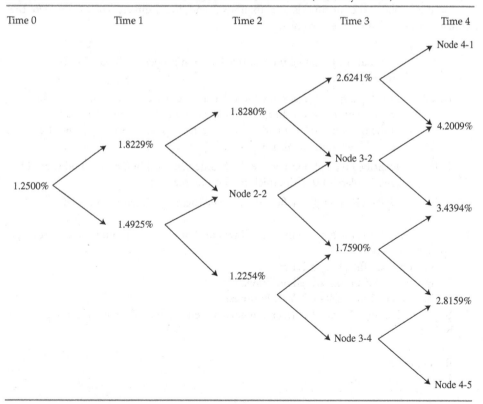

EXHIBIT 4   Implied Values (in Euros) for a 2.5%, Four-Year, Option-Free, Annual Pay Bond Based on Exhibit 3

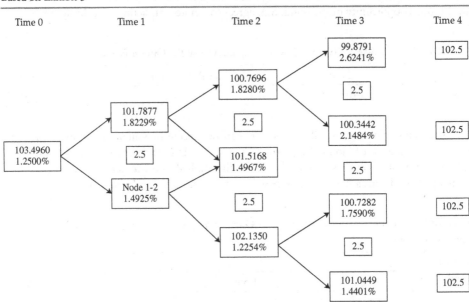

Black asks about the missing data in Exhibits 3 and 4 and directs Sun to complete the following tasks related to those exhibits:

Task 1   Test that the binomial interest tree has been properly calibrated to be arbitrage free.

Task 2   Develop a spreadsheet model to calculate pathwise valuations. To test the accuracy of the spreadsheet, use the data in Exhibit 3 and calculate the value of the bond if it takes a path of lowest rates in Year 1 and Year 2 and the second lowest rate in Year 3.

Task 3   Identify a type of bond where the Monte Carlo calibration method should be used in place of the binomial interest rate method.

Task 4   Update Exhibit 3 to reflect the current volatility, which is now 15%.

1. Based on Exhibit 1, the *best* action that an investor should take to profit from the arbitrage opportunity is to:
   A. buy on Frankfurt, sell on Eurex.
   B. buy on NYSE Euronext, sell on Eurex.
   C. buy on Frankfurt, sell on NYSE Euronext.
2. Based on Exhibits 1 and 2, the exchange that reflects the arbitrage-free price of the bond is:
   A. Eurex.
   B. Frankfurt.
   C. NYSE Euronext.

3. Recall from the chapter that each node is represented by both a time element and a rate change component. Which of the following statements about the missing data in Exhibit 3 is correct?

   A. Node 3–2 can be derived from Node 2–2.

   B. Node 4–1 should be equal to Node 4–5 multiplied by $e^{0.4}$.

   C. Node 2–2 approximates the implied one-year forward rate two years from now.

4. Based on the information in Exhibits 3 and 4, the bond price in euros at Node 1–2 in Exhibit 4 is *closest* to:

   A. 102.7917.

   B. 104.8640.

   C. 105.2917.

5. A benefit of performing Task 1 is that it:

   A. enables the model to price bonds with embedded options.

   B. identifies benchmark bonds that have been mispriced by the market.

   C. allows investors to realize arbitrage profits through stripping and reconstitution.

6. If the assumed volatility is changed as Black requested in Task 4, the forward rates shown in Exhibit 3 will *most likely*:

   A. spread out.

   B. remain unchanged.

   C. converge to the spot rates.

The following information relates to Questions 7–10

Betty Tatton is a fixed-income analyst with the hedge fund Sailboat Asset Management (SAM). SAM invests in a variety of global fixed-income strategies, including fixed-income arbitrage. Tatton is responsible for pricing individual investments and analyzing market data to assess the opportunity for arbitrage. She uses two methods to value bonds:

Method 1:   Discount each year's cash flow separately using the appropriate interest rate curve.

Method 2:   Build and use a binomial interest rate tree.

Tatton compiles pricing data for a list of annual pay bonds (Exhibit 1). Each of the bonds will mature in two years, and Tatton considers the bonds risk-free; both the one-year and two-year benchmark spot rates are 2%. Tatton calculates the arbitrage-free prices and identifies an arbitrage opportunity to recommend to her team.

EXHIBIT 1   Market Data for Selected Bonds

Asset	Coupon	Market Price
Bond A	1%	98.0584
Bond B	3%	100.9641
Bond C	5%	105.8247

Next, Tatton uses the benchmark yield curve provided in Exhibit 2 to consider arbitrage opportunities of both option-free corporate bonds and corporate bonds with embedded options. The benchmark bonds in Exhibit 2 pay coupons annually, and the bonds are priced at par.

EXHIBIT 2   Benchmark Par Curve

Maturity (years)	Yield-to-Maturity (YTM)
1	3.0%
2	4.0%
3	5.0%

Tatton then identifies three mispriced three-year annual coupon bonds and compiles data on the bonds (see Exhibit 3).

EXHIBIT 3   Market Data of Annual Pay Corporate Bonds

Company	Coupon	Market Price	Yield	Embedded Option?
Hutto-Barkley Inc.	3%	94.9984	5.6%	No
Luna y Estrellas Intl.	0%	88.8996	4.0%	Yes
Peaton Scorpio Motors	0%	83.9619	6.0%	No

Lastly, Tatton identifies two mispriced Swiss bonds, Bond X, a three-year bond, and Bond Y, a five-year bond. Both are 6% annual coupon bonds. To calculate the bonds' values, Tatton devises the first three years of the interest rate lognormal tree presented in Exhibit 4 using historical interest rate volatility data. Tatton considers how these data would change if implied volatility, which is higher than historical volatility, were used instead.

EXHIBIT 4   Interest Rate Tree—Forward Rates Based on Swiss Market

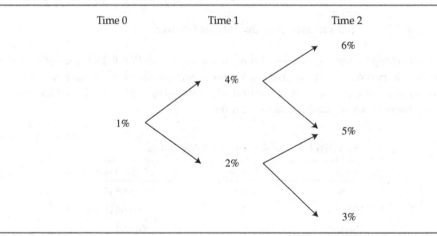

7. Based on Exhibit 1, which of the following bonds *most likely* includes an arbitrage oppor-
   tunity?
   A. Bond A
   B. Bond B
   C. Bond C

8. Based on Exhibits 2 and 3 and using Method 1, the amount (in absolute terms) by which
   the Hutto-Barkley Inc. corporate bond is mispriced is *closest* to:
   A. 0.3368 per 100 of par value.
   B. 0.4682 per 100 of par value.
   C. 0.5156 per 100 of par value.

9. Method 1 would *most likely* not be an appropriate valuation technique for the bond
   issued by:
   A. Hutto-Barkley Inc.
   B. Luna y Estrellas Intl.
   C. Peaton Scorpio Motors.

10. Based on Exhibit 4 and using Method 2, the correct price for Bond X is *closest* to:
    A. 97.2998.
    B. 109.0085.
    C. 115.0085.

The following information relates to Questions 11–18

Meredith Alvarez is a junior fixed-income analyst with Canzim Asset Management. Her supervisor, Stephanie Hartson, asks Alvarez to review the asset price and payoff data shown in
Exhibit 1 to determine whether an arbitrage opportunity exists.

EXHIBIT 1   Price and Payoffs for Two Risk-Free Assets

Asset	Price Today	Payoff in One Year
Asset A	$500	$525
Asset B	$1,000	$1,100

Hartson also shows Alvarez data for a bond that trades in three different markets in the
same currency. These data appear in Exhibit 2.

EXHIBIT 2   2% Coupon, Five-Year Maturity, Annual Pay Bond

	New York	Hong Kong	Mumbai
Yield-to-Maturity	1.9%	2.3%	2.0%

Hartson asks Alvarez to value two bonds (Bond C and Bond D) using the binomial tree
in Exhibit 3. Exhibit 4 presents selected data for both bonds.

EXHIBIT 3   Binomial Interest Rate Tree with Volatility = 25%

Time 0	Time 1	Time 2
		2.7183%
	2.8853%	
1.500%		1.6487%
	1.7500%	
		1.0000%

EXHIBIT 4   Selected Data on Annual Pay Bonds

Bond	Maturity	Coupon Rate
Bond C	2 years	2.5%
Bond D	3 years	3.0%

Hartson tells Alvarez that she and her peers have been debating various viewpoints regarding the conditions underlying binomial interest rate trees. The following statements were made in the course of the debate.

Statement 1: The only requirements needed to create a binomial interest rate tree are current benchmark interest rates and an assumption about interest rate volatility.

Statement 2: Potential interest rate volatility in a binomial interest rate tree can be estimated using historical interest rate volatility or observed market prices from interest rate derivatives.

Statement 3: A bond value derived from a binomial interest rate tree with a relatively high volatility assumption will be different from the value calculated by discounting the bond's cash flows using current spot rates.

Based on data in Exhibit 5, Hartson asks Alvarez to calibrate a binomial interest rate tree starting with the calculation of implied forward rates shown in Exhibit 6.

EXHIBIT 5   Selected Data for a Binomial Interest Rate Tree

Maturity	Par Rate	Spot Rate
1	2.5000%	2.5000%
2	3.5000%	3.5177%

EXHIBIT 6   Calibration of Binomial Interest Rate Tree with Volatility = 25%

Time 0	Time 1
	5.8365%
2.500%	
	Lower one-period forward rate

Hartson mentions pathwise valuations as another method to value bonds using a binomial interest rate tree. Using the binomial interest rate tree in Exhibit 3, Alvarez calculates the possible interest rate paths for Bond D shown in Exhibit 7.

EXHIBIT 7   Interest Rate Paths for Bond D

Path	Time 0	Time 1	Time 2
1	1.500%	2.8853%	2.7183%
2	1.500	2.8853	1.6487
3	1.500	1.7500	1.6487
4	1.500	1.7500	1.0000

Before leaving for the day, Hartson asks Alvarez about the value of using the Monte Carlo method to simulate a large number of potential interest rate paths to value a bond. Alvarez makes the following statements.

Statement 4:   Increasing the number of paths increases the estimate's statistical accuracy.

Statement 5:   The bond value derived from a Monte Carlo simulation will be closer to the bond's true fundamental value.

11. Based on Exhibit 1, Alvarez finds that an arbitrage opportunity is:
   A. not available.
   B. available based on the dominance principle.
   C. available based on the value additivity principle.
12. Based on the data in Exhibit 2, the *most* profitable arbitrage opportunity would be to buy the bond in:
   A. Mumbai and sell it in Hong Kong.
   B. Hong Kong and sell it in New York.
   C. New York and sell it in Hong Kong.
13. Based on Exhibits 3 and 4, the value of Bond C at the upper node at Time 1 is *closest* to:
   A. 97.1957.
   B. 99.6255.
   C. 102.1255.
14. Based on Exhibits 3 and 4, the price for Bond D is *closest* to:
   A. 97.4785.
   B. 103.3230.
   C. 106.3230.
15. Which of the various statements regarding binomial interest rate trees is correct?
   A. Statement 1
   B. Statement 2
   C. Statement 3
16. Based on Exhibits 5 and 6, the value of the lower one-period forward rate is *closest* to:
   A. 3.5122%.
   B. 3.5400%.
   C. 4.8037%.

17. Based on Exhibits 4 and 7, the present value of Bond D's cash flows following Path 2 is *closest* to:
    A. 97.0322.
    B. 102.8607.
    C. 105.8607.
18. Which of the statements regarding Monte Carlo simulation is correct?
    A. Only Statement 4 is correct.
    B. Only Statement 5 is correct.
    C. Both Statement 4 and Statement 5 are correct.

---

19. Which term structure model can be calibrated to closely fit an observed yield curve?
    A. The Ho–Lee model
    B. The Vasicek model
    C. The Cox–Ingersoll–Ross model

The following information relates to Questions 20–21

Keisha Jones is a junior analyst at Sparling Capital. Julie Anderson, a senior partner and Jones's manager, meets with Jones to discuss interest rate models used for the firm's fixed-income portfolio.

Anderson begins the meeting by asking Jones to describe features of equilibrium and arbitrage-free term structure models. Jones responds by making the following statements:

Statement 1: Equilibrium term structure models are factor models that use the observed market prices of a reference set of financial instruments, assumed to be correctly priced, to model the market yield curve.

Statement 2: In contrast, arbitrage-free term structure models seek to describe the dynamics of the term structure by using fundamental economic variables that are assumed to affect interest rates.

Anderson then asks Jones about her preferences concerning term structure models. Jones states:
I prefer arbitrage-free models. Even though equilibrium models require fewer parameters to be estimated relative to arbitrage-free models, arbitrage-free models allow for time-varying parameters. In general, this allowance leads to arbitrage-free models being able to model the market yield curve more precisely than equilibrium models.

20. Which of Jones's statements regarding equilibrium and arbitrage-free term structure models is *incorrect*?
    A. Statement 1 only
    B. Statement 2 only
    C. Both Statement 1 and Statement 2
21. Is Jones correct in describing key differences in equilibrium and arbitrage-free models as they relate to the number of parameters and model accuracy?
    A. Yes
    B. No, she is incorrect about which type of model requires fewer parameter estimates.
    C. No, she is incorrect about which type of model is more precise at modeling market yield curves.

---

22. Which of the following statements comparing the Ho–Lee and Kalotay–Williams–Fabozzi (KWF) equilibrium term structure models is *correct*?
    A. The Ho–Lee model assumes constant volatility, while the KWF model does not.
    B. The KWF model incorporates the possibility of negative rates, while the Ho–Lee model does not.
    C. The KWF model describes the log of the dynamics of the short rate, while the Ho–Lee model does not.

VALUATION AND ANALYSIS OF BONDS WITH EMBEDDED OPTIONS

LEARNING OUTCOMES

The candidate should be able to:

- describe fixed-income securities with embedded options;
- explain the relationships between the values of a callable or putable bond, the underlying option-free (straight) bond, and the embedded option;
- describe how the arbitrage-free framework can be used to value a bond with embedded options;
- explain how interest rate volatility affects the value of a callable or putable bond;
- explain how changes in the level and shape of the yield curve affect the value of a callable or putable bond;
- calculate the value of a callable or putable bond from an interest rate tree;
- explain the calculation and use of option-adjusted spreads;
- explain how interest rate volatility affects option-adjusted spreads;
- calculate and interpret effective duration of a callable or putable bond;
- compare effective durations of callable, putable, and straight bonds;
- describe the use of one-sided durations and key rate durations to evaluate the interest rate sensitivity of bonds with embedded options;
- compare effective convexities of callable, putable, and straight bonds;
- calculate the value of a capped or floored floating-rate bond;
- describe defining features of a convertible bond;
- calculate and interpret the components of a convertible bond's value;
- describe how a convertible bond is valued in an arbitrage-free framework;
- compare the risk–return characteristics of a convertible bond with the risk–return characteristics of a straight bond and of the underlying common stock.

SUMMARY OVERVIEW

- An embedded option represents a right that can be exercised by the issuer, by the bondholder, or automatically depending on the course of interest rates. It is attached to, or embedded in, an underlying option-free bond called a straight bond.
- Simple embedded option structures include call options, put options, and extension options. Callable and putable bonds can be redeemed prior to maturity, at the discretion of the issuer in the former case and of the bondholder in the latter case. An extendible bond gives the bondholder the right to keep the bond for a number of years after maturity. Putable and extendible bonds are equivalent, except that their underlying option-free bonds are different.
- Complex embedded option structures include bonds with other types of options or combinations of options. For example, a convertible bond includes a conversion option that allows the bondholders to convert their bonds into the issuer's common stock. A bond with an estate put can be put by the heirs of a deceased bondholder. Sinking fund bonds make the issuer set aside funds over time to retire the bond issue and are often callable, may have an acceleration provision, and may also contain a delivery option. Valuing and analyzing bonds with complex embedded option structures is challenging.
- According to the arbitrage-free framework, the value of a bond with an embedded option is equal to the arbitrage-free values of its parts—that is, the arbitrage-free value of the straight bond and the arbitrage-free values of each of the embedded options.
- Because the call option is an issuer option, the value of the call option decreases the value of the callable bond relative to an otherwise identical but non-callable bond. In contrast, because the put option is an investor option, the value of the put option increases the value of the putable bond relative to an otherwise identical but non-putable bond.
- In the absence of default and interest rate volatility, the bond's future cash flows are certain. Thus, the value of a callable or putable bond can be calculated by discounting the bond's future cash flows at the appropriate one-period forward rates, taking into consideration the decision to exercise the option. If a bond is callable, the decision to exercise the option is made by the issuer, which will exercise the call option when the value of the bond's future cash flows is higher than the call price. In contrast, if the bond is putable, the decision to exercise the option is made by the bondholder, who will exercise the put option when the value of the bond's future cash flows is lower than the put price.
- In practice, interest rates fluctuate and interest rate volatility affects the value of embedded options. Thus, when valuing bonds with embedded options, it is important to consider the possible evolution of the yield curve over time.
- Interest rate volatility is modeled using a binomial interest rate tree. The higher the volatility, the lower the value of the callable bond and the higher the value of the putable bond.
- Valuing a bond with embedded options assuming an interest rate volatility requires three steps: (1) Generate a tree of interest rates based on the given yield curve and volatility assumptions; (2) at each node of the tree, determine whether the embedded options will be exercised; and (3) apply the backward induction valuation methodology to calculate the present value of the bond.
- The option-adjusted spread is the single spread added uniformly to the one-period forward rates on the tree to produce a value or price for a bond. OAS is sensitive to interest rate volatility: The higher the volatility, the lower the OAS for a callable bond.
- For bonds with embedded options, the best measure to assess the sensitivity of the bond's price to a parallel shift of the benchmark yield curve is effective duration. The effective duration of a callable or putable bond cannot exceed that of the straight bond.

- When the option is near the money, the convexity of a callable bond is negative, indicating that the upside for a callable bond is much smaller than the downside, whereas the convexity of a putable bond is positive, indicating that the upside for a putable bond is much larger than the downside.
- Because the prices of callable and putable bonds respond asymmetrically to upward and downward interest rate changes of the same magnitude, one-sided durations provide a better indication regarding the interest rate sensitivity of bonds with embedded options than (two-sided) effective duration.
- Key rate durations show the effect of shifting only key points, one at a time, rather than the entire yield curve.
- The arbitrage-free framework can be used to value capped and floored floaters. The cap provision in a floater is an issuer option that prevents the coupon rate from increasing above a specified maximum rate. Thus, the value of a capped floater is equal to or less than the value of the straight bond. In contrast, the floor provision in a floater is an investor option that prevents the coupon from decreasing below a specified minimum rate. Thus, the value of a floored floater is equal to or higher than the value of the straight bond.
- The characteristics of a convertible bond include the conversion price, which is the applicable share price at which the bondholders can convert their bonds into common shares, and the conversion ratio, which reflects the number of shares of common stock that the bondholders receive from converting their bonds into shares. The conversion price is adjusted in case of corporate actions, such as stock splits, bonus share issuances, and rights and warrants issuances. Convertible bondholders may receive compensation when the issuer pays dividends to its common shareholders, and they may be given the opportunity to either put their bonds or convert their bonds into shares earlier and at more advantageous terms in the case of a change of control.
- A number of investment metrics and ratios help analyze and value convertible bonds. The conversion value indicates the value of the bond if it is converted at the market price of the shares. The minimum value of a convertible bond sets a floor value for the convertible bond at the greater of the conversion value or the straight value. This floor is moving, however, because the straight value is not fixed. The market conversion premium represents the price investors effectively pay for the underlying shares if they buy the convertible bond and then convert it into shares. Scaled by the market price of the shares, it represents the premium payable when buying the convertible bond rather than the underlying common stock.
- Because convertible bonds combine characteristics of bonds, stocks, and options, as well as potentially other features, their valuation and analysis are challenging. Convertible bond investors should consider the factors that affect not only bond prices but also the underlying share price.
- The arbitrage-free framework can be used to value convertible bonds, including callable and putable ones. Each component (straight bond, call option of the stock, and call and/or put option on the bond) can be valued separately.
- The risk–return characteristics of a convertible bond depend on the underlying share price relative to the conversion price. When the underlying share price is well below the conversion price, the convertible bond is "busted" and exhibits mostly bond risk–return characteristics. Thus, it is mainly sensitive to interest rate movements. In contrast, when the underlying share price is well above the conversion price, the convertible bond exhibits mostly stock risk–return characteristics. Thus, its price follows similar movements to the price of the underlying stock. In between these two extremes, the convertible bond trades like a hybrid instrument.

PROBLEMS

The following information relates to Questions 1–10

Samuel & Sons is a fixed-income specialty firm that offers advisory services to investment management companies. On 1 October 20X0, Steele Ferguson, a senior analyst at Samuel, is reviewing three fixed-rate bonds issued by a local firm, Pro Star, Inc. The three bonds, whose characteristics are given in Exhibit 1, carry the highest credit rating.

EXHIBIT 1   Fixed-Rate Bonds Issued by Pro Star, Inc.

Bond	Maturity	Coupon	Type of Bond
Bond #1	1 October 20X3	4.40% annual	Option-free
Bond #2	1 October 20X3	4.40% annual	Callable at par on 1 October 20X1 and on 1 October 20X2
Bond #3	1 October 20X3	4.40% annual	Putable at par on 1 October 20X1 and on 1 October 20X2

The one-year, two-year, and three-year par rates are 2.250%, 2.750%, and 3.100%, respectively. Based on an estimated interest rate volatility of 10%, Ferguson constructs the binomial interest rate tree shown in Exhibit 2.

EXHIBIT 2   Binomial Interest Rate Tree

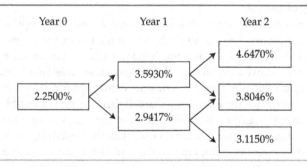

On 19 October 20X0, Ferguson analyzes the convertible bond issued by Pro Star given in Exhibit 3. That day, the option-free value of Pro Star's convertible bond is $1,060 and its stock price $37.50.

EXHIBIT 3   Convertible Bond Issued by Pro Star, Inc.

Issue Date:	6 December 20X0
Maturity Date:	6 December 20X4
Coupon Rate:	2%
Issue Price:	$1,000
Conversion Ratio:	31

1. The call feature of Bond #2 is *best* described as:
   A. European style.
   B. American style.
   C. Bermudan style.
2. The bond that would *most likely* protect investors against a significant increase in interest rates is:
   A. Bond #1.
   B. Bond #2.
   C. Bond #3.
3. A fall in interest rates would *most likely* result in:
   A. a decrease in the effective duration of Bond #3.
   B. Bond #3 having more upside potential than Bond #2.
   C. a change in the effective convexity of Bond #3 from positive to negative.
4. The value of Bond #2 is *closest* to:
   A. 102.103% of par.
   B. 103.121% of par.
   C. 103.744% of par.
5. The value of Bond #3 is *closest* to:
   A. 102.103% of par.
   B. 103.688% of par.
   C. 103.744% of par.
6. All else being equal, a rise in interest rates will *most likely* result in the value of the option embedded in Bond #3:
   A. decreasing.
   B. remaining unchanged.
   C. increasing.
7. All else being equal, if Ferguson assumes an interest rate volatility of 15% instead of 10%, the bond that would *most likely* increase in value is:
   A. Bond #1.
   B. Bond #2.
   C. Bond #3.
8. All else being equal, if the shape of the yield curve changes from upward sloping to flattening, the value of the option embedded in Bond #2 will *most likely*:
   A. decrease.
   B. remain unchanged.
   C. increase.
9. The conversion price of the bond in Exhibit 3 is *closest* to:
   A. $26.67.
   B. $32.26.
   C. $34.19.
10. If the market price of Pro Star's common stock falls from its level on 19 October 20X0, the price of the convertible bond will *most likely*:
    A. fall at the same rate as Pro Star's stock price.
    B. fall but at a slightly lower rate than Pro Star's stock price.
    C. be unaffected until Pro Star's stock price reaches the conversion price.

The following information relates to Questions 11–19

Rayes Investment Advisers specializes in fixed-income portfolio management. Meg Rayes, the owner of the firm, would like to add bonds with embedded options to the firm's bond portfolio. Rayes has asked Mingfang Hsu, one of the firm's analysts, to assist her in selecting and analyzing bonds for possible inclusion in the firm's bond portfolio.

Hsu first selects two corporate bonds that are callable at par and have the same characteristics in terms of maturity, credit quality, and call dates. Hsu uses the option adjusted spread (OAS) approach to analyze the bonds, assuming an interest rate volatility of 10%. The results of his analysis are presented in Exhibit 1.

EXHIBIT 1   Summary Results of Hsu's
Analysis Using the OAS Approach

Bond	OAS (in bps)
Bond #1	25.5
Bond #2	30.3

Hsu then selects the four bonds issued by RW, Inc., given in Exhibit 2. These bonds all have a maturity of three years and the same credit rating. Bonds #4 and #5 are identical to Bond #3, an option-free bond, except that they each include an embedded option.

EXHIBIT 2   Bonds Issued by RW, Inc.

Bond	Coupon	Special Provision
Bond #3	4.00% annual	
Bond #4	4.00% annual	Callable at par at the end of years 1 and 2
Bond #5	4.00% annual	Putable at par at the end of years 1 and 2
Bond #6	One-year reference rate annually, set in arrears	

To value and analyze RW's bonds, Hsu uses an estimated interest rate volatility of 15% and constructs the binomial interest rate tree provided in Exhibit 3.

EXHIBIT 3   Binomial Interest Rate Tree Used to Value RW's Bonds

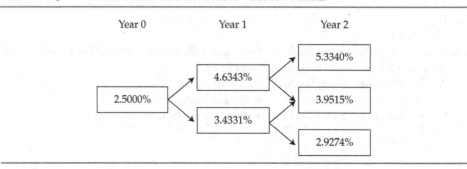

Rayes asks Hsu to determine the sensitivity of Bond #4's price to a 20 bps parallel shift of the benchmark yield curve. The results of Hsu's calculations are shown in Exhibit 4.

EXHIBIT 4   Summary Results of Hsu's Analysis about the Sensitivity of Bond #4's Price to a Parallel Shift of the Benchmark Yield Curve

Magnitude of the Parallel Shift in the Benchmark Yield Curve	+20 bps	−20 bps
Full Price of Bond #4 (% of par)	100.478	101.238

Hsu also selects the two floating-rate bonds issued by Varlep, plc, given in Exhibit 5. These bonds have a maturity of three years and the same credit rating.

EXHIBIT 5   Floating-Rate Bonds Issued by Varlep, plc

Bond	Coupon
Bond #7	One-year reference rate annually, set in arrears, capped at 5.00%
Bond #8	One-year reference rate annually, set in arrears, floored at 3.50%

To value Varlep's bonds, Hsu constructs the binomial interest rate tree provided in Exhibit 6.

EXHIBIT 6   Binomial Interest Rate Tree Used to Value Varlep's Bonds

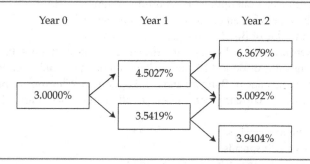

Last, Hsu selects the two bonds issued by Whorton, Inc., given in Exhibit 7. These bonds are close to their maturity date and are identical, except that Bond #9 includes a conversion option. Whorton's common stock is currently trading at $30 per share.

EXHIBIT 7   Bonds Issued by Whorton, Inc.

Bond	Type of Bond
Bond #9	Convertible bond with a conversion price of $50
Bond #10	Identical to Bond #9 except that it does not include a conversion option

11. Based on Exhibit 1, Rayes would *most likely* conclude that relative to Bond #1, Bond #2 is:
    A. overpriced.
    B. fairly priced.
    C. underpriced.

12. The effective duration of Bond #6 is:
    A. close to 1.
    B. higher than 1 but lower than 3.
    C. higher than 3.
13. In Exhibit 2, the bond whose effective duration might lengthen if interest rates rise is:
    A. Bond #3.
    B. Bond #4.
    C. Bond #5.
14. The effective duration of Bond #4 is *closest* to:
    A. 0.76.
    B. 1.88.
    C. 3.77.
15. The value of Bond #7 is *closest* to:
    A. 99.697% of par.
    B. 99.936% of par.
    C. 101.153% of par.
16. The value of Bond #8 is *closest* to:
    A. 98.116% of par.
    B. 100.000% of par.
    C. 100.485% of par.
17. The value of Bond #9 is equal to the value of Bond #10:
    A. plus the value of a put option on Whorton's common stock.
    B. plus the value of a call option on Whorton's common stock.
    C. minus the value of a call option on Whorton's common stock.
18. The minimum value of Bond #9 is equal to the *greater* of:
    A. the conversion value of Bond #9 and the current value of Bond #10.
    B. the current value of Bond #10 and a call option on Whorton's common stock.
    C. the conversion value of Bond #9 and a call option on Whorton's common stock.
19. The factor that is currently *least likely* to affect the risk–return characteristics of Bond #9 is:
    A. interest rate movements.
    B. Whorton's credit spreads.
    C. Whorton's common stock price movements.

The following information relates to Questions 20–27

John Smith, an investment adviser, meets with Lydia Carter to discuss her pending retirement and potential changes to her investment portfolio. Domestic economic activity has been weakening recently, and Smith's outlook is that equity market values will be lower during the next year. He would like Carter to consider reducing her equity exposure in favor of adding more fixed-income securities to the portfolio.

Government yields have remained low for an extended period, and Smith suggests considering investment-grade corporate bonds to provide additional yield above government debt issues. In light of recent poor employment figures and two consecutive quarters of negative GDP growth, the consensus forecast among economists is that the central bank, at its next meeting this month, will take actions that will lead to lower interest rates.

Smith and Carter review par, spot, and one-year forward rates (Exhibit 1) and four fixed-rate investment-grade bonds issued by Alpha Corporation that are being considered for investment (Exhibit 2).

EXHIBIT 1   Par, Spot, and One-Year Forward Rates (annual coupon payments)

Maturity (Years)	Par Rate (%)	Spot Rate (%)	One-Year Forward (%)
1	1.0000	1.0000	1.0000
2	1.2000	1.2012	1.4028
3	1.2500	1.2515	1.3522

EXHIBIT 2   Selected Fixed-Rate Bonds of Alpha Corporation

Bond	Annual Coupon	Type of Bond
Bond 1	1.5500%	Straight bond
Bond 2	1.5500%	Convertible bond: currently trading out of the money
Bond 3	1.5500%	Putable bond: putable at par one year and two years from now
Bond 4	1.5500%	Callable bond: callable at par without any lockout periods

Note: All bonds in Exhibit 2 have remaining maturities of exactly three years.

Carter tells Smith that the local news media have been reporting that housing starts, exports, and demand for consumer credit are all relatively strong, even in light of other poor macroeconomic indicators. Smith explains that the divergence in economic data leads him to believe that volatility in interest rates will increase. Smith also states that he recently read a report issued by Brown and Company forecasting that the yield curve could invert within the next six months.

Smith develops a binomial interest rate tree with a 15% interest rate volatility assumption to assess the value of Alpha Corporation's bonds. Exhibit 3 presents the interest rate tree.

EXHIBIT 3   Binomial Interest Rate Tree for Alpha Corporation with 15% Interest Rate Volatility

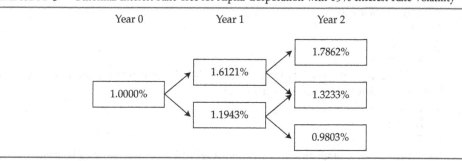

Carter asks Smith about the possibility of analyzing bonds that have lower credit ratings than the investment-grade Alpha bonds. Smith discusses four other corporate bonds with Carter. Exhibit 4 presents selected data on the four bonds.

EXHIBIT 4   Selected Information on Fixed-Rate Bonds for Beta, Gamma, Delta, and Rho Corporations

Bond	Issuer	Bond Features	Credit Rating
Bond 5	Beta Corporation	Coupon 1.70% Callable in Year 2 OAS of 45 bps	B
Bond 6	Gamma Corporation	Coupon 1.70% Callable in Year 2 OAS of 65 bps	B
Bond 7	Delta Corporation	Coupon 1.70% Callable in Year 2 OAS of 85 bps	B
Bond 8	Rho Corporation	Coupon 1.70% Callable in Year 2 OAS of 105 bps	CCC

Notes: All bonds have remaining maturities of three years. OAS stands for option-adjusted spread.

20. Based on Exhibit 2, and assuming that the forecast for interest rates and Smith's outlook for equity returns are validated, which bond's option is *most likely* to be exercised?
    A. Bond 2
    B. Bond 3
    C. Bond 4

21. Based on Exhibit 2, the current price of Bond 1 is *most likely* greater than the current price of:
    A. Bond 2.
    B. Bond 3.
    C. Bond 4.

22. Assuming the forecast for interest rates is proven accurate, which bond in Exhibit 2 will likely experience the smallest price increase?
    A. Bond 1
    B. Bond 3
    C. Bond 4

23. Based on the information in Exhibit 1 and Exhibit 2, the value of the embedded option in Bond 4 is *closest* to:
    A. nil.
    B. 0.1906.
    C. 0.8789.

24. If Smith's interest rate volatility forecast turns out to be true, which bond in Exhibit 2 is likely to experience the greatest price increase?
    A. Bond 2
    B. Bond 3
    C. Bond 4

25. If the Brown and Company forecast comes true, which of the following is *most likely* to occur? The value of the embedded option in:
    A. Bond 3 decreases.
    B. Bond 4 decreases.
    C. both Bond 3 and Bond 4 increases.

26. Based on Exhibit 2 and Exhibit 3, the market price of Bond 4 is *closest* to:
    A. 100.0000.
    B. 100.5123.
    C. 100.8790.
27. Which of the following conclusions regarding the bonds in Exhibit 4 is correct?
    A. Bond 5 is relatively cheaper than Bond 6.
    B. Bond 7 is relatively cheaper than Bond 6.
    C. Bond 8 is relatively cheaper than Bond 7.

The following information relates to Questions 28–36

Jules Bianchi is a bond analyst for Maneval Investments, Inc. Bianchi gathers data on three corporate bonds, as shown in Exhibit 1.

EXHIBIT 1   Selected Bond Data

Issuer	Coupon Rate	Price	Bond Description
Ayrault, Inc. (AI)	5.25%	100.200	Callable at par in one year and two years from today
Blum, Inc. (BI)	5.25%	101.300	Option-free
Cresson Enterprises (CE)	5.25%	102.100	Putable at par in one year from today

Note: Each bond has a remaining maturity of three years, annual coupon payments, and a credit rating of BBB.

To assess the interest rate risk of the three bonds, Bianchi constructs two binomial interest rate trees based on a 10% interest rate volatility assumption and a current one-year rate of 4%. Panel A of Exhibit 2 provides an interest rate tree assuming the benchmark yield curve shifts down by 30 bps, and Panel B provides an interest rate tree assuming the benchmark yield curve shifts up by 30 bps. Bianchi determines that the AI bond is currently trading at an option-adjusted spread (OAS) of 13.95 bps relative to the benchmark yield curve.

EXHIBIT 2   Binomial Interest Rate Trees

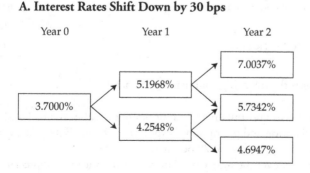

A. Interest Rates Shift Down by 30 bps

Year 0   Year 1   Year 2

3.7000%

5.1968%

4.2548%

7.0037%

5.7342%

4.6947%

(continued)

EXHIBIT 2   (Continued)

B. Interest Rates Shift Up by 30 bps

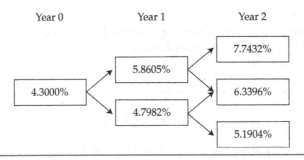

	Year 0	Year 1	Year 2

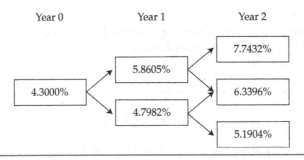

Armand Gillette, a convertible bond analyst, stops by Bianchi's office to discuss two convertible bonds. One is issued by DeLille Enterprises (DE), and the other is issued by Raffarin Incorporated (RI). Selected data for the two bonds are presented in Exhibits 3 and 4.

EXHIBIT 3   Selected Data for DE Convertible Bond

Issue price	€1,000 at par
Conversion period	13 September 20X5 to 12 September 20X8
Initial conversion price	€10.00 per share
Threshold dividend	€0.50 per share
Change of control conversion price	€8.00 per share
Common stock share price on issue date	€8.70
Share price on 17 September 20X5	€9.10
Convertible bond price on 17 September 20X5	€1,123

EXHIBIT 4   Selected Data for RI Convertible Bond

Straight bond value	€978
Value of embedded issuer call option	€43
Value of embedded investor put option	€26
Value of embedded call option on issuer's stock	€147
Conversion price	€12.50
Current common stock share price	€11.75

Gillette makes the following comments to Bianchi:

- "The DE bond does not contain any call or put options, but the RI bond contains both an embedded call option and put option. I expect that DeLille Enterprises will soon announce a common stock dividend of €0.70 per share."
- "My belief is that, over the next year, Raffarin's share price will appreciate toward the conversion price but not exceed it."

28. Based on Exhibits 1 and 2, the effective duration for the AI bond is *closest* to:
    A. 1.98.
    B. 2.15.
    C. 2.73.

29. If benchmark yields were to fall, which bond in Exhibit 1 would *most likely* experience a decline in effective duration?
    A. AI bond
    B. BI bond
    C. CE bond

30. Based on Exhibit 1, for the BI bond, one-sided:
    A. up-duration will be greater than one-sided down-duration.
    B. down-duration will be greater than one-sided up-duration.
    C. up-duration and one-sided down-duration will be about equal.

31. Based on Exhibit 1, which key rate duration is the largest for the BI bond?
    A. One-year key rate duration
    B. Two-year key rate duration
    C. Three-year key rate duration

32. Which bond in Exhibit 1 *most likely* has the lowest effective convexity?
    A. AI bond
    B. BI bond
    C. CE bond

33. Based on Exhibit 3, if DeLille Enterprises pays the dividend expected by Gillette, the conversion price of the DE bond will:
    A. be adjusted downward.
    B. not be adjusted.
    C. be adjusted upward.

34. Based on Exhibit 3, the market conversion premium per share for the DE bond on 17 September 20X5 is *closest* to:
    A. €0.90.
    B. €2.13.
    C. €2.53.

35. Based on Exhibit 4, the arbitrage-free value of the RI bond is *closest* to:
    A. €814.
    B. €1,056.
    C. €1,108.

36. Based on Exhibit 4 and Gillette's forecast regarding Raffarin's share price, the return on the RI bond over the next year is *most likely* to be:
    A. lower than the return on Raffarin's common shares.
    B. the same as the return on Raffarin's common shares.
    C. higher than the return on Raffarin's common shares.

CHAPTER 10

CREDIT ANALYSIS MODELS

LEARNING OUTCOMES

The candidate should be able to:

- explain expected exposure, the loss given default, the probability of default, and the credit valuation adjustment;
- explain credit scores and credit ratings;
- calculate the expected return on a bond given transition in its credit rating;
- explain structural and reduced-form models of corporate credit risk, including assumptions, strengths, and weaknesses;
- calculate the value of a bond and its credit spread, given assumptions about the credit risk parameters;
- interpret changes in a credit spread;
- explain the determinants of the term structure of credit spreads and interpret a term structure of credit spreads;
- compare the credit analysis required for securitized debt to the credit analysis of corporate debt.

SUMMARY OVERVIEW

We have covered several important topics in credit analysis. Among the points made are the following:

- Three factors important to modeling credit risk are the expected exposure to default, the recovery rate, and the loss given default.
- These factors permit the calculation of a credit valuation adjustment that is subtracted from the (hypothetical) value of the bond, if it were default risk free, to get the bond's fair value given its credit risk. The credit valuation adjustment is calculated as the sum of the present values of the expected loss for each period in the remaining life of the bond. Expected values are computed using risk-neutral probabilities, and discounting is done at the risk-free rates for the relevant maturities.

- The CVA captures investors' compensation for bearing default risk. The compensation can also be expressed in terms of a credit spread.
- Credit scores and credit ratings are third-party evaluations of creditworthiness used in distinct markets.
- Analysts may use credit ratings and a transition matrix of probabilities to adjust a bond's yield to maturity to reflect the probabilities of credit migration. Credit spread migration typically reduces expected return.
- Credit analysis models fall into two broad categories: structural models and reduced-form models.
- Structural models are based on an option perspective of the positions of the stakeholders of the company. Bondholders are viewed as owning the assets of the company; shareholders have call options on those assets.
- Reduced-form models seek to predict *when* a default may occur, but they do not explain the *why* as structural models do. Reduced-form models, unlike structural models, are based only on observable variables.
- When interest rates are assumed to be volatile, the credit risk of a bond can be estimated in an arbitrage-free valuation framework.
- The discount margin for floating-rate notes is similar to the credit spread for fixed-coupon bonds. The discount margin can also be calculated using an arbitrage-free valuation framework.
- Arbitrage-free valuation can be applied to judge the sensitivity of the credit spread to changes in credit risk parameters.
- The term structure of credit spreads depends on macro and micro factors.
- As it concerns macro factors, the credit spread curve tends to become steeper and to widen in conditions of weak economic activity. Market supply and demand dynamics are important. The most frequently traded securities tend to determine the shape of this curve.
- Issuer- or industry-specific factors, such as the chance of a future leverage-decreasing event, can cause the credit spread curve to flatten or invert.
- When a bond is very likely to default, it often trades close to its recovery value at various maturities; moreover, the credit spread curve is less informative about the relationship between credit risk and maturity.
- For securitized debt, the characteristics of the asset portfolio themselves suggest the best approach for a credit analyst to take when deciding among investments. Important considerations include the relative concentration of assets and their similarity or heterogeneity as it concerns credit risk.

PROBLEMS

The following information relates to Questions 1–15

Daniela Ibarra is a senior analyst in the fixed-income department of a large wealth management firm. Marten Koning is a junior analyst in the same department, and David Lok is a member of the credit research team.

The firm invests in a variety of bonds. Ibarra is presently analyzing a set of bonds with some similar characteristics, such as four years until maturity and a par value of €1,000. Exhibit 1 includes details of these bonds.

EXHIBIT 1   A Brief Description of the Bonds Being Analyzed

Bond	Description
B1	A zero-coupon, four-year corporate bond with a par value of €1,000. The wealth management firm's research team has estimated that the risk-neutral probability of default for each date for the bond is 1.50%, and the recovery rate is 30%.
B2	A bond similar to B1, except that it has a fixed annual coupon rate of 6% paid annually.
B3	A bond similar to B2 but rated AA.
B4	A bond similar to B2 but the coupon rate is the one-year benchmark rate plus 4%.

Ibarra asks Koning to assist her with analyzing the bonds. She wants him to perform the analysis with the assumptions that there is no interest rate volatility and that the government bond yield curve is flat at 3%.

Ibarra performs the analysis assuming an upward-sloping yield curve and volatile interest rates. Exhibit 2 provides the data on annual payment benchmark government bonds.

She uses these data to construct a binomial interest rate tree based on an assumption of future interest rate volatility of 20%.

EXHIBIT 2   Par Curve for Annual Payment Benchmark Government Bonds

Maturity	Coupon Rate	Price	Discount Factor	Spot Rate	Forward Rate
1	−0.25%	€100	1.002506	−0.2500%	
2	0.75%	€100	0.985093	0.7538%	1.7677%
3	1.50%	€100	0.955848	1.5166%	3.0596%
4	2.25%	€100	0.913225	2.2953%	4.6674%

Answer the first five questions (1–5) based on the assumptions made by Marten Koning, the junior analyst. Answer Questions 8–12 based on the assumptions made by Daniela Ibarra, the senior analyst.

Note: All calculations in this problem set are carried out on spreadsheets to preserve precision. The rounded results are reported in the solutions.

1. The market price of Bond B1 is €875. The bond is:
   A. fairly valued.
   B. overvalued.
   C. undervalued.

2. Koning realizes that an increase in the recovery rate would lead to an increase in the bond's fair value, whereas an increase in the probability of default would lead to a decrease in the bond's fair value. He is not sure, however, which effect would be greater. So, he increases both the recovery rate and the probability of default by 25% of their existing estimates and recomputes the bond's fair value. The recomputed fair value is closest to:
   A. €843.14.
   B. €848.00.
   C. €855.91.

3. The fair value of Bond B2 is closest to:
   A. €1,069.34.
   B. €1,111.51.
   C. €1,153.68.

4. The market price of Bond B2 is €1,090. If the bond is purchased at this price and there is a default on Date 3, the rate of return to the bond buyer would be closest to:
   A. −28.38%.
   B. −41.72%.
   C. −69.49%.

5. Bond B3 will have a modified duration of 2.75 at the end of the year. Based on the representative one-year corporate transition matrix in Exhibit 3 and assuming no default, how should the analyst adjust the bond's yield to maturity to assess the expected return on the bond over the next year?

EXHIBIT 3   Representative One-Year Corporate Transition Matrix (entries are in %)

From/To	AAA	AA	A	BBB	BB	B	CCC, CC, C	D
AAA	**90.00**	9.00	0.60	0.15	0.10	0.10	0.05	0.00
AA	1.50	**88.00**	9.50	0.75	0.15	0.05	0.03	0.02
A	0.05	2.50	**87.50**	8.40	0.75	0.60	0.12	0.08
BBB	0.02	0.30	4.80	**85.50**	6.95	1.75	0.45	0.23
BB	0.01	0.06	0.30	7.75	**79.50**	8.75	2.38	1.25
B	0.00	0.05	0.15	1.40	9.15	**76.60**	8.45	4.20
CCC, CC, C	0.00	0.01	0.12	0.87	1.65	18.50	**49.25**	29.60
Credit Spread	0.60%	0.90%	1.10%	1.50%	3.40%	6.50%	9.50%	

   A. Add 7.7 bps to YTM.
   B. Subtract 7.7 bps from YTM.
   C. Subtract 9.0 bps from YTM.

6. David Lok has estimated the probability of default of Bond B1 to be 1.50%. He is presenting the approach the research team used to estimate the probability of default. Which of the following statements is Lok likely to make in his presentation if the team used a reduced-form credit model?
   A. Option pricing methodologies were used, with the volatility of the underlying asset estimated based on historical data on the firm's stock price.
   B. Regression analysis was used, with the independent variables including both firm-specific variables, such as the debt ratio and return on assets, and macroeconomic variables, such as the rate of inflation and the unemployment rate.
   C. The default barrier was first estimated, followed by the estimation of the probability of default as the portion of the probability distribution that lies below the default barrier.

7. In the presentation, Lok is asked why the research team chose to use a reduced-form credit model instead of a structural model. Which statement is he likely to make in reply?
   A. Structural models are outdated, having been developed in the 1970s; reduced-form models are more modern, having been developed in the 1990s.
   B. Structural models are overly complex because they require the use of option pricing models, whereas reduced-form models use regression analysis.
   C. Structural models require "inside" information known to company management, whereas reduced-form models can use publicly available data on the firm.

8. As previously mentioned, Ibarra is considering a future interest rate volatility of 20% and an upward-sloping yield curve, as shown in Exhibit 2. Based on her analysis, the fair value of Bond B2 is closest to:

    A. €1,101.24.

    B. €1,141.76.

    C. €1,144.63.

9. Ibarra wants to know the credit spread of Bond B2 over a theoretical comparable-maturity government bond with the same coupon rate as this bond. The foregoing credit spread is closest to:

    A. 108 bps.

    B. 101 bps.

    C. 225 bps.

10. Ibarra is interested in analyzing how a simultaneous decrease in the recovery rate and the probability of default would affect the fair value of Bond B2. She decreases both the recovery rate and the probability of default by 25% of their existing estimates and recomputes the bond's fair value. The recomputed fair value is closest to:

    A. €1,096.59.

    B. €1,108.40.

    C. €1,111.91.

11. The wealth management firm has an existing position in Bond B4. The market price of B4, a floating-rate note, is €1,070. Senior management has asked Ibarra to make a recommendation regarding the existing position. Based on the assumptions used to calculate the estimated fair value only, her recommendation should be to:

    A. add to the existing position.

    B. hold the existing position.

    C. reduce the existing position.

12. The issuer of the floating-rate note, B4, is in the energy industry. Ibarra believes that oil prices are likely to increase significantly in the next year, which will lead to an improvement in the firm's financial health and a decline in the probability of default from 1.50% in Year 1 to 0.50% in Years 2, 3, and 4. Based on these expectations, which of the following statements is correct?

    A. The CVA will decrease to €22.99.

    B. The note's fair value will increase to €1,177.26.

    C. The value of the FRN, assuming no default, will increase to €1,173.55.

13. The floating-rate note, B4, is currently rated BBB by Standard & Poor's and Fitch Ratings (and Baa by Moody's Investors Service). Based on the research department assumption about the probability of default in Question 10 and her own assumption in Question 11, which action does Ibarra *most likely* expect from the credit rating agencies?

    A. Downgrade from BBB to BB.

    B. Upgrade from BBB to AAA.

    C. Place the issuer on watch with a positive outlook.

14. During the presentation about how the research team estimates the probability of default for a particular bond issuer, Lok is asked for his thoughts on the shape of the term structure of credit spreads. Which statement is he most likely to include in his response?

    A. The term structure of credit spreads typically is flat or slightly upward sloping for high-quality investment-grade bonds. High-yield bonds are more sensitive to the credit cycle, however, and can have a more upwardly sloped term structure of credit spreads than investment-grade bonds or even an inverted curve.

    B. The term structure of credit spreads for corporate bonds is always upward sloping— more so the weaker the credit quality because probabilities of default are positively correlated with the time to maturity.

    C. There is no consistent pattern for the term structure of credit spreads. The shape of the credit term structure depends entirely on industry factors.

15. The final question for Lok is about covered bonds. The person asking says, "I've heard about them but don't know what they are." Which statement is Lok most likely to make to describe a covered bond?

    A. A covered bond is issued in a non-domestic currency. The currency risk is then fully hedged using a currency swap or a package of foreign exchange forward contracts.

    B. A covered bond is issued with an attached credit default swap. It essentially is a "risk-free" government bond.

    C. A covered bond is a senior debt obligation giving recourse to the issuer as well as a predetermined underlying collateral pool, often commercial or residential mortgages.

The following information relates to Questions 16–22

Anna Lebedeva is a fixed-income portfolio manager. Paulina Kowalski, a junior analyst, and Lebedeva meet to review several positions in Lebedeva's portfolio.

Lebedeva begins the meeting by discussing credit rating migration. Kowalski asks Lebedeva about the typical impact of credit rating migration on the expected return on a bond. Lebedeva asks Kowalski to estimate the expected return over the next year on a bond issued by Entre Corp. The BBB rated bond has a yield to maturity of 5.50% and a modified duration of 7.54. Kowalski calculates the expected return on the bond over the next year given the partial credit transition and credit spread data in Exhibit 1. She assumes that market spreads and yields will remain stable over the year.

EXHIBIT 1   One-Year Transition Matrix for BBB Rated Bonds and Credit Spreads

	AAA	AA	A	BBB	BB	B	CCC, CC, C
Probability (%)	0.02	0.30	4.80	85.73	6.95	1.75	0.45
Credit spread	0.60%	0.90%	1.10%	1.50%	3.40%	6.50%	9.50%

Lebedeva next asks Kowalski to analyze a three-year bond, issued by VraiRive S.A., using an arbitrage-free framework. The bond's coupon rate is 5%, with interest paid annually and a par value of 100. In her analysis, she makes the following three assumptions:

- The annual interest rate volatility is 10%.
- The recovery rate is one-third of the exposure each period.
- The annual probability of default each year is 2.00%.

Selected information on benchmark government bonds for the VraiRive bond is presented in Exhibit 2, and the relevant binomial interest rate tree is presented in Exhibit 3.

EXHIBIT 2   Par Curve Rates for Annual Payment Benchmark Government Bonds

Maturity	Coupon Rate	Price	Discount Factor	Spot Rate	Forward Rate
1	3.00%	100	0.970874	3.0000%	3.0000%
2	4.20%	100	0.920560	4.2255%	5.4656%
3	5.00%	100	0.862314	5.0618%	6.7547%

EXHIBIT 3   One-Year Binomial Interest Rate Tree for 10% Volatility (risk-neutral probabilities in parentheses)

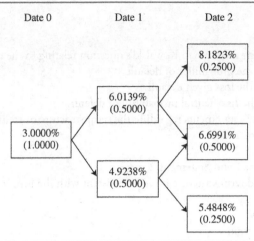

	Date 0	Date 1	Date 2

8.1823% (0.2500)

6.0139% (0.5000)

3.0000% (1.0000)

6.6991% (0.5000)

4.9238% (0.5000)

5.4848% (0.2500)

Kowalski estimates the value of the VraiRive bond assuming no default (VND) as well as the fair value of the bond. She then estimates the bond's yield to maturity and the bond's credit spread over the benchmark in Exhibit 2. Kowalski asks Lebedeva, "What might cause the bond's credit spread to decrease?"

Lebedeva and Kowalski next discuss the drivers of the term structure of credit spreads. Kowalski tells Lebedeva the following:

Statement 1: The credit term structure for the most highly rated securities tends to be either flat or slightly upward sloping.
Statement 2: The credit term structure for lower-rated securities is often steeper, and credit spreads widen with expectations of strong economic growth.

Next, Kowalski analyzes the outstanding bonds of DLL Corporation, a high-quality issuer with a strong, competitive position. Her focus is to determine the rationale for a positive-sloped credit spread term structure.

Lebedeva ends the meeting by asking Kowalski to recommend a credit analysis approach for a securitized asset-backed security (ABS) held in the portfolio. This non-static asset pool is made up of many medium-term auto loans that are homogeneous, and each loan is small relative to the total value of the pool.

16. The *most appropriate* response to Kowalski's question regarding credit rating migration is that it has:
    A. a negative impact.
    B. no impact.
    C. a positive impact.
17. Based on Exhibit 1, the one-year expected return on the Entre Corp. bond is *closest* to:
    A. 3.73%.
    B. 5.50%.
    C. 7.27%.

18. Based on Kowalski's assumptions and Exhibits 2 and 3, the credit spread on the VraiRive bond is *closest* to:
    A. 0.6949%.
    B. 0.9388%.
    C. 1.4082%.

19. The *most appropriate* response to Kowalski's question relating to the credit spread is:
    A. an increase in the probability of default.
    B. an increase in the loss given default.
    C. a decrease in the risk-neutral probability of default.

20. Which of Kowalski's statements regarding the term structure of credit spreads is correct?
    A. Only Statement 1
    B. Only Statement 2
    C. Both Statement 1 and Statement 2

21. DLL's credit spread term structure is *most* consistent with the firm having:
    A. low leverage.
    B. weak cash flow.
    C. a low profit margin.

22. Given the description of the asset pool of the ABS, Kowalski should recommend a:
    A. loan-by-loan approach.
    B. portfolio-based approach.
    C. statistics-based approach.

The following information relates to Questions 23–30

Lena Liecken is a senior bond analyst at Taurus Investment Management. Kristel Kreming, a junior analyst, works for Liecken in helping conduct fixed-income research for the firm's portfolio managers. Liecken and Kreming meet to discuss several bond positions held in the firm's portfolios.

Bonds I and II both have a maturity of one year, an annual coupon rate of 5%, and a market price equal to par value. The risk-free rate is 3%. Historical default experiences of bonds comparable to Bonds I and II are presented in Exhibit 1.

EXHIBIT 1   Credit Risk Information for Comparable Bonds

Bond	Recovery Rate	Percentage of Bonds That Survive and Make Full Payment
I	40%	98%
II	35%	99%

Bond III is a zero-coupon bond with three years to maturity. Liecken evaluates similar bonds and estimates a recovery rate of 38% and a risk-neutral default probability of 2%, assuming conditional probabilities of default. Kreming creates Exhibit 2 to compute Bond III's credit valuation adjustment. She assumes a flat yield curve at 3%, with exposure, recovery, and loss given default values expressed per 100 of par value.

EXHIBIT 2   Analysis of Bond III

Date	Exposure	Recovery	Loss Given Default	Probability of Default	Probability of Survival	Expected Loss	Present Value of Expected Loss
0							
1	94.2596	35.8186	58.4410	2.0000%	98.0000%	1.1688	1.1348
2	97.0874	36.8932	60.1942	1.9600%	96.0400%	1.1798	1.1121
3	100.0000	38.0000	62.0000	1.9208%	94.1192%	1.1909	1.0898
Sum				5.8808%		3.5395	3.3367

Bond IV is an AA rated bond that matures in five years, has a coupon rate of 6%, and a modified duration of 4.2. Liecken is concerned about whether this bond will be downgraded to an A rating, but she does not expect the bond to default during the next year. Kreming constructs a partial transition matrix, which is presented in Exhibit 3, and suggests using a model to predict the rating change of Bond IV using leverage ratios, return on assets, and macroeconomic variables.

EXHIBIT 3   Partial One-Year Corporate Transition Matrix (entries in %)

From/To	AAA	AA	A
AAA	92.00	6.00	1.00
AA	2.00	89.00	8.00
A	0.05	1.00	85.00
Credit Spread (%)	0.50	1.00	1.75

Kreming calculates the risk-neutral probabilities, compares them with the actual default probabilities of bonds evaluated over the past 10 years, and observes that the actual and risk-neutral probabilities differ. She makes two observations regarding the comparison of these probabilities:

- Observation 1: Actual default probabilities include the default risk premium associated with the uncertainty in the timing of the possible default loss.
- Observation 2: The observed spread over the yield on a risk-free bond in practice includes liquidity and tax considerations, in addition to credit risk.

23. The expected exposure to default loss for Bond I is:
    A. less than the expected exposure for Bond II.
    B. the same as the expected exposure for Bond II.
    C. greater than the expected exposure for Bond II.
24. Based on Exhibit 1, the loss given default for Bond II is:
    A. less than that for Bond I.
    B. the same as that for Bond I.
    C. greater than that for Bond I.

25. Based on Exhibit 1, the expected future value of Bond I at maturity is *closest* to:
    A. 98.80.
    B. 103.74.
    C. 105.00.
26. Based on Exhibit 1, the risk-neutral default probability for Bond I is *closest* to:
    A. 2.000%.
    B. 3.175%.
    C. 4.762%.
27. Based on Exhibit 2, the credit valuation adjustment for Bond III is *closest* to:
    A. 3.3367.
    B. 3.5395.
    C. 5.8808.
28. Based on Exhibit 3, if Bond IV's credit rating changes during the next year to an A rating, its expected price change would be *closest* to:
    A. −8.00%.
    B. −7.35%.
    C. −3.15%.
29. Kreming's suggested model for Bond IV is a:
    A. structural model.
    B. reduced-form model.
    C. term structure model.
30. Which of Kreming's observations regarding actual and risk-neutral default probabilities is correct?
    A. Only Observation 1
    B. Only Observation 2
    C. Both Observation 1 and Observation 2

CHAPTER 11

CREDIT DEFAULT SWAPS

LEARNING OUTCOMES

The candidate should be able to:

- describe credit default swaps (CDS), single-name and index CDS, and the parameters that define a given CDS product;
- describe credit events and settlement protocols with respect to CDS;
- explain the principles underlying and factors that influence the market's pricing of CDS;
- describe the use of CDS to manage credit exposures and to express views regarding changes in the shape and/or level of the credit curve;
- describe the use of CDS to take advantage of valuation disparities among separate markets, such as bonds, loans, equities, and equity-linked instruments.

SUMMARY OVERVIEW

- A credit default swap (CDS) is a contract between two parties in which one party purchases protection from another party against losses from the default of a borrower for a defined period of time.
- A CDS is written on the debt of a third party, called the reference entity, whose relevant debt is called the reference obligation, typically a senior unsecured bond.
- A CDS written on a particular reference obligation normally provides coverage for all obligations of the reference entity that have equal or higher seniority.
- The two parties to the CDS are the credit protection buyer, who is said to be short the reference entity's credit, and the credit protection seller, who is said to be long the reference entity's credit.
- The CDS pays off upon occurrence of a credit event, which includes bankruptcy, failure to pay, and, in some countries, involuntary restructuring.
- Settlement of a CDS can occur through a cash payment from the credit protection seller to the credit protection buyer as determined by the cheapest-to-deliver obligation of the reference entity or by physical delivery of the reference obligation from the protection buyer to the protection seller in exchange for the CDS notional.

- A cash settlement payoff is determined by an auction of the reference entity's debt, which gives the market's assessment of the likely recovery rate. The credit protection buyer must accept the outcome of the auction even though the ultimate recovery rate could differ.
- CDS can be constructed on a single entity or as indexes containing multiple entities. Bespoke CDS or baskets of CDS are also common.
- The fixed payments made from CDS buyer to CDS seller are customarily set at a fixed annual rate of 1% for investment-grade debt or 5% for high-yield debt.
- Valuation of a CDS is determined by estimating the present value of the payment leg, which is the series of payments made from the protection buyer to the protection seller, and the present value of the protection leg, which is the payment from the protection seller to the protection buyer in event of default. If the present value of the payment leg is greater than the present value of the protection leg, the protection buyer pays an upfront premium to the seller. If the present value of the protection leg is greater than the present value of the payment leg, the seller pays an upfront premium to the buyer.
- An important determinant of the value of the expected payments is the hazard rate, the probability of default given that default has not already occurred.
- CDS prices are often quoted in terms of credit spreads, the implied number of basis points that the credit protection seller receives from the credit protection buyer to justify providing the protection.
- Credit spreads are often expressed in terms of a credit curve, which expresses the relationship between the credit spreads on bonds of different maturities for the same borrower.
- CDS change in value over their lives as the credit quality of the reference entity changes, which leads to gains and losses for the counterparties, even though default may not have occurred or may never occur. CDS spreads approach zero as the CDS approaches maturity.
- Either party can monetize an accumulated gain or loss by entering into an offsetting position that matches the terms of the original CDS.
- CDS are used to increase or decrease credit exposures or to capitalize on different assessments of the cost of credit among different instruments tied to the reference entity, such as debt, equity, and derivatives of debt and equity.

PROBLEMS

The following information relates to Questions 1–6

UNAB Corporation

On 1 January 20X2, Deem Advisors purchased a $10 million six-year senior unsecured bond issued by UNAB Corporation. Six months later (1 July 20X2), concerned about the portfolio's credit exposure to UNAB, Doris Morrison, the chief investment officer at Deem Advisors, buys $10 million protection on UNAB with a standardized coupon rate of 5%. The reference obligation of the CDS is the UNAB bond owned by Deem Advisors. UNAB adheres to the ISDA CDS protocols.

On 1 January 20X3, Morrison asks Bill Watt, a derivatives analyst, to assess the current credit quality of UNAB bonds and the value of Deem Advisors' CDS on UNAB debt. Watt gathers the following information on UNAB's debt issues currently trading in the market:

Bond 1: A two-year senior unsecured bond trading at 40% of par
Bond 2: A five-year senior unsecured bond trading at 50% of par
Bond 3: A five-year subordinated unsecured bond trading at 20% of par

With respect to the credit quality of UNAB, Watt makes the following statement:

> "There is severe near-term stress in the financial markets, and UNAB's credit curve clearly reflects the difficult environment."

On 1 July 20X3, UNAB fails to make a scheduled interest payment on the outstanding subordinated unsecured obligation after a grace period; however, the company does not file for bankruptcy. Morrison asks Watt to determine if UNAB experienced a credit event and, if so, to recommend a settlement preference.

Kand Corporation

Morrison is considering purchasing protection on Kand Corporation debt to hedge the portfolio's position in Kand. She instructs Watt to determine if an upfront payment would be required and, if so, the amount of the premium. Watt presents the information for the CDS in Exhibit 1.

EXHIBIT 1   Summary Data for 10-year CDS on Kand Corporation

Credit spread	700 bps
Duration	7 years
Coupon rate	5%

Morrison purchases 10-year protection on Kand Corporation debt. Two months later the credit spread for Kand Corporation has increased by 200 bps. Morrison asks Watt to close out the firm's CDS position on Kand Corporation by entering into a new, offsetting contract.

Tollunt Corporation

Deem Advisors' chief credit analyst recently reported that Tollunt Corporation's five-year bond is currently yielding 7% and a comparable CDS contract has a credit spread of 4.25%. Since the current market reference rate is 2.5%, Watt has recommended executing a basis trade to take advantage of the pricing of Tollunt's bonds and CDS. The basis trade would consist of purchasing both the bond and the CDS contract.

1. If UNAB experienced a credit event on 1 July, Watt should recommend that Deem Advisors:
   A. prefer a cash settlement.
   B. prefer a physical settlement.
   C. be indifferent between a cash or a physical settlement.
2. According to Watt's statement, the shape of UNAB's credit curve is *most likely*:
   A. flat.
   B. upward-sloping.
   C. downward-sloping.
3. Should Watt conclude that UNAB experienced a credit event?
   A. Yes
   B. No, because UNAB did not file for bankruptcy
   C. No, because the failure to pay occurred on a subordinated unsecured bond
4. Based on Exhibit 1, the upfront premium as a percent of the notional for the CDS protection on Kand Corporation would be *closest* to:
   A. 2.0%.
   B. 9.8%.
   C. 14.0%.

5. If Deem Advisors enters into a new offsetting contract two months after purchasing protection on Kand Corporation, this action will most likely result in:
   A. a loss on the CDS position.
   B. a profit on the CDS position.
   C. neither a loss nor a profit on the CDS position.
6. If convergence occurs in the bond and CDS markets for Tollunt Corporation, a basis trade will capture a profit *closest* to:
   A. 0.25%.
   B. 1.75%.
   C. 2.75%.

The following information relates to Questions 7–14

John Smith, a fixed-income portfolio manager at a €10 billion sovereign wealth fund (the Fund), meets with Sofia Chan, a derivatives strategist with Shire Gate Securities (SGS), to discuss investment opportunities for the Fund. Chan notes that SGS adheres to ISDA (International Swaps and Derivatives Association) protocols for credit default swap (CDS) transactions and that any contract must conform to ISDA specifications. Before the Fund can engage in trading CDS products with SGS, the Fund must satisfy compliance requirements.

Smith explains to Chan that fixed-income derivatives strategies are being contemplated for both hedging and trading purposes. Given the size and diversified nature of the Fund, Smith asks Chan to recommend a type of CDS that would allow the Fund to simultaneously fully hedge multiple fixed-income exposures.

Smith and Chan discuss opportunities to add trading profits to the Fund. Smith asks Chan to determine the probability of default associated with a five-year investment-grade bond issued by Orion Industrial. Selected data on the Orion Industrial bond are presented in Exhibit 1.

EXHIBIT 1   Selected Data on Orion Industrial Five-Year Bond

Year	Hazard Rate
1	0.22%
2	0.35%
3	0.50%
4	0.65%
5	0.80%

Chan explains that a single-name CDS can also be used to add profit to the Fund over time. Chan describes a hypothetical trade in which the Fund sells £6 million of five-year CDS protection on Orion, where the CDS contract has a duration of 3.9 years. Chan assumes that the Fund closes the position six months later, after Orion's credit spread narrowed from 150 bps to 100 bps.

Chan discusses the mechanics of a long/short trade. In order to structure a number of potential trades, Chan and Smith exchange their respective views on individual companies and global economies. Chan and Smith agree on the following outlooks.

Outlook 1: The European economy will weaken.
Outlook 2: The US economy will strengthen relative to that of Canada.
Outlook 3: The credit quality of electric car manufacturers will improve relative to that of traditional car manufacturers.

Chan believes US macroeconomic data are improving and that the general economy will strengthen in the short term. Chan suggests that a curve trade could be used by the Fund to capitalize on her short-term view of a steepening of the US credit curve.

Another short-term trading opportunity that Smith and Chan discuss involves the merger and acquisition market. SGS believes that Delta Corporation may make an unsolicited bid at a premium to the market price for all of the publicly traded shares of Zega, Inc. Zega's market capitalization and capital structure are comparable to Delta's; both firms are highly levered. It is anticipated that Delta will issue new equity along with 5- and 10-year senior unsecured debt to fund the acquisition, which will significantly increase its debt ratio.

7. To satisfy the compliance requirements referenced by Chan, the Fund is *most likely* required to:
   A. set a notional amount.
   B. post an upfront payment.
   C. sign an ISDA master agreement.

8. Which type of CDS should Chan recommend to Smith?
   A. CDS index
   B. Tranche CDS
   C. Single-name CDS

9. Based on Exhibit 1, the probability of Orion defaulting on the bond during the first three years is *closest* to:
   A. 1.07%.
   B. 2.50%.
   C. 3.85%.

10. To close the position on the hypothetical Orion trade, the Fund:
    A. sells protection at a higher premium than it paid at the start of the trade.
    B. buys protection at a lower premium than it received at the start of the trade.
    C. buys protection at a higher premium than it received at the start of the trade.

11. The hypothetical Orion trade generated an approximate:
    A. loss of £117,000.
    B. gain of £117,000.
    C. gain of £234,000.

12. Based on the three economic outlook statements, a profitable long/short trade would be to:
    A. sell protection using a Canadian CDX IG and buy protection using a US CDX IG.
    B. buy protection using an iTraxx Crossover and sell protection using an iTraxx Main.
    C. buy protection using an electric car CDS and sell protection using a traditional car CDS.

13. The curve trade that would *best* capitalize on Chan's view of the US credit curve is to:
    A. buy protection using a 20-year CDX and buy protection using a 2-year CDX.
    B. buy protection using a 20-year CDX and sell protection using a 2-year CDX.
    C. sell protection using a 20-year CDX and buy protection using a 2-year CDX.

14. A profitable equity-versus-credit trade involving Delta and Zega is to:
    A. short Zega shares and buy protection on Delta using the 10-year CDS.
    B. go long Zega shares and buy protection on Delta using 5-year CDS.
    C. go long Delta shares and buy protection on Delta using 5-year CDS.

CHAPTER 12

OVERVIEW OF FIXED-INCOME PORTFOLIO MANAGEMENT

LEARNING OUTCOMES

The candidate should be able to:

- discuss roles of fixed-income securities in portfolios and how fixed-income mandates may be classified;
- describe fixed-income portfolio measures of risk and return as well as correlation characteristics;
- describe bond market liquidity, including the differences among market sub-sectors, and discuss the effect of liquidity on fixed-income portfolio management;
- describe and interpret a model for fixed-income returns;
- discuss the use of leverage, alternative methods for leveraging, and risks that leverage creates in fixed-income portfolios;
- discuss differences in managing fixed-income portfolios for taxable and tax-exempt investors.

SUMMARY OVERVIEW

- Fixed-income investments provide diversification benefits in a portfolio context. These benefits arise from the generally low correlations of fixed-income investments with other major asset classes, such as equities.
- Floating-rate and inflation-linked bonds can be used to hedge inflation risk.
- Fixed-income investments have regular cash flows, which is beneficial for the purposes of funding future liabilities.

- For liability-based fixed-income mandates, portfolio construction follows two main approaches—cash flow matching and duration matching—to match fixed-income assets with future liabilities.
- Total return mandates are generally structured to either track or outperform a benchmark.
- Total return mandates can be classified into various approaches according to their target active return and active risk levels. Approaches range from pure indexing to enhanced indexing to active management.
- Bond Portfolio Duration is the sensitivity of a portfolio of bonds to small changes in interest rates. It can be calculated as the weighted average of time to receipt of the aggregate cash flows or, more commonly, as the weighted average of the individual bond durations that comprise the portfolio.
- Modified Duration of a Bond Portfolio indicates the percentage change in the market value given a change in yield-to-maturity. Modified duration of a portfolio comprising j fixed income securities can be estimated as

$$AvgModDur = \sum_{j=1}^{J} ModDur_j \left(\frac{MV_j}{MV} \right)$$

where MV stands for market value of the portfolio and MV_j is the market value of a specific bond.
- Convexity of a bond portfolio is a second-order effect; it operates behind duration in importance and can largely be ignored for small yield changes. When convexity is added with the use of derivatives, however, it can be extremely important to returns.
- Effective duration and convexity of a portfolio are the relevant summary statistics when future cash flows of bonds in a portfolio are contingent on interest rate changes.
- Spread duration is a useful measure for determining a portfolio's sensitivity to changes in credit spreads. It provides the approximate percentage increase (decrease) in bond price expected for a 1% decrease (increase) in credit spread.
- Duration times spread is a modification of the spread duration definition to incorporate the empirical observation that spread changes across the credit spectrum tend to occur on a *proportional percentage* basis rather than being based on *absolute* basis point changes.
- Portfolio dispersion captures the variance of the times to receipt of cash flows around the duration. It is used in measuring interest rate immunization for liabilities.
- Duration management is the primary tool used by fixed-income portfolio managers.
- Convexity supplements duration as a measure of a bond's price sensitivity for larger movements in interest rates. Adjusting convexity can be an important portfolio management tool.
- For two portfolios with the same duration, the portfolio with higher convexity has higher sensitivity to large declines in yields to maturity and lower sensitivity to large increases in yields to maturity.
- Interest rate derivatives can be used effectively to increase or decrease duration and convexity in a bond portfolio.
- Liquidity is an important consideration in fixed-income portfolio management. Bonds are generally less liquid than equities, and liquidity varies greatly across sectors.
- Liquidity affects pricing in fixed-income markets because many bonds either do not trade or trade infrequently.
- Liquidity affects portfolio construction because there is a trade-off between liquidity and yield to maturity. Less liquid bonds have higher yields to maturity, all else being equal, and

may be more desirable for buy-and-hold investors. Investors anticipating liquidity needs may forgo higher yields to maturity for more liquid bonds.

- Investors can obtain exposure to the bond market using mutual funds and ETFs that track a bond index. Shares in mutual funds are redeemable at the net asset value with a one-day time lag. ETF shares have the advantage of trading on an exchange.
- A total return swap, an over-the-counter derivative, allows an institutional investor to transform an asset or liability from one asset category to another—for instance, from variable-rate cash flows referencing the market reference rate to the total return on a particular bond index.
- A total return swap can have some advantages over a direct investment in a bond mutual fund or ETF. As a derivative, it requires less initial cash outlay than direct investment in the bond portfolio for similar performance but carries counterparty risk.
- As a customized over-the-counter product, a TRS can offer exposure to assets that are difficult to access directly, such as some high-yield and commercial loan investments.
- When evaluating fixed-income investment strategies, it is important to consider expected returns and to understand the various components of expected returns.
- Decomposing expected fixed-income returns allows investors to understand the different sources of returns given expected changes in bond market conditions.
- A model for expected fixed-income returns can decompose them into the following components: coupon income, rolldown return, expected change in price based on investor's views of yields to maturity and yield spreads, and expected currency gains or losses.
- Leverage is the use of borrowed capital to increase the magnitude of portfolio positions. By using leverage, fixed-income portfolio managers may be able to increase portfolio returns relative to what they can achieve in unleveraged portfolios. The potential for increased returns, however, comes with increased risk.
- Methods for leveraging fixed-income portfolios include the use of futures contracts, swap agreements, repurchase agreements, structured financial instruments, and security lending.
- Taxes can complicate investment decisions in fixed-income portfolio management. Complications result from the differences in taxation among investor types, countries, and income sources.
- The two primary sources of investment income that affect taxes for fixed-income securities are coupon payments (interest income) and capital gains or losses. Tax is usually payable only on capital gains and interest income that have actually been received.
- Capital gains are frequently taxed at a lower effective tax rate than interest income. If capital losses exceed capital gains in the year, they can often be "carried forward" and applied to gains in future years.

PROBLEMS

The following information relates to Questions 1–6

Cécile is a junior analyst for an international wealth management firm. Her supervisor, Margit, asks Cécile to evaluate three fixed-income funds as part of the firm's global fixed-income offerings. Selected financial data for the funds Aschel, Permot, and Rosaiso are presented in Exhibit 1. In Cécile's initial review, she assumes that there is no reinvestment income and that the yield curve remains unchanged.

EXHIBIT 1   Selected Data on Fixed-Income Funds

	Aschel	Permot	Rosaiso
Current average bond price	$117.00	$91.50	$94.60
Expected average bond price in one year (end of Year 1)	$114.00	$96.00	$97.00
Average modified duration	7.07	7.38	6.99
Average annual coupon payment	$3.63	$6.07	$6.36
Present value of portfolio's assets (millions)	$136.33	$68.50	$74.38
Bond type*			
Fixed-coupon bonds	95%	38%	62%
Floating-coupon bonds	2%	34%	17%
Inflation-linked bonds	3%	28%	21%
Quality*			
AAA	65%	15%	20%
BBB	35%	65%	50%
B	0%	20%	20%
Not rated	0%	0%	10%
Value of portfolio's equity (millions)	$94.33		
Value of borrowed funds (millions)	$42.00		
Borrowing rate	2.80%		
Return on invested funds	6.20%		

*Bond type and quality are shown as a percentage of total for each fund.

After further review of the composition of each of the funds, Cécile makes the following notes:

Note 1:   Aschel is the only fund of the three that uses leverage.
Note 2:   Rosaiso is the only fund of the three that holds a significant number of bonds with embedded options.

Margit asks Cécile to analyze liability-based mandates for a meeting with Villash Foundation. Villash Foundation is a tax-exempt client. Prior to the meeting, Cécile identifies what she considers to be two key features of a liability-based mandate.

Feature 1   It can minimize the risk of deficient cash inflows for a company.
Feature 2   It matches expected liability payments with future projected cash inflows.

Two years later, Margit learns that Villash Foundation needs $5 million in cash to meet liabilities. She asks Cécile to analyze two bonds for possible liquidation. Selected data on the two bonds are presented in Exhibit 2.

EXHIBIT 2   Selected Data for Bonds 1 and 2

	Bond 1	Bond 2
Current market value	$5,000,000	$5,000,000
Capital gain/loss	400,000	−400,000
Coupon rate	2.05%	2.05%
Remaining maturity	8 years	8 years
Investment view	Overvalued	Undervalued
Income tax rate		39%
Capital gains tax rate		30%

1. Based on Exhibit 1, which fund provides the highest level of protection against inflation for coupon payments?
   A. Aschel
   B. Permot
   C. Rosaiso
2. Based on Exhibit 1, the rolling yield of Aschel over a one-year investment horizon is *closest* to:
   A. −2.56%.
   B. 0.54%.
   C. 5.66%.
3. The leveraged portfolio return for Aschel is *closest* to:
   A. 7.25%.
   B. 7.71%.
   C. 8.96%.
4. Based on Note 2, Rosaiso is the only fund for which the expected change in price based on the investor's views of yields to maturity and yield spreads should be calculated using:
   A. convexity.
   B. modified duration.
   C. effective duration.
5. Is Cécile correct with respect to key features of liability-based mandates?
   A. Yes
   B. No, only Feature 1 is correct.
   C. No, only Feature 2 is correct.
6. Based on Exhibit 2, the optimal strategy to meet Villash Foundation's cash needs is the sale of:
   A. 100% of Bond 1.
   B. 100% of Bond 2.
   C. 50% of Bond 1 and 50% of Bond 2.

The following information relates to Questions 7–12

Celia is chief investment officer for the Topanga Investors Fund, which invests in equities and fixed income. The clients in the fund are all taxable investors. The fixed-income allocation includes a domestic (US) bond portfolio and an externally managed global bond portfolio.

The domestic bond portfolio has a total return mandate, which specifies a long-term return objective of 25 basis points (bps) over the benchmark index. Relative to the benchmark, small deviations in sector weightings are permitted, such risk factors as duration must closely match, and tracking error is expected to be less than 50 bps per year.

The objectives for the domestic bond portfolio include the ability to fund future liabilities, protect interest income from short-term inflation, and minimize the correlation with the fund's equity portfolio. The correlation between the fund's domestic bond portfolio and equity portfolio is currently 0.14. Celia plans to reduce the fund's equity allocation and increase the allocation to the domestic bond portfolio. She reviews two possible investment strategies.

Strategy 1   Purchase AAA rated fixed-coupon corporate bonds with a modified duration of two years and a correlation coefficient with the equity portfolio of −0.15.

Strategy 2   Purchase US government agency floating-coupon bonds with a modified duration of one month and a correlation coefficient with the equity portfolio of −0.10.

Celia realizes that the fund's return may decrease if the equity allocation of the fund is reduced. Celia decides to liquidate $20 million of US Treasuries that are currently owned and to invest the proceeds in the US corporate bond sector. To fulfill this strategy, Celia asks Dan, a newly hired analyst for the fund, to recommend specific Treasuries to sell and corporate bonds to purchase.

Dan recommends Treasuries from the existing portfolio that he believes are overvalued and will generate capital gains. Celia asks Dan why he chose only overvalued bonds with capital gains and did not include any bonds with capital losses. Dan responds with two statements.

Statement 1:   Taxable investors should prioritize selling overvalued bonds and always sell them before selling bonds that are viewed as fairly valued or undervalued.
Statement 2:   Taxable investors should never intentionally realize capital losses.

Regarding the purchase of corporate bonds, Dan collects relevant data, which are presented in Exhibit 1.

EXHIBIT 1   Selected Data on Three US Corporate Bonds

Bond Characteristics	Bond 1	Bond 2	Bond 3
Credit quality	AA	AA	A
Issue size ($ millions)	100	75	75
Maturity (years)	5	7	7
Total issuance outstanding ($ millions)	1,000	1,500	1,000
Months since issuance	New issue	3	6

Celia and Dan review the total expected 12-month return (assuming no reinvestment income) for the global bond portfolio. Selected financial data are presented in Exhibit 2.

EXHIBIT 2   Selected Data on Global Bond Portfolio

Notional principal of portfolio (in millions)	€200
Average bond coupon payment (per €100 par value)	€2.25
Coupon frequency	Annual
Investment horizon	1 year
Current average bond price	€98.45
Expected average bond price in one year (assuming an unchanged yield curve)	€98.62
Average bond convexity	22
Average bond modified duration	5.19
Expected average benchmark yield-to-maturity change	0.15%
Expected change in credit spread (widening)	0.13%
Expected currency gains (€ appreciation vs. $)	0.65%

Celia contemplates adding a new manager to the global bond portfolio. She reviews three proposals and determines that each manager uses the same index as its benchmark but pursues a different total return approach, as presented in Exhibit 3.

EXHIBIT 3   New Manager Proposals: Fixed-Income Portfolio Characteristics

Sector Weights (%)	Manager A	Manager B	Manager C	Index
Government	53.5	52.5	47.8	54.1
Agency/quasi-agency	16.2	16.4	13.4	16.0
Corporate	20.0	22.2	25.1	19.8
MBS	10.3	8.9	13.7	10.1
Risk and Return Characteristics	Manager A	Manager B	Manager C	Index
Average maturity (years)	7.63	7.84	8.55	7.56
Modified duration (years)	5.23	5.25	6.16	5.22
Average yield to maturity (%)	1.98	2.08	2.12	1.99
Turnover (%)	207	220	290	205

7. Which approach to its total return mandate is the fund's domestic bond portfolio *most likely* to use?
   A. Pure indexing
   B. Enhanced indexing
   C. Active management
8. Strategy 2 is *most likely* preferred to Strategy 1 for meeting the objective of:
   A. protecting against inflation.
   B. funding future liabilities.
   C. minimizing the correlation of the fund's domestic bond portfolio and equity portfolio.
9. Are Dan's statements to Celia that support Dan's choice of bonds to sell correct?
   A. Only Statement 1 is correct.
   B. Only Statement 2 is correct.
   C. Neither Statement 1 nor Statement 2 is correct.

10. Based on Exhibit 1, which bond *most likely* has the highest liquidity premium?
    A. Bond 1
    B. Bond 2
    C. Bond 3
11. Based on Exhibit 2, the total expected return of the fund's global bond portfolio is *closest* to:
    A. 0.90%.
    B. 1.66%.
    C. 3.76%.
12. Based on Exhibit 3, which manager is *most likely* to have an active management total return mandate?
    A. Manager A
    B. Manager B
    C. Manager C

CHAPTER 13

LIABILITY-DRIVEN AND INDEX-BASED STRATEGIES

LEARNING OUTCOMES

The candidate should be able to:

- describe liability-driven investing;
- evaluate strategies for managing a single liability;
- compare strategies for a single liability and for multiple liabilities, including alternative means of implementation;
- describe construction, benefits, limitations, and risk–return characteristics of a laddered bond portfolio;
- evaluate liability-based strategies under various interest rate scenarios and select a strategy to achieve a portfolio's objectives;
- explain risks associated with managing a portfolio against a liability structure;
- discuss bond indexes and the challenges of managing a fixed-income portfolio to mimic the characteristics of a bond index;
- compare alternative methods for establishing bond market exposure passively;
- discuss criteria for selecting a benchmark and justify the selection of a benchmark.

SUMMARY OVERVIEW

- Structured fixed-income investing requires a frame of reference, such as a balance sheet, to structure the bond portfolio. This frame of reference can be as simple as the time to retirement for an individual or as complex as a balance sheet of rate-sensitive assets and liabilities for a company.
- Assets and liabilities can be categorized by the degree of certainty surrounding the amount and timing of cash flows. Type I assets and liabilities, such as traditional fixed-rate bonds with no embedded options, have known amounts and payment dates. For Type I assets and liabilities, such yield duration statistics as Macaulay, modified, and money duration apply.

- Type II, III, and IV assets and liabilities have uncertain amounts and/or uncertain timing of payment. For Type II, III, and IV assets and liabilities, curve duration statistics, such as effective duration, are needed. A model is used to obtain the estimated values when the yield curve shifts up and down by the same amount.
- Immunization is the process of structuring and managing a fixed-income portfolio to minimize the variance in the realized rate of return over a known investment horizon.
- In the case of a single liability, immunization is achieved by matching the Macaulay duration of the bond portfolio to the horizon date. As time passes and bond yields change, the duration of the bonds changes and the portfolio needs to be rebalanced. This rebalancing can be accomplished by buying and selling bonds or using interest rate derivatives, such as futures contracts and interest rate swaps.
- An immunization strategy aims to lock in the cash flow yield on the portfolio, which is the internal rate of return on the cash flows. It is not the weighted average of the yields to maturity on the bonds that constitute the portfolio.
- The risk to immunization is that as the yield curve shifts and twists, the cash flow yield on the bond portfolio does not match the change in the yield on the zero-coupon bond that would provide for perfect immunization.
- A sufficient, but not necessary, condition for immunization is a parallel (or shape-preserving) shift whereby all yields change by the same amount in the same direction. If the change in the cash flow yield is the same as that on the zero-coupon bond being replicated, immunization can be achieved even with a non-parallel shift to the yield curve.
- Structural risk to immunization arises from some non-parallel shifts and twists to the yield curve. This risk is reduced by minimizing the dispersion of cash flows in the portfolio, which can be accomplished by minimizing the convexity statistic for the portfolio. Concentrating the cash flows around the horizon date makes the immunizing portfolio closely track the zero-coupon bond that provides for perfect immunization.
- For multiple liabilities, one method of immunization is cash flow matching. A portfolio of high-quality zero-coupon or fixed-income bonds is purchased to match as closely as possible the amount and timing of the liabilities.
- A motive for cash flow matching can be accounting defeasance, whereby both the assets and liabilities are removed from the balance sheet.
- A laddered bond portfolio is a common investment strategy in the wealth management industry. The laddered portfolio offers "diversification" over the yield curve compared with "bullet" or "barbell" portfolios. This structure is especially attractive in stable, upwardly sloped yield curve environments as maturing short-term debt is replaced with higher-yielding long-term debt at the back of the ladder.
- A laddered portfolio offers an increase in convexity because the cash flows have greater dispersions than a more concentrated (bullet) portfolio.
- A laddered portfolio provides liquidity in that it always contains a soon-to-mature bond that could provide high-quality, low-duration collateral on a repo contract if needed.
- Immunization of multiple liabilities can be achieved by structuring and managing a portfolio of fixed-income bonds. Because the market values of the assets and liabilities differ, the strategy is to match the money durations. The money duration is the modified duration multiplied by the market value. The basis point value is a measure of money duration calculated by multiplying the money duration by 0.0001.
- The conditions to immunize multiple liabilities are that (1) the market value of assets is greater than or equal to the market value of the liabilities, (2) the asset basis point value

(BPV) equals the liability BPV, and (3) the dispersion of cash flows and the convexity of assets are greater than those of the liabilities.

- A derivatives overlay—for example, interest rate futures contracts—can be used to immunize single or multiple liabilities.

- The number of futures contracts needed to immunize is the liability BPV minus the asset BPV, divided by the futures BPV. If the result is a positive number, the entity buys, or goes long, futures contracts. If the result is a negative number, the entity sells, or goes short, futures contracts. The futures BPV can be approximated by the BPV for the cheapest-to-deliver security divided by the conversion factor for the cheapest-to-deliver security.

- Contingent immunization adds active management of the surplus, which is the difference between the asset and liability market values, with the intent to reduce the overall cost of retiring the liabilities. In principle, any asset classes can be used for the active investment. The entity can choose to over-hedge or under-hedge the number of futures contracts needed for passive immunization.

- Liability-driven investing (LDI) often is used for complex rate-sensitive liabilities, such as those for a defined benefit pension plan. The retirement benefits for covered employees depend on many variables, such as years of employment, age at retirement, wage level at retirement, and expected lifetime. There are different measures for the liabilities: for instance, the accumulated benefit obligation (ABO) that is based on current wages and the projected benefit obligation (PBO) that is based on expected future wages. For each liability measure (ABO or PBO), a model is used to extract the effective duration and BPV.

- Interest rate swap overlays can be used to reduce the duration gap as measured by the asset and liability BPVs. There often is a large gap because pension funds hold sizable asset positions in equities that have low or zero effective durations and their liability durations are high.

- The hedging ratio is the percentage of the duration gap that is closed with the derivatives. A hedging ratio of zero implies no hedging. A hedging ratio of 100% implies immunization— that is, complete removal of interest rate risk.

- Strategic hedging is the active management of the hedging ratio. Because asset BPVs are less than liability BPVs in typical pension funds, the derivatives overlay requires the use of receive-fixed interest rate swaps. Because receive-fixed swaps gain value as current swap market rates fall, the fund manager could choose to raise the hedging ratio when lower rates are anticipated. If rates are expected to go up, the manager could strategically reduce the hedging ratio.

- An alternative to the receive-fixed interest rate swap is a purchased receiver swaption. This swaption confers to the buyer the right to enter the swap as the fixed-rate receiver. Because of its negative duration gap (asset BPV is less than liability BPV), the typical pension plan suffers when interest rates fall and could become underfunded. The gain on the receiver swaption as rates decline offsets the losses on the balance sheet.

- Another alternative is a swaption collar, the combination of buying the receiver swaption and writing a payer swaption. The premium received on the payer swaption that is written offsets the premium needed to buy the receiver swaption.

- The choice among hedging with the receive-fixed swap, the purchased receiver swaption, and the swaption collar depends in part on the pension fund manager's view on future interest rates. If rates are expected to be low, the receive-fixed swap typically is the preferred derivative. If rates are expected to go up, the swaption collar can become attractive. And if rates are projected to reach a certain threshold that depends on the option costs and the strike rates, the purchased receiver swaption can become the favored choice.

- Model risks arise in LDI strategies because of the many assumptions in the models and approximations used to measure key parameters. For example, the liability BPV for the defined benefit pension plan depends on the choice of measure (ABO or PBO) and the assumptions that go into the model regarding future events (e.g., wage levels, time of retirement, and time of death).

- Spread risk in LDI strategies arises because it is common to assume equal changes in asset, liability, and hedging instrument yields when calculating the number of futures contracts, or the notional principal on an interest rate swap, to attain a particular hedging ratio. The assets and liabilities are often on corporate securities, however, and their spreads to benchmark yields can vary over time.

- Investing in a fund that tracks a bond market index offers the benefits of both diversification and low administrative costs. Tracking risk arises when the fund manager chooses to buy only a subset of the index, a strategy called enhanced indexing, because fully replicating the index can be impractical as a result of the large number of bonds in the fixed-income universe.

- Corporate bonds are often illiquid. Matrix pricing uses available data on comparable securities to estimate the fair value of the illiquid bonds.

- The primary risk factors encountered by an investor tracking a bond index include decisions regarding duration (option-adjusted duration for callable bonds, convexity for possible large yield shifts, and key rate durations for non-parallel shifts) and portfolio weights (assigned by sector, credit quality, maturity, coupon rate, and issuer).

- Index replication is one method to establish a passive exposure to the bond market. The manager buys or sells bonds only when there are changes to the index. Full replication can be expensive, however, as well as infeasible for broad-based fixed-income indexes that include many illiquid bonds.

- Several enhancement strategies can reduce the costs to track a bond index: lowering trading costs, using models to identify undervalued bonds and to gauge relative value at varying points along the yield curve, over/under weighting specific credit sectors over the business cycle, and evaluating specific call features to identify value given large yield changes.

- Investors can obtain passive exposure to the bond market using ETFs or mutual funds. Exchange-traded fund (ETF) shares have the advantage of trading on an exchange throughout the day.

- A total return swap, an over-the-counter derivative, allows an institutional investor to transform an asset or liability from one asset category to another—for instance, from variable-rate cash flows referencing the MRR to the total return on a particular bond index.

- A total return swap (TRS) can have some advantages over a direct investment in a bond mutual fund or ETF. As a derivative, it requires less initial cash outlay than direct investment in the bond portfolio for similar performance. A TRS also carries counterparty credit risk, however. As a customized over-the-counter product, a TRS can offer exposure to assets that are difficult to access directly, such as some high-yield and commercial loan investments.

- Selecting a particular bond index is a major decision for a fixed-income investment manager. Selection is guided by the specified goals and objectives for the investment. The decision should recognize several features of bond indexes: (1) Given that bonds have finite maturities, the duration of the index drifts down over time; (2) the composition of the index changes over time with the business cycle and maturity preferences of issuers.

PROBLEMS

The following information relates to Questions 1–8

Serena is a risk management specialist with Liability Protection Advisors. Trey, CFO of Kiest Manufacturing, enlists Serena's help with three projects. The first project is to defease some of Kiest's existing fixed-rate bonds that are maturing in each of the next three years. The bonds have no call or put provisions and pay interest annually. Exhibit 1 presents the payment schedule for the bonds.

EXHIBIT 1   Kiest Manufacturing Bond Payment Schedule (as of beginning of Year 1)

Maturity Date	Payment Amount
End of Year 1	$9,572,000
End of Year 2	$8,392,000
End of Year 3	$8,200,000

The second project for Serena is to help Trey immunize a $20 million portfolio of liabilities. The liabilities range from 3.00 years to 8.50 years with a Macaulay duration of 5.34 years, cash flow yield of 3.25%, portfolio convexity of 33.05, and basis point value (BPV) of $10,505. Serena suggested employing a duration-matching strategy using one of the three AAA rated bond portfolios presented in Exhibit 2.

EXHIBIT 2   Possible AAA Rated Duration-Matching Portfolios

	Portfolio A	Portfolio B	Portfolio C
Bonds (term, coupon)	4.5 years, 2.63%	3.0 years, 2.00%	1.5 years, 1.25%
	7.0 years, 3.50%	6.0 years, 3.25%	11.5 years, 4.38%
		8.5 years, 3.88%	
Macaulay duration	5.35	5.34	5.36
Cash flow yield	3.16%	3.33%	3.88%
Convexity	31.98	34.51	50.21
BPV	$10,524	$10,506	$10,516

Serena explains to Trey that the underlying duration-matching strategy is based on the following three assumptions.

1. Yield curve shifts in the future will be parallel.
2. Bond types and quality will closely match those of the liabilities.
3. The portfolio will be rebalanced by buying or selling bonds rather than using derivatives.

The third project for Serena is to make a significant direct investment in broadly diversified global bonds for Kiest's pension plan. Kiest has a young workforce, and thus, the plan has a long-term investment horizon. Trey needs Serena's help to select a benchmark index that is appropriate for Kiest's young workforce. Serena discusses three benchmark candidates, presented in Exhibit 3.

EXHIBIT 3   Global Bond Index Benchmark Candidates

Index Name	Effective Duration	Index Characteristics
Global Aggregate	7.73	Market cap weighted; Treasuries, corporates, agency, securitized debt
Global Aggregate GDP Weighted	7.71	Same as Global Aggregate, except GDP weighted
Global High Yield	4.18	GDP weighted; sovereign, agency, corporate debt

With the benchmark selected, Trey provides guidelines to Serena directing her to (1) use the most cost-effective method to track the benchmark and (2) provide low tracking error.

After providing Trey with advice on direct investment, Serena offered him additional information on alternative indirect investment strategies using (1) bond mutual funds, (2) exchange-traded funds (ETFs), and (3) total return swaps. Trey expresses interest in using bond mutual funds rather than the other strategies for the following reasons.

- **Reason 1:** Total return swaps have much higher transaction costs and initial cash outlay than bond mutual funds.
- **Reason 2:** Unlike bond mutual funds, bond ETFs can trade at discounts to their underlying indexes, and those discounts can persist.
- **Reason 3:** Bond mutual funds can be traded throughout the day at the net asset value of the underlying bonds.

1. Based on Exhibit 1, Kiest's liabilities would be classified as:
   A. Type I.
   B. Type II.
   C. Type III.
2. Based on Exhibit 2, the portfolio with the greatest structural risk is:
   A. Portfolio A.
   B. Portfolio B.
   C. Portfolio C.
3. Which portfolio in Exhibit 2 fails to meet the requirements to achieve immunization for multiple liabilities?
   A. Portfolio A
   B. Portfolio B
   C. Portfolio C
4. Based on Exhibit 2, relative to Portfolio C, Portfolio B:
   A. has higher cash flow reinvestment risk.
   B. is a more desirable portfolio for liquidity management.
   C. provides less protection from yield curve shifts and twists.
5. Serena's three assumptions regarding the duration-matching strategy indicate the presence of:
   A. model risk.
   B. spread risk.
   C. counterparty credit risk.
6. The global bond benchmark in Exhibit 3 that is least appropriate for Kiest to use is the:
   A. Global Aggregate Index.
   B. Global High Yield Index.
   C. Global Aggregate GDP Weighted Index.

7. To meet both of Trey's guidelines for the pension's bond fund investment, Serena should recommend:
   A. pure indexing.
   B. enhanced indexing.
   C. active management.
8. Which of Trey's reasons for choosing bond mutual funds as an investment vehicle is correct?
   A. Reason 1
   B. Reason 2
   C. Reason 3

The following information relates to questions 9–16

SD&R Capital (SD&R), a global asset management company, specializes in fixed-income investments. Molly, chief investment officer, is meeting with a prospective client, Leah of DePuy Financial Company (DFC).

Leah informs Molly that DFC's previous fixed-income manager focused on the interest rate sensitivities of assets and liabilities when making asset allocation decisions. Molly explains that, in contrast, SD&R's investment process first analyzes the size and timing of client liabilities, and then it builds an asset portfolio based on the interest rate sensitivity of those liabilities.

Molly notes that SD&R generally uses actively managed portfolios designed to earn a return in excess of the benchmark portfolio. For clients interested in passive exposure to fixed-income instruments, SD&R offers two additional approaches.

- **Approach 1:** Seeks to fully replicate a small range of benchmarks consisting of government bonds.
- **Approach 2:** Follows an enhanced indexing process for a subset of the bonds included in the Bloomberg Barclays US Aggregate Bond Index. Approach 2 may also be customized to reflect client preferences.

To illustrate SD&R's immunization approach for controlling portfolio interest rate risk, Molly discusses a hypothetical portfolio composed of two non-callable, investment-grade bonds. The portfolio has a weighted average yield-to-maturity of 9.55%, a weighted average coupon rate of 10.25%, and a cash flow yield of 9.85%.

Leah informs Molly that DFC has a single $500 million liability due in nine years, and she wants SD&R to construct a bond portfolio that earns a rate of return sufficient to pay off the obligation. Leah expresses concern about the risks associated with an immunization strategy for this obligation. In response, Molly makes the following statements about liability-driven investing:

- **Statement 1:** Although the amount and date of SD&R's liability is known with certainty, measurement errors associated with key parameters relative to interest rate changes may adversely affect the bond portfolios.
- **Statement 2:** A cash flow matching strategy will mitigate the risk from non-parallel shifts in the yield curve.

Molly provides the four US dollar–denominated bond portfolios in Exhibit 1 for consideration. Molly explains that the portfolios consist of non-callable, investment-grade corporate and government bonds of various maturities because zero-coupon bonds are unavailable.

EXHIBIT 1   Proposed Bond Portfolios to Immunize SD&R Single Liability

	Portfolio 1	Portfolio 2	Portfolio 3	Portfolio 4
Cash flow yield	7.48%	7.50%	7.53%	7.51%
Average time to maturity	11.2 years	9.8 years	9.0 years	10.1 years
Macaulay duration	9.8	8.9	8.0	9.1
Market value-weighted duration	9.1	8.5	7.8	8.6
Convexity	154.11	131.75	130.00	109.32

The discussion turns to benchmark selection. DFC's previous fixed-income manager used a custom benchmark with the following characteristics:

- **Characteristic 1:** The benchmark portfolio invests only in investment-grade bonds of US corporations with a minimum issuance size of $250 million.
- **Characteristic 2:** Valuation occurs on a weekly basis, because many of the bonds in the index are valued weekly.
- **Characteristic 3:** Historical prices and portfolio turnover are available for review.

Molly explains that, in order to evaluate the asset allocation process, fixed-income portfolios should have an appropriate benchmark. Leah asks for benchmark advice regarding DFC's portfolio of short-term and intermediate-term bonds, all denominated in US dollars. Molly presents three possible benchmarks in Exhibit 2.

EXHIBIT 2   Proposed Benchmark Portfolios

Benchmark	Index	Composition	Duration
1	Bloomberg Barclays US Bond Index	80% US government bonds 20% US corporate bonds	8.7
2 Index Blend	50% Bloomberg Barclays US Corporate Bond Index	100% US corporate bonds	7.5
	50% Bloomberg Barclays Short-Term Treasury Index	100% short-term US government debt	0.5
3	Bloomberg Barclays Global Aggregate Bond Index	60% EUR-denominated corporate bonds 40% US-denominated corporate debt	12.3

9. The investment process followed by DFC's previous fixed-income manager is *best* described as:
    A. asset-driven liabilities.
    B. liability-driven investing.
    C. asset–liability management.

10. Relative to Approach 1 of gaining passive exposure, an advantage of Approach 2 is that it:
    A. minimizes tracking error.
    B. requires less risk analysis.
    C. is more appropriate for socially responsible investors.

11. The two-bond hypothetical portfolio's immunization goal is to lock in a rate of return equal to:
    A. 9.55%.
    B. 9.85%.
    C. 10.25%.
12. Which of Molly's statements about liability-driven investing is (are) correct?
    A. Statement 1 only.
    B. Statement 2 only.
    C. Both Statement 1 and Statement 2.
13. Based on Exhibit 1, which of the portfolios will *best* immunize SD&R's single liability?
    A. Portfolio 1
    B. Portfolio 2
    C. Portfolio 3
14. Which of the portfolios in Exhibit 1 *best* minimizes the structural risk to a single-liability immunization strategy?
    A. Portfolio 1
    B. Portfolio 3
    C. Portfolio 4
15. Which of the custom benchmark's characteristics violates the requirements for an appropriate benchmark portfolio?
    A. Characteristic 1
    B. Characteristic 2
    C. Characteristic 3
16. Based on DFC's bond holdings and Exhibit 2, Molly should recommend:
    A. Benchmark 1.
    B. Benchmark 2.
    C. Benchmark 3.

The following information relates to Questions 17–22

Doug, the newly hired chief financial officer for the City of Radford, asks the deputy financial manager, Hui, to prepare an analysis of the current investment portfolio and the city's current and future obligations. The city has multiple liabilities of different amounts and maturities relating to the pension fund, infrastructure repairs, and various other obligations.

Hui observes that the current fixed-income portfolio is structured to match the duration of each liability. Previously, this structure caused the city to access a line of credit for temporary mismatches resulting from changes in the term structure of interest rates.

Doug asks Hui for different strategies to manage the interest rate risk of the city's fixed-income investment portfolio against one-time shifts in the yield curve. Hui considers two different strategies:

- Strategy 1: Immunization of the single liabilities using zero-coupon bonds held to maturity.
- Strategy 2: Immunization of the single liabilities using coupon-bearing bonds while continuously matching duration.

The city also manages a separate, smaller bond portfolio for the Radford School District. During the next five years, the school district has obligations for school expansions and renovations. The funds needed for those obligations are invested in the Bloomberg Barclays US Aggregate Index. Doug asks Hui which portfolio management strategy would be most efficient in mimicking this index.

A Radford School Board member has stated that she prefers a bond portfolio structure that provides diversification over time, as well as liquidity. In addressing the board member's inquiry, Hui examines a bullet portfolio, a barbell portfolio, and a laddered portfolio.

17. A disadvantage of Strategy 1 is that:
   A. price risk still exists.
   B. interest rate volatility introduces risk to effective matching.
   C. there may not be enough bonds available to match all liabilities.

18. Which duration measure should be matched when implementing Strategy 2?
   A. Key rate
   B. Modified
   C. Macaulay

19. An upward shift in the yield curve on Strategy 2 will *most likely* result in the:
   A. price effect canceling the coupon reinvestment effect.
   B. price effect being greater than the coupon reinvestment effect.
   C. coupon reinvestment effect being greater than the price effect.

20. The effects of a non-parallel shift in the yield curve on Strategy 2 can be reduced by:
   A. minimizing the convexity of the bond portfolio.
   B. maximizing the cash flow yield of the bond portfolio.
   C. minimizing the difference between liability duration and bond-portfolio duration.

21. Hui's response to Doug's question about the most efficient portfolio management strategy should be:
   A. full replication.
   B. active management.
   C. an enhanced indexing strategy.

22. Which portfolio structure should Hui recommend that would satisfy the school board member's preference?
   A. Bullet portfolio
   B. Barbell portfolio
   C. Laddered portfolio

The following information relates to Questions 23–25

Chaopraya is an investment advisor for high-net-worth individuals. One of her clients, Schuylkill, plans to fund her grandson's college education and considers two options:

- Option 1: Contribute a lump sum of $300,000 in 10 years.
- Option 2: Contribute four level annual payments of $76,500 starting in 10 years.

The grandson will start college in 10 years. Schuylkill seeks to immunize the contribution today.

For Option 1, Chaopraya calculates the present value of the $300,000 as $234,535. To immunize the future single outflow, Chaopraya considers three bond portfolios given that no zero-coupon government bonds are available. The three portfolios consist of non-callable, fixed-rate, coupon-bearing government bonds considered free of default risk. Chaopraya prepares a comparative analysis of the three portfolios, presented in Exhibit 1.

EXHIBIT 1   Results of Comparative Analysis of Potential Portfolios

	Portfolio A	Portfolio B	Portfolio C
Market value	$235,727	$233,428	$235,306
Cash flow yield	2.504%	2.506%	2.502%
Macaulay duration	9.998	10.002	9.503
Convexity	119.055	121.498	108.091

Chaopraya evaluates the three bond portfolios and selects one to recommend to Schuylkill.

23. Recommend the portfolio in Exhibit 1 that would *best* achieve the immunization. Justify your response.

Template for Question 23

Recommend the portfolio in Exhibit 1 that would *best* achieve the immunization. (circle one)	**Justify** your response.
Portfolio A	
Portfolio B	
Portfolio C	

Schuylkill and Chaopraya now discuss Option 2.

Chaopraya estimates the present value of the four future cash flows as $230,372, with a money duration of $2,609,700 and convexity of 135.142. She considers three possible portfolios to immunize the future payments, as presented in Exhibit 2.

EXHIBIT 2   Data for Bond Portfolios to Immunize Four Annual Contributions

	Portfolio 1	Portfolio 2	Portfolio 3
Market value	$245,178	$248,230	$251,337
Cash flow yield	2.521%	2.520%	2.516%
Money duration	2,609,981	2,609,442	2,609,707
Convexity	147.640	139.851	132.865

24. Determine the *most appropriate* immunization portfolio in Exhibit 2. Justify your decision.

Template for Question 24

Determine the *most appropriate* immunization portfolio in Exhibit 2. (circle one)	**Justify** your decision.
Portfolio 1	
Portfolio 2	
Portfolio 3	

After selecting a portfolio to immunize Schuylkill's multiple future outflows, Chaopraya prepares a report on how this immunization strategy would respond to various interest rate scenarios. The scenario analysis is presented in Exhibit 3.

EXHIBIT 3 Projected Portfolio Response to Interest Rate Scenarios

	Immunizing Portfolio	Outflow Portfolio	Difference
Upward parallel shift			
Δ Market value	−6,410	−6,427	18
Δ Cash flow yield	0.250%	0.250%	0.000%
Δ Portfolio BPV	−9	−8	−1
Downward parallel shift			
Δ Market value	6,626	6,622	4
Δ Cash flow yield	−0.250%	−0.250%	0.000%
Δ Portfolio BPV	9	8	1
Steepening twist			
Δ Market value	−1,912	347	−2,259
Δ Cash flow yield	0.074%	−0.013%	0.087%
Δ Portfolio BPV	−3	0	−3
Flattening twist			
Δ Market value	1,966	−343	2,309
Δ Cash flow yield	−0.075%	0.013%	−0.088%
Δ Portfolio BPV	3	0	3

25. Discuss the effectiveness of Chaopraya's immunization strategy in terms of duration gaps.

CHAPTER 14

YIELD CURVE STRATEGIES

LEARNING OUTCOMES

The candidate should be able to:

- describe the factors affecting fixed-income portfolio returns due to a change in benchmark yields;
- formulate a portfolio positioning strategy given forward interest rates and an interest rate view that coincides with the market view;
- formulate a portfolio positioning strategy given forward interest rates and an interest rate view that diverges from the market view in terms of rate level, slope, and shape;
- formulate a portfolio positioning strategy based upon expected changes in interest rate volatility;
- evaluate a portfolio's sensitivity using key rate durations of the portfolio and its benchmark;
- discuss yield curve strategies across currencies;
- evaluate the expected return and risks of a yield curve strategy.

SUMMARY OVERVIEW

This chapter addresses active fixed-income yield curve management using cash- and derivative-based strategies to generate returns, which exceed those of a benchmark index due to yield curve changes. The following are the main points in the chapter:

- A par yield curve is a stylized representation of yields-to-maturity available to investors at various maturities, which often does not consist of traded securities but must be extracted from available bond yields using a model.
- Primary yield curve risk factors may be categorized by changes in level (or a parallel "shift"), slope (a flatter or steeper yield curve), and shape or curvature.
- Yield curve slope measures the difference between the yield-to-maturity on a long-maturity bond and the yield-to-maturity on a shorter-maturity bond. Curvature is the relationship between short-, intermediate-, and long-term yields-to-maturity.
- Fixed-income portfolio managers can approximate actual and anticipated bond portfolio value changes using portfolio duration and convexity measures. Duration measures the linear relationship between bond prices and yield-to-maturity. Convexity is a second-order effect describing a bond's price behavior for larger rate movements and is affected by cash flow dispersion.

- A barbell portfolio combining short- and long-term bond positions will have greater convexity than a bullet portfolio concentrated in a single maturity for a given duration.
- Active managers seeking excess return in an expected static yield curve environment that is upward-sloping can use a buy-and-hold strategy to increase duration, roll down the yield curve, or use leverage via a carry trade in cash markets. Receive-fixed swaps and long futures positions replicate this exposure in the derivatives market.
- Derivatives offer the opportunity to synthetically change exposure with a far smaller initial cash outlay than cash strategies but require managers to maintain sufficient cash or eligible securities to fulfill margin or collateral requirements.
- Active fixed-income managers with a divergent rate level view increase duration exposure above a target if yields-to-maturity are expected to decline and reduce duration if expecting higher yields-to-maturity to minimize losses.
- Yield curve steepeners seek to gain from a greater spread between short- and long-term yields-to-maturity by combining a "long" short-dated bond position with a "short" long-dated bond position, while a flattener involves sale of short-term bonds and purchase of long-term bonds.
- Steepener and flattener strategies may be net duration neutral or net long or short duration depending upon a manager's view of how the yield curve slope will change—that is, the relative contribution of short- and long-term yield-to-maturity changes to the expected yield curve slope change.
- The butterfly strategy combining a long bullet with a short barbell portfolio (or vice versa) is commonly used to capitalize on expected yield curve shape changes.
- Active managers capitalize on a view as to whether future realized interest rate volatility will be greater or less than implied volatility by purchasing or selling bonds with embedded options or by using stand-alone interest rate options.
- Stand-alone interest rate put and call options are generally based upon a bond's price, not yield-to-maturity.
- Interest rate swaptions and options on bond futures are among the common tools used by active managers to alter portfolio duration and convexity subject to yield-to-maturity changes. An interest rate swaption involves the right to enter into an interest rate swap at a specific strike price in the future, while an option on a bond future involves the right, not the obligation, to buy or sell a futures contract.
- Key rate durations can be used in active fixed-income management to identify a bond portfolio's sensitivity to changes in the shape of the benchmark yield curve, allowing an active manager to quantify exposures along the curve.
- Fixed-income managers engaged in active yield curve strategies across currencies measure excess return from active management in functional currency terms—that is, considering domestic currency returns on foreign currency assets within a portfolio.
- Interest rate parity establishes the fundamental relationship between spot and forward exchange rates, with a higher-yielding currency trading at a forward discount and a lower-yielding currency trading at a premium.
- Covered interest rate parity involves the use of a forward contract to lock in domestic currency proceeds, while uncovered interest rate parity suggests that over time, the returns on unhedged foreign currency exposure will be the same as on a domestic currency investment.
- Active investors use the carry trade across currencies to take advantage of divergence from interest rate parity by borrowing in a lower-yield currency and investing in a higher-yield currency.
- A cross-currency swap enables investors to fully hedge the domestic currency value of cash flows associated with foreign currency bonds.

- Active managers deviate from fully hedged foreign currency bond cash flows by entering overweight and underweight bond positions denominated in different currencies, often using an underweight position in one currency to fund an overweight position in another.
- Investors evaluate the expected return on an active fixed-income portfolio strategy by combining coupon income and rolldown return with expected portfolio changes based on benchmark yield-to-maturity, credit, and currency value changes over the investment horizon.
- Unexpected market changes or risks to portfolio value are frequently evaluated using scenario analysis.

PROBLEMS

The following information relates to Questions 1–8

A Sydney-based fixed-income portfolio manager is considering the following Commonwealth of Australia government bonds traded on the ASX (Australian Stock Exchange):

Tenor	Coupon	Yield	Price	Modified Duration	Convexity
2y	5.75%	0.28%	110.90	1.922	4.9
4.5y	3.25%	0.55%	111.98	4.241	22.1
9y	2.50%	1.10%	111.97	8.175	85.2

The manager is considering portfolio strategies based upon various interest rate scenarios over the next 12 months. She is considering three long-only government bond portfolio alternatives, as follows:

Bullet: Invest solely in 4.5-year government bonds
Barbell: Invest equally in 2-year and 9-year government bonds
Equal weights: Invest equally in 2-year, 4.5-year, and 9-year bonds

1. The portfolio alternative with the *highest* modified duration is the:
   A. bullet portfolio.
   B. barbell portfolio.
   C. equally weighted portfolio.
2. The manager estimates that accelerated economic growth in Australia will increase the *level* of government yields-to-maturity by 50 bps. Under this scenario, which of the three portfolios experiences the *smallest* decline in market value?
   A. Bullet portfolio
   B. Barbell portfolio
   C. Equally weighted portfolio
3. Assume the manager is able to extend her mandate by adding derivatives strategies to the three portfolio alternatives. The best way to position her portfolio to benefit from a *bear flattening* scenario is to combine a:
   A. 2-year receive-fixed Australian dollar (AUD) swap with the *same* money duration as the bullet portfolio.
   B. 2-year pay-fixed AUD swap with *twice* the money duration as the 2-year government bond in the barbell portfolio.
   C. 9-year receive-fixed AUD swap with *twice* the money duration as the 9-year government bond position in the equally weighted portfolio.

4. In her market research, the manager learns that ASX 3-year and 10-year Treasury bond futures are the most liquid products for investors trading and hedging medium- to long-term Australian dollar (AUD) interest rates. Although neither contract matches the exact characteristics of the cash bonds of her choice, which of the following additions to a barbell portfolio *best* positions her to gain under a *bull flattening* scenario?
   A. Purchase a 3-year Treasury bond future matching the money duration of the short-term (2-year) position.
   B. Sell a 3-year Treasury bond future matching the money duration of the short-term bond position.
   C. Purchase a 10-year Treasury bond future matching the money duration of the long-term bond position.

5. An economic slowdown is expected to result in a 25 bp decline in Australian yield *levels*. Which portfolio alternative will experience the largest gain under this scenario?
   A. Bullet portfolio
   B. Barbell portfolio
   C. Equally weighted portfolio

6. The portfolio alternative with the *least* exposure to convexity is the:
   A. bullet portfolio.
   B. barbell portfolio.
   C. equally weighted portfolio.

7. The current butterfly spread for the Australian government yield curve based upon the manager's portfolio choices is:
   A. 83 bps.
   B. 28 bps.
   C. −28 bps.

8. If the manager has a positive butterfly view on Australian government yields-to-maturity, the *best* portfolio position strategy to pursue is to:
   A. purchase the bullet portfolio and sell the barbell portfolio.
   B. sell the bullet portfolio and sell the barbell portfolio.
   C. purchase the equally weighted portfolio and sell the barbell portfolio.

---

9. An analyst manages an active fixed-income fund that is benchmarked to the Bloomberg Barclays US Treasury Index. This index of US government bonds currently has a modified portfolio duration of 7.25 and an average maturity of 8.5 years. The yield curve is upward-sloping and expected to remain unchanged. Which of the following is the *least* attractive portfolio positioning strategy in a static curve environment?
   A. Purchasing a 10-year zero-coupon bond with a yield of 2% and a price of 82.035
   B. Entering a pay-fixed, 30-year USD interest rate swap
   C. Purchasing a 20-year Treasury and financing it in the repo market

10. A Dutch investor considering a 5-year EUR government bond purchase expects yields-to-maturity to decline by 25 bps in the next six months. Which of the following statements about the rolldown return is *correct*?
   A. The rolldown return equals the difference between the price of the 5-year bond and that of a 4.5-year bond at the lower yield-to-maturity.
   B. The rolldown return consists of the 5-year bond's basis point value multiplied by the expected 25 bp yield-to-maturity change over the next six months.

    C. The rolldown return will be negative if the 5-year bond has a zero coupon and is trading at a premium.

11. An investment manager is considering decreasing portfolio duration versus a benchmark index given her expectations of an upward parallel shift in the yield curve. If she has a choice between a callable, putable, or option-free bond with otherwise comparable characteristics, the most profitable position would be to:
    A. own the callable bond.
    B. own the putable bond.
    C. own the option-free bond.

12. An active fixed-income manager holds a portfolio of commercial and residential mortgage-backed securities that tracks the Bloomberg Barclays US Mortgage-Backed Securities Index. Which of the following choices is the most relevant portfolio statistic for evaluating the first-order change in his portfolio's value for a given change in benchmark yield?
    A. Effective duration
    B. Macaulay duration
    C. Modified duration

13. An active fund trader seeks to capitalize on an expected steepening of the current upward-sloping yield curve using option-based fixed-income instruments. Which of the following portfolio positioning strategies *best* positions her to gain if her interest rate view is realized?
    A. Sell a 30-year receiver swaption and a 2-year bond put option.
    B. Purchase a 30-year receiver swaption and a 2-year bond put option.
    C. Purchase a 30-year payer swaption and a 2-year bond call option.

The following information relates to Questions 14–17

A financial analyst at an in-house asset manager fund has created the following spreadsheet of key rate durations to compare her active position to that of a benchmark index so she can compare the rate sensitivities across maturities.

Tenor	KeyRateDur^{Active}	KeyRateDur^{Index}	Difference
2y	−0.532	0.738	−1.270
5y	0.324	1.688	−1.364
10y	5.181	2.747	2.434
30y	1.142	2.162	−1.020
Portfolio	6.115	7.335	−1.220

14. Which of the following statements is true if yield *levels* increase by 50 bps?
    A. The active portfolio will outperform the index portfolio by approximately 61 bps.
    B. The index portfolio will outperform the active portfolio by approximately 61 bps.
    C. The index portfolio will outperform the active portfolio by approximately 21 bps.

15. Which of the following statements best characterizes how the active portfolio is positioned for yield curve changes *relative* to the index portfolio?
    A. The active portfolio is positioned to benefit from a bear steepening of the yield curve versus the benchmark portfolio.

  B. The active portfolio is positioned to benefit from a positive butterfly movement in the shape of the yield curve versus the index.
  C. The active portfolio is positioned to benefit from yield curve flattening versus the index.
16. Which of the following derivatives strategies would *best* offset the yield curve exposure difference between the active and index portfolios?
  A. Add a pay-fixed 10-year swap and long 2-year, 5-year, and 30-year bond futures positions to the active portfolio.
  B. Add a receive-fixed 30-year swap, a pay-fixed 10-year swap, and short positions in 2-year and 5-year bond futures to the active portfolio.
  C. Add a pay-fixed 10-year swap, a short 30-year bond futures, and long 2-year and 5-year bond futures positions to the active portfolio.
17. Which of the following statements best describes the forward rate bias?
  A. Investors tend to favor fixed-income investments in currencies that trade at a premium on a forward basis.
  B. Investors tend to hedge fixed-income investments in higher-yielding currencies given the potential for lower returns due to currency depreciation.
  C. Investors tend to favor unhedged fixed-income investments in higher-yielding currencies that are sometimes enhanced by borrowing in lower-yielding currencies.

The following information relates to Questions 18–20

A US-based fixed-income portfolio manager is examining unhedged investments in Thai baht (THB) zero-coupon government bonds issued in Thailand and is considering two investment strategies:

1. **Buy-and-hold:** Purchase a 1-year, THB zero-coupon bond with a current yield-to-maturity of 1.00%.
2. **Roll down the THB yield curve:** Purchase a 2-year zero-coupon note with a current yield-to-maturity of 2.00% and sell it in a year.

THB proceeds under each strategy will be converted into USD at the end of the 1-year investment horizon. The manager expects a stable THB yield curve and that THB will appreciate by 1.5% relative to USD. The following information is used to analyze these two investment strategies:

Statistic	Buy and Hold	Yield Curve Rolldown
Investment horizon (years)	1.0	1.0
Bond maturity at purchase (years)	1.0	2.0
Yield-to-maturity (today)	1.00%	2.00%
Average portfolio bond price (today)	99.0090	96.1169
Expected average portfolio bond price (in 1 year)	100.00	99.0090
Expected currency gains (in 1 year)	1.5%	1.5%

18. The *rolldown returns* over the 1-year investment horizon for the Buy-and-Hold and Yield Curve Rolldown portfolios are closest to:
    A. 1.00% for the Buy-and-Hold portfolio and 3.01% for the Yield Curve Rolldown portfolio, respectively.
    B. 0.991% for the Buy-and-Hold portfolio and 3.01% for the Yield Curve Rolldown portfolio, respectively.
    C. 0.991% for the Buy-and-Hold portfolio and 2.09% for the Yield Curve Rolldown portfolio, respectively.

19. The *total expected return* over the 1-year investment horizon for the Buy-and-Hold and Yield Curve Rolldown portfolios are closest to:
    A. 2.515% for the Buy-and-Hold portfolio and 4.555% for the Yield Curve rolldown portfolio, respectively.
    B. 2.42% for the Buy-and-Hold portfolio and 4.51% for the Yield Curve Rolldown portfolio, respectively.
    C. 2.491% for the Buy-and-Hold portfolio and 3.59% for the Yield Curve Rolldown portfolio, respectively.

20. Which of the following statements best describes how the expected total return results would *change* if THB yields were to rise significantly over the investment horizon?
    A. Both the Buy-and-Hold and Yield Curve Rolldown expected portfolio returns would *increase* due to higher THB yields.
    B. Both the Buy-and-Hold and Yield Curve Rolldown expected portfolio returns would *decrease* due to higher THB yields.
    C. The Buy-and-Hold expected portfolio returns would be *unchanged* and the Yield Curve Rolldown expected portfolio returns would *decrease* due to the rise in yields.

---

21. An active investor enters a duration-neutral yield curve flattening trade that combines 2-year and 10-year Treasury positions. Under which of the following yield curve scenarios would you expect the investor to realize the *greatest* portfolio gain?
    A. Bear flattening
    B. Bull flattening
    C. Yield curve inversion

CHAPTER 15

FIXED-INCOME ACTIVE MANAGEMENT: CREDIT STRATEGIES

LEARNING OUTCOMES

The candidate should be able to:

- describe risk considerations for spread-based fixed-income portfolios;
- discuss the advantages and disadvantages of credit spread measures for spread-based fixed-income portfolios, and explain why option-adjusted spread is considered the most appropriate measure;
- discuss bottom-up approaches to credit strategies;
- discuss top-down approaches to credit strategies;
- discuss liquidity risk in credit markets and how liquidity risk can be managed in a credit portfolio;
- describe how to assess and manage tail risk in credit portfolios;
- discuss the use of credit default swap strategies in active fixed-income portfolio management;
- discuss various portfolio positioning strategies that managers can use to implement a specific credit spread view;
- discuss considerations in constructing and managing portfolios across international credit markets;
- describe the use of structured financial instruments as an alternative to corporate bonds in credit portfolios;
- describe key inputs, outputs, and considerations in using analytical tools to manage fixed-income portfolios.

SUMMARY OVERVIEW

Active spread-based, fixed-income portfolio management involves taking positions in credit and other risk factors that differ from those of an index to generate excess return. The main points of the reading are as follows:

- Yield spreads compensate investors for the risk that they will not receive expected interest and principal cash flows and for the bid–offer cost of buying or selling a bond under current market conditions.
- Two key components of a bond's credit risk are the POD and the LGD.
- Credit spread changes are driven by the credit cycle, or the expansion and contraction of credit over the business cycle, which causes asset prices to change based on default and recovery expectations.
- High-yield issuers experience greater changes in the POD over the credit cycle than investment-grade issuers, with bond prices approaching the recovery rate for distressed debt.
- While fixed-rate bond yield spread measures use actual, interpolated, or zero curve–based benchmark rates to capture relative credit risk, OAS allow comparison between risky option-free bonds and bonds with embedded options.
- FRNs pay periodic interest based on an MRR plus a yield spread.
- Spread duration measures the change in a bond's price for a given change in yield spread, while spread changes for lower-rated bonds tend to be proportional on a percentage rather than an absolute basis.
- Bottom-up credit strategies include the use of financial ratio analysis, reduced form credit models (such as the Z-score model), and structural credit models, including Bloomberg's DRSK model.
- Top-down credit strategies are often based on macro factors and group investment choices by credit rating and industry sector categories.
- Fixed-income factor investing incorporates such factors as size, value, and momentum to target active returns and also increasingly include ESG factors.
- Liquidity risk in credit markets is higher than in equities because of market structure differences and is often addressed using liquid bonds for short-term tactical positioning, less liquid positions for buy-and-hold strategies, and liquid alternatives where active management adds little value.
- Credit market tail risk is usually quantified using VaR or expected shortfall measures and is frequently managed using position limits, risk budgeting, or derivative strategies.
- Credit derivative strategies offer a synthetic liquid alternative to active portfolio managers as a means of over- or underweighting issuers, sectors, and/or maturities across the credit spectrum.
- Credit spread levels and curve slopes change over the credit cycle, with credit curve steepening usually indicating low near-term default expectations and higher growth expectations, while curve flattening, or inversion, suggests rising default expectations and lower future growth.
- Active credit managers can benefit under a stable credit curve scenario by adding spread duration for existing exposures and/or increasing average portfolio credit risk and can capitalize on divergent market views using cash- or derivative-based strategies related to specific issuers, sectors, or the overall credit market.
- Investors in international credit markets distinguish between developed and emerging markets. Developed markets face common macro factors, with market and credit cycle

differences affecting relative interest rates, foreign exchange rates, and credit spreads. Emerging markets usually exhibit higher growth combined with greater sovereign and geopolitical risk, currency restrictions, and capital controls.

- Structured financial instruments offer active credit managers access to liquid bond portfolios, fixed-income cash flows derived from real estate and consumer loans, and enhanced returns by adding volatility and/or debt exposure via tranching across the credit spectrum.
- Key considerations for fixed-income analytical tools include the accuracy of model inputs and assumptions as well as alignment between model outputs and fixed-income manager objectives.

PROBLEMS

1. Which of the following statements best describes empirical duration?
   A. A common way to calculate a bond's empirical duration is to run a regression of its price returns on changes in a benchmark interest rate.
   B. A bond's empirical duration tends to be larger than its effective duration.
   C. The price sensitivity of high-yield bonds to interest rate changes is typically higher than that of investment-grade bonds.
2. A junior analyst considers a 10-year high-yield bond issued by EKN Corporation (EKN) position in a high-yield portfolio. The bond has a price of 91.82, a modified duration of 8.47, and a spread duration of 8.47. The analyst speculates on the effects of an interest rate increase of 20 bps and, because of a change in its credit risk, an increase in the EKN bond's credit spread of 20 bps. The analyst comments that because the modified duration and the credit spread duration of the EKN bond are equal, the bond's price will not change (all else being equal) in response to the interest rate and credit spread changes.

   Is the analyst's prediction correct that the EKN bond price will not change in response to the interest rate and credit spread changes, all else being equal?
   A. Yes.
   B. No, the bond price should decrease.
   C. No, the bond price should increase.
3. Which of the following outcomes is most likely if the junior analyst revises the bond's original recovery rate higher?
   A. An increase in the bond's POD
   B. A decrease in the bond's POD
   C. A decrease in the bond's credit spread
4. Which of the following observations on the risks of spread-based fixed-income portfolios is the most accurate?
   A. Because credit spreads equal the product of the LGD and the POD, distinguishing between the credit risk and liquidity risk components of yield spread across all market scenarios is straightforward.
   B. Given that frequent issuers with many bonds outstanding across maturities have their own issuer-specific credit curve, distinguishing between the credit spread and liquidity spread of all bonds for these issuers is straightforward.
   C. The yield spread of a particular bond comprises both credit and liquidity risk and depends on market conditions and the specific supply-and-demand dynamics of each fixed-income security.

The following information relates to Questions 5–8

An active portfolio manager observes the following market information related to an outstand-ing corporate bond and two on-the-run government bonds that pay annual coupons:

Issuer	Term	Coupon	Yield	ModDur
Corporate	12y	3.00%	2.80%	9.99
Government	10y	1.75%	1.85%	9.09
Government	20y	2.25%	2.30%	15.94

The portfolio manager also observes 10-year and 20-year swap spreads of 0.20% and 0.25%, respectively.

5. Calculate the G-spread of the corporate bond.
   A. 0.860%
   B. 0.725%
   C. 0.950%
6. Calculate the I-spread of the corporate bond.
   A. 0.85%
   B. 0.65%
   C. 0.95%
7. Calculate the ASW of the corporate bond.
   A. 0.65%
   B. 0.95%
   C. 0.85%
8. Estimate the corporate bond's percentage price change if the government yield curve steepens, assuming a 0.20% increase in the 20-year YTM and no change to the 10-year government YTM or corporate G-spread.
   A. −0.40%
   B. 0.40%
   C. −0.04%

9. Which of the following statements about credit spread measures is most accurate?
   A. The DM is the yield spread over the MRR established upon issuance to compensate investors for assuming an issuer's credit risk.
   B. The Z-DM will be above the DM if the MRR is expected to remain constant over time.
   C. The yield spread for a corporate bond will be equal to the G-spread if the government benchmark yield curve is flat.

The following information relates to Questions 10–12

An active fixed-income manager is considering two corporate bond positions for an active portfolio. The first bond has a BBB rating with a credit spread of 2.75% and an effective spread duration of 6, and the second bond has a BB rating with a credit spread of 3.50% and an effective spread duration of five years.

10. What is the approximate excess return if the BBB rated bond is held for six months and the credit spread narrows by 40 bps, ignoring spread duration changes and assuming no default losses?
    A. 3.775%
    B. 2.35%
    C. 2.40%
11. What is the instantaneous (holding period of zero) excess return for the BB rated bond if the spread widens by 50 bps?
    A. 3.00%
    B. −2.50%
    C. 2.50%
12. What is the expected excess spread of the BBB rated bond for an instantaneous 50 bp decline in yields if the bond's LGD is 40% and the POD is 0.75%?
    A. 1.95%
    B. 2.45%
    C. 2.70%

---

13. An active manager is considering the senior bonds of one of several corporate issuers. Holding other factors constant, which of the following key financial ratio changes would lead the manager to expect a decrease in the POD for that issuer?
    A. An increase in the issuer's coverage ratio
    B. An increase in the issuer's stock price volatility
    C. An increase in the issuer's leverage ratio
14. Which of the following statements about statistical credit analysis models is most accurate?
    A. Structural credit models solve for the POD using observable company-specific variables such as financial ratios and macroeconomic variables.
    B. Reduced-form credit models use market-based variables to estimate an issuer's asset value and the volatility of asset value.
    C. Structural credit models define the likelihood of default as the probability of the asset value falling below that of liabilities.

The following information relates to Questions 15–17

An investor is faced with an active portfolio decision across three bond rating categories based on the following current market information:

Rating Category	Current OAS	Expected Loss (POD × LGD)	EffSpreadDur
A	1.00%	0.10%	7
BBB	1.75%	0.75%	6
BB	2.75%	2.50%	5

15. Which bond rating category offers the highest expected excess return if credit spreads remain stable under current market conditions?
    A. A rated bond category
    B. BBB rated bond category
    C. BB rated bond category

16. Which active bond portfolio maximizes expected excess return under a stable credit market assumption versus an equally weighted benchmark portfolio across the three rating categories?
    A. 50% A rated bonds, 50% BBB rated bonds
    B. 50% BBB rated bonds, 50% BB rated bonds
    C. 50% A rated bonds, 50% B rated bonds
17. Which bond rating category offers the highest expected excess return if spreads instantaneously rise 10% across all ratings categories?
    A. A rated bond category
    B. BBB rated bond category
    C. BB rated bond category

---

18. Which of the following strategies best addresses the liquidity risk of a less frequently traded bond position in an active manager's portfolio?
    A. Enter into a receive fixed, pay floating asset swap, unwinding the swap position once the illiquid bond position is sold.
    B. Sell single-name CDS protection on the illiquid bond issuer, unwinding the CDS contract when the bond is sold.
    C. Allocate the illiquid bond to the buy-and-hold portion of the investment portfolio.
19. Which of the following statements best describes methods for assessing portfolio tail risk?
    A. Parametric methods use expected value and standard deviation of risk factors under a normal distribution and are well suited for option-based portfolios.
    B. Historical simulation methods use historical parameters and ranking results and are not well suited for option-based portfolios.
    C. Monte Carlo methods generate random outcomes using portfolio measures and sensitivities and are well suited for option-based portfolios.

The following information relates to Questions 20 and 21

An investor is considering the portfolio impact of a new 12-year corporate bond position with a $75 million face value, a 3.25% coupon, current YTM of 2.85%, modified duration of 9.887, and a price of 104.0175 per 100 of face value.
20. Which of the following VaR measures is most appropriate for the portfolio manager to use to evaluate how this position would affect portfolio tail risk?
    A. CVaR
    B. Relative VaR
    C. Incremental VaR
21. What is the approximate VaR for the bond position at a 99% confidence interval (equal to 2.33 standard deviations) for one month (with 21 trading days) if daily yield volatility is 1.50% and returns are normally distributed?
    A. $1,234,105
    B. $2,468,210
    C. $5,413,133

---

22. Which of the following statements best describes how a single-name CDS contract is priced at inception?
    A. If the reference entity's credit spread trades below the standard coupon rate, the CDS contract will be priced at a premium above par because the protection buyer pays a "below market" periodic coupon.

B. If the reference entity's credit spread trades above the standard coupon rate, the CDS contract will be priced at a discount to par because the protection seller effectively receives a "below market" periodic premium.

C. Similar to fixed-rate bonds, CDS contracts are initially priced at par with a fixed coupon and a price that changes over time as the reference entity's credit spreads change.

The following information relates to Questions 23 and 24

An active portfolio manager seeking to purchase single-name CDS protection observes a 1.75% 10-year market credit spread for a private investment-grade issuer. The effective spread duration is 8.75 and CDS basis is close to zero.

23. What should the protection buyer expect to pay or receive to enter a new 10-year CDS contract?
   A. The buyer should receive approximately 6.5625% of the notional.
   B. The buyer should pay approximately 15.3125% of the notional.
   C. The buyer should pay approximately 6.5625% of the notional.

24. Once the manager purchases CDS protection, the issuer's CDS spread immediately falls to 1.60%. What is the investor's approximate mark-to-market gain or loss for a contract notional of €10,000,000?
   A. The manager realizes an approximate loss of €131,250.
   B. The manager realizes an approximate gain of €131,250.
   C. The manager realizes an approximate gain of €525,000.

25. Which of the following credit portfolio positioning strategies is the most appropriate to underweight the financial sector versus an index?
   A. Purchase protection on the CDX and sell protection on the CDX Financials subindex.
   B. Sell protection on the CDX and purchase protection on the CDX Financials subindex.
   C. Purchase a payer option on the CDX and sell protection on the CDX Financials subindex.

26. Which of the following phases of the credit cycle typically involves a decline in the number of issuer defaults?
   A. Late expansion phase
   B. Early expansion phase
   C. Peak phase

27. Which of the following regarding the shape of the credit spread curve for high-yield issuers is most accurate?
   A. High-yield credit spread curves change shape more over the cycle than investment-grade ones do and usually invert during the peak phase.
   B. Investors should exercise caution in interpreting credit spread curve shape for distressed debt issuers because their bonds tend to trade on a price rather than credit spread basis as the likelihood of default increases.
   C. High-yield credit spread curves often invert because of the empirical observation that DTS is the best way to measure high-yield bond price changes.

28. Which of the following statements best describes a credit curve roll-down strategy?
   A. Returns from a credit curve roll-down strategy can be estimated by combining the incremental coupon from a longer maturity corporate bond with price appreciation due to the passage of time.

    B. A synthetic credit curve roll-down strategy involves purchasing protection using a single-name CDS contract for a longer maturity.

    C. A credit curve roll-down strategy is expected to generate a positive return if the credit spread curve is upward sloping.

The following information relates to Questions 29 and 30

An investor observes the following current CDS market information:

CDX Contract	Tenor (years)	CDS Spread	EffSpreadDur$_{CDS}$
CDX IG Index	5	85 bps	4.9
CDX IG Index	10	135 bps	8.9
CDX HY Index	5	175 bps	4.7
CDX HY Index	10	275 bps	8.7

29. Select the most appropriate credit portfolio positioning strategy to capitalize on an expected steepening of the investment-grade credit spread curve.

    A. Sell protection on the 10-year CDX IG index and purchase protection on the 5-year CDX IG index using contracts of equal notional value.

    B. Sell protection on the 10-year CDX IG index and purchase protection on the 5-year CDX IG index using a contract with a notional amount equal to 1.82 times that of the 10-year contract.

    C. Buy protection on the 10-year CDX IG index and sell protection on the 5-year CDX IG index using a contract with a notional amount equal to 1.82 times that of the 10-year contract.

30. Which of the following is the most appropriate credit portfolio positioning strategy to capitalize on an expected economic contraction?

    A. Buy protection on the 5-year CDX HY index and sell protection on the 5-year CDX IG index in approximately equal notional amounts.

    B. Buy protection on the 10-year CDX IG index and sell protection on the 5-year CDX IG index using a contract with a notional amount equal to 1.82 times that of the 10-year contract.

    C. Buy protection on the 10-year CDX HY index and sell protection on the 5-year CDX HY index using a contract with a notional amount equal to 1.85 times that of the 10-year contract.

31. Which of the following is the most accurate statement related to international credit markets?

    A. Fixed exchange-rate regimes among emerging markets usually reduce the likelihood of financial distress because the domestic currency is tied to a major foreign currency.

    B. Although many emerging economies have domestic bond markets that include sovereign, financial, and corporate issuers, investments across these bonds offer less diversification than similar investments in developed markets.

    C. Higher domestic currency YTMs among emerging versus developed markets are due to expected currency appreciation resulting from higher economic growth.

The following information relates to Questions 32 and 33

An active United States–based credit manager faces the following US and European investment-grade and high-yield corporate bond portfolio choices:

Rating Category	OAS	EffSpreadDur	Expected Loss
USD IG	1.25%	4.50	0.40%
USD HY	3.00%	5.50	2.25%
EUR IG	1.15%	4.75	0.50%
EUR HY	3.25%	6.00	2.50%

The EUR IG and EUR HY allocations are denominated in euros, and the euro is expected to depreciate by 2% versus the US dollar over the next year.

32. What is the approximate unhedged excess return to the United States–based credit manager for an international credit portfolio index equally weighted across the four portfolio choices, assuming no change to spread duration and no default losses occur?
    A. −0.257%
    B. −0.850%
    C. 0.750%

33. Which of the following active portfolios is expected to have the highest excess return versus the index if European economies are expected to experience an earlier and much stronger credit cycle recovery than the United States?
    A. EUR HY 50.0%, EUR IG 25.0%, USD IG 12.5%, USD HY 12.5%
    B. EUR IG 50.0%, EUR HY 25.0%, USD IG 12.5%, USD HY 12.5%
    C. EUR HY 33.3%, US HY 33.3%, EUR IG 16.7%, USD IG 16.7%

---

34. Which of the following statements about the role of structured products in an active credit portfolio is most accurate?
    A. Covered bonds perform relatively well in a downturn versus other fixed-income bonds with real estate exposure because a covered bond investor also has recourse to the issuer.
    B. Higher-rated ABS tranches are attractive for active investors seeking to overweight default risk when the credit cycle is in recovery.
    C. CLO tranches are more advantageous than CDO tranches with similar ratings under an economic slowdown scenario.

35. An active fixed-income manager is evaluating the relative performance of an investment-grade corporate versus a high-yield corporate debt allocation in a fixed-income portfolio. Which of the following analytical model assumption changes is most likely to reduce the future value of the high-yield portfolio relative to the investment-grade holdings?
    A. Steepening of the benchmark yield volatility curve
    B. Decreased likelihood of an economic slowdown
    C. Increased likelihood of a flight to quality associated with bullish benchmark yield curve flattening (long-term rates fall by more than short-term rates do)

PART II

SOLUTIONS

CHAPTER 1

FIXED-INCOME SECURITIES: DEFINING ELEMENTS

SOLUTIONS

1. A is correct. The tenor of the bond is the time remaining until the bond's maturity date. Although the bond had a maturity of ten years at issuance (original maturity), it was issued four years ago. Thus, there are six years remaining until the maturity date.

   B is incorrect because the nominal rate is the coupon rate (i.e., the interest rate that the issuer agrees to pay each year until the maturity date). Although interest is paid semi-annually, the nominal rate is 10%, not 5%. C is incorrect because it is the bond's price, not its redemption value (also called principal amount, principal value, par value, face value, nominal value, or maturity value), that is equal to 102% of the par value.

2. C is correct. A capital market security has an original maturity longer than one year.

   A is incorrect because a perpetual bond does not have a stated maturity date. Thus, the sovereign bond, which has a maturity of 15 years, cannot be a perpetual bond. B is incorrect because a pure discount bond is a bond issued at a discount to par value and redeemed at par. Some sovereign bonds (e.g., Treasury bills) are pure discount bonds, but others are not.

3. C is correct. The coupon rate that applies to the interest payment due on 30 June is based on the three-month MRR rate prevailing on 31 March. Thus, the coupon rate is 1.55% + 0.65% = 2.20%.

4. B is correct. The indenture, also referred to as trust deed, is the legal contract that describes the form of the bond, the obligations of the issuer, and the rights of the bondholders.

   A is incorrect because covenants are only one element of a bond's indenture. Covenants are clauses that specify the rights of the bondholders and any actions that the issuer is obligated to perform or prohibited from performing. C is incorrect because a debenture is a type of bond.

5. B is correct. A surety bond is an external credit enhancement (i.e., a guarantee received from a third party). If the issuer defaults, the guarantor who provided the surety bond will reimburse investors for any losses, usually up to a maximum amount called the penal sum.

A is incorrect because covenants are legally enforceable rules that borrowers and lenders agree upon when the bond is issued. C is incorrect because overcollateralization is an internal, not external, credit enhancement. Collateral is a guarantee underlying the debt above and beyond the issuer's promise to pay, and overcollateralization refers to the process of posting more collateral than is needed to obtain or secure financing. Collateral, such as assets or securities pledged to ensure debt payments, is not provided by a third party. Thus, overcollateralization is not an external credit enhancement.

6. B is correct. Affirmative (or positive) covenants enumerate what issuers are required to do and are typically administrative in nature. A common affirmative covenant describes what the issuer intends to do with the proceeds from the bond issue.

   A and C are incorrect because imposing a limit on the issuer's leverage ratio or on the percentage of the issuer's gross assets that can be sold are negative covenants. Negative covenants prevent the issuer from taking actions that could reduce its ability to make interest payments and repay the principal.

7. B is correct. Prohibiting the issuer from investing in risky projects restricts the issuer's potential business decisions. These restrictions are referred to as negative bond covenants.

   A and C are incorrect because paying taxes as they come due and maintaining the current lines of business are positive covenants.

8. C is correct. Bonds sold in a country and denominated in that country's currency by an entity from another country are referred to as foreign bonds.

   A is incorrect because Eurobonds are bonds issued outside the jurisdiction of any single country. B is incorrect because global bonds are bonds issued in the Eurobond market and at least one domestic country simultaneously.

9. A is correct. Eurobonds are typically issued as bearer bonds (i.e., bonds for which the trustee does not keep records of ownership). In contrast, domestic and foreign bonds are typically registered bonds for which ownership is recorded by either name or serial number.

   B is incorrect because Eurobonds are typically issued as bearer bonds, not registered bonds. C is incorrect because Eurobonds are typically subject to lower, not greater, regulation than domestic and foreign bonds.

10. C is correct. The original issue discount tax provision requires the investor to include a prorated portion of the original issue discount in his taxable income every tax year until maturity. The original issue discount is equal to the difference between the bond's par value and its original issue price.

    A is incorrect because the original issue discount tax provision allows the investor to increase his cost basis in the bond so that when the bond matures, he faces no capital gain or loss. B is incorrect because the original issue discount tax provision does not require any tax deduction in the year the bond is purchased or afterwards.

11. C is correct. A fully amortized bond calls for equal cash payments by the bond's issuer prior to maturity. Each fixed payment includes both an interest payment component and a principal repayment component such that the bond's outstanding principal amount is reduced to zero by the maturity date.

    A and B are incorrect because a bullet bond or plain vanilla bond only make interest payments prior to maturity. The entire principal repayment occurs at maturity.

12. C is correct. A cap in a floating-rate note (capped FRN) prevents the coupon rate from increasing above a specified maximum rate. This feature benefits the issuer in a rising interest rate environment because it sets a limit to the interest rate paid on the debt.

A is incorrect because a bond with a step-up coupon is one in which the coupon, which may be fixed or floating, increases by specified margins at specified dates. This feature benefits the bondholders, not the issuer, in a rising interest rate environment because it allows bondholders to receive a higher coupon in line with the higher market interest rates. B is incorrect because inflation-linked bonds have their coupon payments and/or principal repayment linked to an index of consumer prices. If interest rates increase as a result of inflation, this feature is a benefit for the bondholders, not the issuer.

13. C is correct. In contrast to fixed-rate bonds that decline in value in a rising interest rate environment, floating-rate notes (FRNs) are less affected when interest rates increase because their coupon rates vary with market interest rates and are reset at regular, short-term intervals. Consequently, FRNs are favored by investors who believe that interest rates will rise.

    A is incorrect because an inverse floater is a bond whose coupon rate has an inverse relationship to the reference rate, so when interest rates rise, the coupon rate on an inverse floater decreases. Thus, inverse floaters are favored by investors who believe that interest rates will decline, not rise. B is incorrect because fixed rate-bonds decline in value in a rising interest rate environment. Consequently, investors who expect interest rates to rise will likely avoid investing in fixed-rate bonds.

14. C is correct. Capital-indexed bonds pay a fixed coupon rate that is applied to a principal amount that increases in line with increases in the index during the bond's life. If the consumer price index increases by 2%, the coupon rate remains unchanged at 6%, but the principal amount increases by 2% and the coupon payment is based on the inflation-adjusted principal amount. On the first coupon payment date, the inflation-adjusted principal amount is $1{,}000 \times (1 + 0.02) = 1{,}020$ and the semi-annual coupon payment is equal to $(0.06 \times 1{,}020) \div 2 = 30.60$.

15. A is correct. A put provision provides bondholders the right to sell the bond back to the issuer at a predetermined price prior to the bond's maturity date.

    B is incorrect because a make-whole call provision is a form of call provision (i.e., a provision that provides the issuer the right to redeem all or part of the bond before its maturity date). A make-whole call provision requires the issuer to make a lump sum payment to the bondholders based on the present value of the future coupon payments and principal repayments not paid because of the bond being redeemed early by the issuer. C is incorrect because an original issue discount provision is a tax provision relating to bonds issued at a discount to par value. The original issue discount tax provision typically requires the bondholders to include a prorated portion of the original issue discount (i.e., the difference between the par value and the original issue price) in their taxable income every tax year until the bond's maturity date.

16. B is correct. A call provision (callable bond) gives the issuer the right to redeem all or part of the bond before the specified maturity date. If market interest rates decline or the issuer's credit quality improves, the issuer of a callable bond can redeem it and replace it by a cheaper bond. Thus, the call provision is beneficial to the issuer.

    A is incorrect because a put provision (putable bond) is beneficial to the bondholders. If interest rates rise, thus lowering the bond's price, the bondholders have the right to sell the bond back to the issuer at a predetermined price on specified dates. C is incorrect because a conversion provision (convertible bond) is beneficial to the bondholders. If the issuing company's share price increases, the bondholders have the right to exchange the bond for a specified number of common shares in the issuing company.

17. A is correct. A put feature is beneficial to the bondholders. Thus, the price of a putable bond will typically be higher than the price of an otherwise similar non-putable bond.

    B is incorrect because a call feature is beneficial to the issuer. Thus, the price of a callable bond will typically be lower, not higher, than the price of an otherwise similar non-callable bond. C is incorrect because a conversion feature is beneficial to the bondholders. Thus, the price of a convertible bond will typically be higher, not lower, than the price of an otherwise similar non-convertible bond.

18. C is correct. A zero-coupon, or pure discount, bond pays no interest; instead, it is issued at a discount to par value and redeemed at par. As a result, the interest earned is implied and equal to the difference between the par value and the purchase price.

19. A is correct. Covenants specify the rights of the bondholders and any actions that the issuer is obligated to perform or is prohibited from performing.

20. A is correct. A covered bond is a debt obligation backed by a segregated pool of assets called a "cover pool." When the assets that are included in the cover pool become non-performing (i.e., the assets are not generating the promised cash flows), the issuer must replace them with performing assets.

21. C is correct. Negative covenants enumerate what issuers are prohibited from doing. Restrictions on debt, including maintaining a minimum interest coverage ratio or a maximum debt usage ratio, are typical examples of negative covenants.

22. A is correct. Affirmative covenants typically do not impose additional costs to the issuer, while negative covenants are frequently costly. B is incorrect because all bond covenants are legally enforceable rules, so there is no difference in this regard between positive and negative bond covenants. C is incorrect because borrowers and lenders agree on all bond covenants at the time of a new bond issue, so there is no difference in this regard between positive and negative bond covenants.

23. B is correct. A bond that is fully amortized is characterized by a fixed periodic payment schedule that reduces the bond's outstanding principal amount to zero by the maturity date. The stream of £230.97 payments reflects the cash flows of a fully amortized bond with a coupon rate of 5% and annual interest payments.

24. B is correct. A credit-linked coupon bond has a coupon that changes when the bond's credit rating changes. Because credit ratings tend to decline the most during recessions, credit-linked coupon bonds may thus provide some general protection against a poor economy by offering increased coupon payments when credit ratings decline.

25. B is correct. Deferred coupon bonds pay no coupon for their first few years but then pay higher coupons than they otherwise normally would for the remainder of their life. Deferred coupon bonds are common in project financing when the assets being developed may not generate any income during the development phase, thus not providing cash flows to make interest payments. A deferred coupon bond allows the issuer to delay interest payments until the project is completed and the cash flows generated by the assets can be used to service the debt.

26. C is correct. A putable bond is beneficial for the bondholder by guaranteeing a prespecified selling price at the redemption date, thus offering protection when interest rates rise and bond prices decline. Relative to a one-time put bond that incorporates a single sellback opportunity, a multiple put bond offers more frequent sellback opportunities, thus providing the most benefit to bondholders.

27. C is correct. An American call option gives the issuer the right to call the bond at any time starting on the first call date.

28. A is correct. The conversion premium is the difference between the convertible bond's price and its conversion value.

CHAPTER 2

FIXED-INCOME MARKETS: ISSUANCE, TRADING, AND FUNDING

SOLUTIONS

1. B is correct. The distinction between investment-grade and non-investment-grade debt relates to differences in credit quality, not tax status or maturity dates. Debt markets are classified based on the issuer's creditworthiness as judged by the credit ratings agencies. Ratings of Baa3 or above by Moody's Investors Service or BBB– or above by Standard & Poor's and Fitch Ratings are considered investment grade, whereas ratings below these levels are referred to as non–investment grade (also called high yield, speculative, or junk).

2. A is correct. Eurobonds are issued internationally, outside the jurisdiction of any single country. B is incorrect because foreign bonds are considered international bonds, but they are issued in a specific country, in the currency of that country, by an issuer domiciled in another country. C is incorrect because municipal bonds are US domestic bonds issued by a state or local government.

3. B is correct. Asset-backed securities are securitized debt instruments created by securitization, a process that involves transferring ownership of assets from the original owners to a special legal entity. The special legal entity then issues securities backed by the transferred assets. The assets' cash flows are used to pay interest and repay the principal owed to the holders of the securities. Assets that are typically used to create securitized debt instruments include loans (such as mortgage loans) and receivables (such as credit card receivables). The structured finance sector includes such securitized debt instruments (also called asset-backed securities).

4. B is correct. Many emerging countries lag developed countries in the areas of political stability, property rights, and contract enforcement. Consequently, emerging market bonds usually exhibit higher risk than developed market bonds. A is incorrect because emerging market bonds typically offer higher (not lower) yields than developed market bonds to compensate investors for the higher risk. C is incorrect because emerging market bonds usually benefit from higher (not lower) growth prospects than developed market bonds.

5. B is correct. The coupon rate of a floating-rate bond is expressed as a reference rate plus a spread. Different reference rates are used depending on where the bond is issued and its currency denomination, but one of the most widely used set of reference rates is Libor. A and C are incorrect because a bond's spread and frequency of coupon payments are typically set when the bond is issued and do not change during the bond's life.

6. A is correct. Changes in the coupon rate of interest on a floating-rate bond that uses a Libor reference rate result from changes in the reference rate (for example, 90-day Libor), which resets periodically. Therefore, the coupon rate adjusts to the level of market interest rates (plus the spread) each time the reference rate is reset.

7. C is correct. Interbank offered rates are used as reference rates not only for floating-rate bonds but also for other debt instruments, including mortgages, derivatives such as interest rate and currency swaps, and many other financial contracts and products. A and B are incorrect because an interbank offered rate such as Libor or Euribor is a set of reference rates (not a single reference rate) for different borrowing periods of up to one year (not 10 years).

8. A is correct. In an underwritten offering (also called firm commitment offering), the investment bank (called the underwriter) guarantees the sale of the bond issue at an offering price that is negotiated with the issuer. Thus, the underwriter takes the risk of buying the newly issued bonds from the issuer and then reselling them to investors or to dealers, which then sell them to investors. B and C are incorrect because the bond issuing mechanism in which an investment bank acts as a broker and receives a commission for selling the bonds to investors, and incurs less risk associated with selling the bonds, is a best-efforts offering (not an underwritten offering).

9. A is correct. In major developed bond markets, newly issued sovereign bonds are sold to the public via an auction. B and C are incorrect because sovereign bonds are rarely issued via private placements or best-efforts offerings.

10. A is correct. Private placements are typically non-underwritten, unregistered bond offerings that are sold only to a single investor or a small group of investors.

11. B is correct. A shelf registration allows certain authorized issuers to offer additional bonds to the general public without having to prepare a new and separate offering circular. The issuer can offer multiple bond issuances under the same master prospectus and only has to prepare a short document when additional bonds are issued. A is incorrect because the grey market is a forward market for bonds about to be issued. C is incorrect because a private placement is a non-underwritten, unregistered offering of bonds that are not sold to the general public but directly to an investor or a small group of investors.

12. B is correct. In secondary bond markets, bonds are traded between investors. A is incorrect because newly issued bonds (whether from corporate issuers or other types of issuers) are issued in primary (not secondary) bond markets. C is incorrect because the major participants in secondary bond markets globally are large institutional investors and central banks (not retail investors).

13. C is correct. In over-the-counter (OTC) markets, buy and sell orders are initiated from various locations and then matched through a communications network. Most bonds are traded in OTC markets. A is incorrect because on organized exchanges, buy and sell orders may come from anywhere, but the transactions must take place at the exchange according to the rules imposed by the exchange. B is incorrect because open market operations refer to central bank activities in secondary bond markets. Central banks buy and sell bonds, usually sovereign bonds issued by the national government, as a means to implement monetary policy.

14. C is correct. Liquidity in secondary bond markets refers to the ability to buy or sell bonds quickly at prices close to their fair market value. A and B are incorrect because a liquid secondary bond market does not guarantee that a bond will sell at the price sought by the investor, or that the investor will not face a loss on his or her investment.

15. A is correct. The vast majority of corporate bonds are traded in over-the-counter (OTC) markets that use electronic trading platforms through which users submit buy and sell orders. Settlement of trades in the OTC markets occurs by means of a simultaneous exchange of bonds for cash on the books of the clearing system "on a paperless, computerized book-entry basis."

16. C is correct. Sovereign bonds are usually unsecured obligations of the national government issuing the bonds; they are backed not by collateral but by the taxing authority of the national government. A is incorrect because bonds issued by local governments are non-sovereign (not sovereign) bonds. B is incorrect because sovereign bonds are typically unsecured (not secured) obligations of a national government.

17. C is correct. Bonds issued in the sovereign's currency and a strong domestic savings base are both favorable sovereign rating factors. It is common to observe a higher credit rating for sovereign bonds issued in local currency because of the sovereign's ability to tax its citizens and print its own currency. Although there are practical limits to the sovereign's taxing and currency-printing capacities, each tends to support a sovereign's ability to repay debt. A strong domestic savings base is advantageous because it supports the sovereign's ability to issue debt in local currency to domestic investors.

18. A is correct. Floaters are bonds with a floating rate of interest that resets periodically based on changes in the level of a reference rate, such as Libor. Because changes in the reference rate reflect changes in market interest rates, price changes of floaters are far less pronounced than those of fixed-rate bonds, such as coupon bonds and discount bonds. Thus, investors holding floaters are less exposed to interest rate risk than investors holding fixed-rate discount or coupon bonds.

19. C is correct. Agency bonds are issued by quasi-government entities. These entities are agencies and organizations usually established by national governments to perform various functions for them. A and B are incorrect because local and national governments issue non-sovereign and sovereign bonds, respectively.

20. B is correct. The IMF is a multilateral agency that issues supranational bonds. A and C are incorrect because sovereign bonds and quasi-government bonds are issued by national governments and by entities that perform various functions for national governments, respectively.

21. C is correct. Bonds issued by levels of government below the national level—such as provinces, regions, states, cities, and local government authorities—are classified as non-sovereign government bonds. These bonds are typically not guaranteed by the national government.

22. C is correct. Companies use commercial paper not only as a source of funding working capital and seasonal demand for cash but also as a source of interim financing for long-term projects until permanent financing can be arranged. A is incorrect because there is a secondary market for trading commercial paper, although trading is limited except for the largest issues. B is incorrect because commercial paper is issued by companies across the risk spectrum, although only the strongest, highly rated companies issue *low-cost* commercial paper.

23. A is correct. Commercial paper, whether US commercial paper or Eurocommercial paper, is negotiable—that is, investors can buy and sell commercial paper on secondary markets.

B is incorrect because Eurocommercial paper can be denominated in any currency. C is incorrect because Eurocommercial paper may be issued on an interest-bearing (or yield) basis or a discount basis.

24. B is correct. With a serial maturity structure, a stated number of bonds mature and are paid off on a pre-determined schedule before final maturity. With a sinking fund arrangement, the issuer is required to set aside funds over time to retire the bond issue. Both result in a pre-determined portion of the issue being paid off according to a pre-determined schedule.

25. A is correct. A sinking fund arrangement is a way to reduce credit risk by making the issuer set aside funds over time to retire the bond issue. B and C are incorrect because a sinking fund arrangement has no effect on inflation risk or interest rate risk.

26. C is correct. Wholesale funds available for banks include central bank funds, interbank funds, and negotiable certificates of deposit. A and B are incorrect because demand deposits (also known as checking accounts) and money market accounts are retail deposits, not wholesale funds.

27. B is correct. A negotiable certificate of deposit (CD) allows any depositor (initial or subsequent) to sell the CD in the open market prior to maturity. A is incorrect because negotiable CDs are mostly available in large (not small) denominations. Large-denomination negotiable CDs are an important source of wholesale funds for banks, whereas small-denomination CDs are not. C is incorrect because a penalty is imposed if the depositor withdraws funds prior to maturity for non-negotiable (instead of negotiable) CDs.

28. B is correct. A repurchase agreement (repo) can be viewed as a collateralized loan in which the security sold and subsequently repurchased represents the collateral posted. A and C are incorrect because interbank deposits and negotiable certificates of deposit are unsecured deposits—that is, there is no collateral backing the deposit.

29. A is correct. Repo margins vary by transaction and are negotiated bilaterally between the counterparties.

30. A is correct. The repo margin (the difference between the market value of the underlying collateral and the value of the loan) is a function of the supply and demand conditions of the collateral. The repo margin is typically lower if the underlying collateral is in short supply or if there is a high demand for it. B and C are incorrect because the repo margin is usually higher (not lower) when the maturity of the repurchase agreement is long and when the credit risk associated with the underlying collateral is high.

CHAPTER 3

INTRODUCTION TO FIXED-INCOME VALUATION

SOLUTIONS

1. B is correct. The bond price is closest to 101.36. The price is determined in the following manner:

$$PV = \frac{PMT}{(1+r)^1} + \frac{PMT}{(1+r)^2} + \frac{PMT+FV}{(1+r)^3}$$

where

PV = present value, or the price of the bond
PMT = coupon payment per period
FV = future value paid at maturity, or the par value of the bond
r = market discount rate, or required rate of return per period

$$PV = \frac{5.5}{(1+0.05)^1} + \frac{5.5}{(1+0.05)^2} + \frac{5.5+100}{(1+0.05)^3}$$

$$PV = 5.24 + 4.99 + 91.13 = 101.36$$

2. C is correct. The bond price is closest to 98.11. The formula for calculating the price of this bond is

$$PV = \frac{PMT}{(1+r)^1} + \frac{PMT+FV}{(1+r)^2}$$

where

PV = present value, or the price of the bond
PMT = coupon payment per period
FV = future value paid at maturity, or the par value of the bond
r = market discount rate, or required rate of return per period

$$PV = \frac{3}{(1+0.04)^1} + \frac{3+100}{(1+0.04)^2} = 2.88 + 95.23 = 98.11$$

3. A is correct. The bond price is closest to 95.00. The bond has six semiannual periods. Half of the annual coupon is paid in each period with the required rate of return also being halved. The price is determined in the following manner:

$$PV = \frac{PMT}{(1+r)^1} + \frac{PMT}{(1+r)^2} + \frac{PMT}{(1+r)^3} + \frac{PMT}{(1+r)^4} + \frac{PMT}{(1+r)^5} + \frac{PMT+FV}{(1+r)^6}$$

where

PV = present value, or the price of the bond
PMT = coupon payment per period
FV = future value paid at maturity, or the par value of the bond
r = market discount rate, or required rate of return per period

$$PV = \frac{4.5}{(1+0.055)^1} + \frac{4.5}{(1+0.055)^2} + \frac{4.5}{(1+0.055)^3} + \frac{4.5}{(1+0.055)^4} +$$
$$\frac{4.5}{(1+0.055)^5} + \frac{4.5+100}{(1+0.055)^6}$$

$$PV = 4.27 + 4.04 + 3.83 + 3.63 + 3.44 + 75.79 = 95.00$$

4. B is correct. The bond price is closest to 96.28. The formula for calculating this bond price is

$$PV = \frac{PMT}{(1+r)^1} + \frac{PMT}{(1+r)^2} + \frac{PMT}{(1+r)^3} + \frac{PMT+FV}{(1+r)^4}$$

where

PV = present value, or the price of the bond
PMT = coupon payment per period
FV = future value paid at maturity, or the par value of the bond
r = market discount rate, or required rate of return per period

$$PV = \frac{2}{(1+0.03)^1} + \frac{2}{(1+0.03)^2} + \frac{2}{(1+0.03)^3} + \frac{2+100}{(1+0.03)^4}$$

$$PV = 1.94 + 1.89 + 1.83 + 90.62 = 96.28$$

5. B is correct. The bond price is closest to 112.54. The formula for calculating this bond price is

$$PV = \frac{PMT}{(1+r)^1} + \frac{PMT}{(1+r)^2} + \frac{PMT}{(1+r)^3} + \cdots + \frac{PMT+FV}{(1+r)^{14}}$$

where

PV = present value, or the price of the bond
PMT = coupon payment per period
FV = future value paid at maturity, or the par value of the bond
r = market discount rate, or required rate of return per period

$$PV = \frac{2.5}{(1+0.015)^1} + \frac{2.5}{(1+0.015)^2} + \frac{2.5}{(1+0.015)^3} + \cdots + \frac{2.5}{(1+0.015)^{13}} +$$
$$\frac{2.5+100}{(1+0.015)^{14}}$$

$$PV = 2.46 + 2.43 + 2.39 + \cdots + 2.06 + 83.21 = 112.54$$

6. B is correct. The price of the zero-coupon bond is closest to 51.67. The price is determined in the following manner:

$$PV = \frac{100}{(1+r)^N}$$

where

PV = present value, or the price of the bond
r = market discount rate, or required rate of return per period
N = number of evenly spaced periods to maturity

$$PV = \frac{100}{(1+0.045)^{15}}$$

$$PV = 51.67$$

7. B is correct. The price difference between Bonds A and B is closest to 3.77. One method for calculating the price difference between two bonds with identical terms to maturity is to use the following formula:

$$PV = \frac{PMT}{(1+r)^1} + \frac{PMT}{(1+r)^2}$$

where

PV = price difference
PMT = coupon difference per period
r = market discount rate, or required rate of return per period

In this case, the coupon difference is (5% − 3%), or 2%.

$$PV = \frac{2}{(1+0.04)^1} + \frac{2}{(1+0.04)^2} = 1.92 + 1.85 = 3.77$$

8. A is correct. Bond A offers the lowest yield-to-maturity. When a bond is priced at a premium above par value, the yield-to-maturity (YTM), or market discount rate, is less than the coupon rate. Bond A is priced at a premium, so its YTM is below its 5% coupon rate. Bond B is priced at par value, so its YTM is equal to its 6% coupon rate. Bond C is priced at a discount below par value, so its YTM is above its 5% coupon rate.

9. B is correct. Bond B will most likely experience the smallest percentage change in price if market discount rates increase by 100 bps. A higher-coupon bond has a smaller percentage price change than a lower-coupon bond when their market discount rates change by the same amount (the coupon effect). Also, a shorter-term bond generally has a smaller percentage price change than a longer-term bond when their market discount rates change by the same amount (the maturity effect). Bond B will experience a smaller percentage change in price than Bond A because of the coupon effect. Bond B will also experience a smaller percentage change in price than Bond C because of the coupon effect and the maturity effect.

10. B is correct. The bond price is most likely to change by less than 5%. The relationship between bond prices and market discount rate is not linear. The percentage price change is greater in absolute value when the market discount rate goes down than when it goes up by the same amount (the convexity effect). If a 100 bp decrease in the market discount rate will cause the price of the bond to increase by 5%, then a 100 bp increase in the market discount rate will cause the price of the bond to decline by an amount less than 5%.

11. B is correct. Generally, for two bonds with the same time-to-maturity, a lower-coupon bond will experience a greater percentage price change than a higher-coupon bond when their market discount rates change by the same amount. Bond B and Bond C have the same time-to-maturity (five years); however, Bond B offers a lower coupon rate. Therefore, Bond B will likely experience a greater percentage change in price in comparison to Bond C.

12. A is correct. Bond A will likely experience the greatest percentage change in price due to the coupon effect and the maturity effect. For two bonds with the same time-to-maturity, a lower-coupon bond has a greater percentage price change than a higher-coupon bond when their market discount rates change by the same amount. Generally, for the same coupon rate, a longer-term bond has a greater percentage price change than a shorter-term bond when their market discount rates change by the same amount. Relative to Bond C, Bond A and Bond B offer a lower coupon rate of 6%; however, Bond A has a longer time-to-maturity than Bond B. Therefore, Bond A will likely experience the greater percentage change in price if the market discount rates for all three bonds increase by 100 bps.

13. A is correct. The bond price is closest to 101.93. The price is determined in the following manner:

$$PV = \frac{PMT}{(1+Z_1)^1} + \frac{PMT+FV}{(1+Z_2)^2}$$

where

$\quad\quad PV$ = present value, or the price of the bond

$\quad PMT$ = coupon payment per period

$\quad\quad FV$ = future value paid at maturity, or the par value of the bond

$\quad\quad Z_1$ = spot rate, or the zero-coupon yield, for Period 1

$\quad\quad Z_2$ = spot rate, or the zero-coupon yield, for Period 2

$$PV = \frac{5}{(1+0.03)^1} + \frac{5+100}{(1+0.04)^2}$$

$$PV = 4.85 + 97.08 = 101.93$$

14. B is correct. The bond price is closest to 101.46. The price is determined in the following manner:

$$PV = \frac{PMT}{(1+Z_1)^1} + \frac{PMT}{(1+Z_2)^2} + \frac{PMT+FV}{(1+Z_3)^3}$$

where

$\quad\quad PV$ = present value, or the price of the bond

$\quad PMT$ = coupon payment per period

$\quad\quad FV$ = future value paid at maturity, or the par value of the bond

$\quad\quad Z_1$ = spot rate, or the zero-coupon yield or zero rate, for Period 1

$\quad\quad Z_2$ = spot rate, or the zero-coupon yield or zero rate, for Period 2

$\quad\quad Z_3$ = spot rate, or the zero-coupon yield or zero rate, for Period 3

$$PV = \frac{10}{(1+0.08)^1} + \frac{10}{(1+0.09)^2} + \frac{10+100}{(1+0.095)^3}$$

$$PV = 9.26 + 8.42 + 83.78 = 101.46$$

15. B is correct. The bond price is closest to 95.28. The formula for calculating this bond price is

$$PV = \frac{PMT}{(1 + Z_1)^1} + \frac{PMT}{(1 + Z_2)^2} + \frac{PMT + FV}{(1 + Z_3)^3}$$

where

$\qquad PV$ = present value, or the price of the bond
$\quad PMT$ = coupon payment per period
$\qquad FV$ = future value paid at maturity, or the par value of the bond
$\qquad Z_1$ = spot rate, or the zero-coupon yield or zero rate, for Period 1
$\qquad Z_2$ = spot rate, or the zero-coupon yield or zero rate, for Period 2
$\qquad Z_3$ = spot rate, or the zero-coupon yield or zero rate, for Period 3

$$PV = \frac{8}{(1 + 0.08)^1} + \frac{8}{(1 + 0.09)^2} + \frac{8 + 100}{(1 + 0.10)^3}$$

$$PV = 7.41 + 6.73 + 81.14 = 95.28$$

16. C is correct. The bond price is closest to 92.76. The formula for calculating this bond price is

$$PV = \frac{PMT}{(1 + Z_1)^1} + \frac{PMT}{(1 + Z_2)^2} + \frac{PMT + FV}{(1 + Z_3)^3}$$

where

$\qquad PV$ = present value, or the price of the bond
$\quad PMT$ = coupon payment per period
$\qquad FV$ = future value paid at maturity, or the par value of the bond
$\qquad Z_1$ = spot rate, or the zero-coupon yield or zero rate, for Period 1
$\qquad Z_2$ = spot rate, or the zero-coupon yield or zero rate, for Period 2
$\qquad Z_3$ = spot rate, or the zero-coupon yield or zero rate, for Period 3

$$PV = \frac{7}{(1 + 0.08)^1} + \frac{7}{(1 + 0.09)^2} + \frac{7 + 100}{(1 + 0.10)^3}$$

$$PV = 6.48 + 5.89 + 80.39 = 92.76$$

17. B is correct. The yield-to-maturity is closest to 9.92%. The formula for calculating the price of Bond Z is

$$PV = \frac{PMT}{(1 + Z_1)^1} + \frac{PMT}{(1 + Z_2)^2} + \frac{PMT + FV}{(1 + Z_3)^3}$$

where

$\qquad PV$ = present value, or the price of the bond
$\quad PMT$ = coupon payment per period
$\qquad FV$ = future value paid at maturity, or the par value of the bond
$\qquad Z_1$ = spot rate, or the zero-coupon yield or zero rate, for Period 1
$\qquad Z_2$ = spot rate, or the zero-coupon yield or zero rate, for Period 2
$\qquad Z_3$ = spot rate, or the zero-coupon yield or zero rate, for Period 3

$$PV = \frac{6}{(1 + 0.08)^1} + \frac{6}{(1 + 0.09)^2} + \frac{6 + 100}{(1 + 0.10)^3}$$

$$PV = 5.56 + 5.05 + 79.64 = 90.25$$

Using this price, the bond's yield-to-maturity can be calculated as

$$PV = \frac{PMT}{(1+r)^1} + \frac{PMT}{(1+r)^2} + \frac{PMT+FV}{(1+r)^3}$$

$$90.25 = \frac{6}{(1+r)^1} + \frac{6}{(1+r)^2} + \frac{6+100}{(1+r)^3}$$

$$r = 9.92\%$$

18. A is correct. Bond dealers usually quote the flat price. When a trade takes place, the accrued interest is added to the flat price to obtain the full price paid by the buyer and received by the seller on the settlement date. The reason for using the flat price for quotation is to avoid misleading investors about the market price trend for the bond. If the full price were to be quoted by dealers, investors would see the price rise day after day even if the yield-to-maturity did not change. That is because the amount of accrued interest increases each day. After the coupon payment is made, the quoted price would drop dramatically. Using the flat price for quotation avoids that misrepresentation. The full price, flat price plus accrued interest, is not usually quoted by bond dealers. Accrued interest is included in the full price, and bond dealers do not generally quote the full price.

19. B is correct. The bond's full price is 103.10. The price is determined in the following manner:

As of the beginning of the coupon period on 10 April 2020, there are 2.5 years (five semi-annual periods) to maturity. These five semiannual periods occur on 10 October 2020, 10 April 2021, 10 October 2021, 10 April 2022, and 10 October 2022.

$$PV = \frac{PMT}{(1+r)^1} + \frac{PMT}{(1+r)^2} + \frac{PMT}{(1+r)^3} + \frac{PMT}{(1+r)^4} + \frac{PMT+FV}{(1+r)^5}$$

where

   PV = present value
   PMT = coupon payment per period
   FV = future value paid at maturity, or the par value of the bond
   r = market discount rate, or required rate of return per period

$$PV = \frac{2.5}{(1+0.02)^1} + \frac{2.5}{(1+0.02)^2} + \frac{2.5}{(1+0.02)^3} + \frac{2.5}{(1+0.02)^4} + \frac{2.5+100}{(1+0.02)^5}$$

$$PV = 2.45 + 2.40 + 2.36 + 2.31 + 92.84 = 102.36$$

The accrued interest period is identified as 66/180. The number of days between 10 April 2020 and 16 June 2020 is 66 days, based on the 30/360 day-count convention (20 days remaining in April + 30 days in May + 16 days in June = 66 days total). The number of days between coupon periods is assumed to be 180 days using the 30/360 day convention.

$$PV^{Full} = PV \times (1+r)^{66/180}$$

$$PV^{Full} = 102.36 \times (1.02)^{66/180} = 103.10$$

20. C is correct. The accrued interest per 100 of par value is closest to 0.92. The accrued interest is determined in the following manner: The accrued interest period is identified as 66/180. The number of days between 10 April 2020 and 16 June 2020 is 66 days, based on the 30/360 day-count convention (20 days remaining in April + 30 days in May + 16 days in June = 66 days total). The number of days between coupon periods is assumed to be 180 days using the 30/360 day convention.

$$\text{Accrued interest} = \frac{t}{T} \times PMT$$

where

t = number of days from the last coupon payment to the settlement date

T = number of days in the coupon period

t/T = fraction of the coupon period that has gone by since the last payment

PMT = coupon payment per period

$$\text{Accrued interest} = \frac{66}{180} \times \frac{5.00}{2} = 0.92$$

21. A is correct. The flat price of 102.18 is determined by subtracting the accrued interest (from Question 20) from the full price (from Question 19).

$$PV^{Flat} = PV^{Full} - \text{Accrued interest}$$
$$PV^{Flat} = 103.10 - 0.92 = 102.18$$

22. B is correct. For bonds not actively traded or not yet issued, matrix pricing is a price estimation process that uses market discount rates based on the quoted prices of similar bonds (similar times-to-maturity, coupon rates, and credit quality).

23. A is correct. Matrix pricing is used in underwriting new bonds to get an estimate of the required yield spread over the benchmark rate. The benchmark rate is typically the yield-to-maturity on a government bond having the same or close to the same time-to-maturity. The spread is the difference between the yield-to-maturity on the new bond and the benchmark rate. The yield spread is the additional compensation required by investors for the difference in the credit risk, liquidity risk, and tax status of the bond relative to the government bond.

In matrix pricing, the market discount rates of comparable bonds and the yield-to-maturity on a government bond having a similar time-to-maturity are not estimated. Rather, they are known and are used to estimate the required yield spread of a new bond.

24. B is correct. The formula for calculating this bond's yield-to-maturity is

$$PV = \frac{PMT}{(1+r)^1} + \frac{PMT}{(1+r)^2} + \frac{PMT}{(1+r)^3} + \cdots + \frac{PMT}{(1+r)^{39}} + \frac{PMT+FV}{(1+r)^{40}}$$

where

PV = present value, or the price of the bond

PMT = coupon payment per period

FV = future value paid at maturity, or the par value of the bond

r = market discount rate, or required rate of return per period

$$111 = \frac{2.5}{(1+r)^1} + \frac{2.5}{(1+r)^2} + \frac{2.5}{(1+r)^3} + \cdots + \frac{2.5}{(1+r)^{39}} + \frac{2.5+100}{(1+r)^{40}}$$

$$r = 0.0209$$

To arrive at the annualized yield-to-maturity, the semiannual rate of 2.09% must be multiplied by two. Therefore, the yield-to-maturity is equal to $2.09\% \times 2 = 4.18\%$.

25. B is correct. The annual yield-to-maturity, stated for a periodicity of 12, is 7.21%. It is calculated as follows:

$$PV = \frac{FV}{(1+r)^N}$$

$$75 = \left(\frac{100}{(1+r)^{4 \times 12}} \right)$$

$$\frac{100}{75} = (1 + r)^{48}$$

$$1.33333 = (1 + r)^{48}$$

$$(1.33333)1/48 = [(1 + r)^{48}]^{1/48}$$

$$1.33333^{02083} = (1 + r)$$

$$1.00601 = (1 + r)$$

$$1.00601 - 1 = r$$

$$0.00601 = r$$

$$r \times 12 = 0.07212, \text{ or approximately } 7.21\%$$

26. A is correct. The yield-to-maturity, stated for a periodicity of 12 (monthly periodicity), is 3.87%. The formula to convert an annual percentage rate (annual yield-to-maturity) from one periodicity to another is as follows:

$$\left(1 + \frac{APR_m}{m}\right)^m = \left(1 + \frac{APR_n}{n}\right)^n$$

$$\left(1 + \frac{0.03897}{2}\right)^2 = \left(1 + \frac{APR_{12}}{12}\right)^{12}$$

$$(1.01949)^2 = \left(1 + \frac{APR_{12}}{12}\right)^{12}$$

$$1.03935 = \left(1 + \frac{APR_{12}}{12}\right)^{12}$$

$$(1.03935)^{1/12} = \left[\left(1 + \frac{APR_{12}}{12}\right)^{12}\right]^{1/12}$$

$$1.00322 = \left(1 + \frac{APR_{12}}{12}\right)$$

$$1.00322 - 1 = \left(\frac{APR_{12}}{12}\right)$$

$$APR_{12} = 0.00322 \times 12 = 0.03865, \text{ or approximately } 3.87\%$$

27. B is correct. The yield-to-maturity is 5.77%. The formula for calculating this bond's yield-to-maturity is

$$PV = \frac{PMT}{(1 + r)^1} + \frac{PMT}{(1 + r)^2} + \frac{PMT}{(1 + r)^3} + \cdots + \frac{PMT}{(1 + r)^9} + \frac{PMT + FV}{(1 + r)^{10}}$$

where

      PV = present value, or the price of the bond

  PMT = coupon payment per period

     FV = future value paid at maturity, or the par value of the bond

       r = market discount rate, or required rate of return per period

$$101 = \frac{3}{(1 + r)^1} + \frac{3}{(1 + r)^2} + \frac{3}{(1 + r)^3} + \cdots + \frac{3}{(1 + r)^9} + \frac{3 + 100}{(1 + r)^{10}}$$

$$r = 0.02883$$

To arrive at the annualized yield-to-maturity, the semiannual rate of 2.883% must be multiplied by two. Therefore, the yield-to-maturity is equal to 2.883% × 2 = 5.77% (rounded).

28. C is correct. The yield-to-first-call is 6.25%. Given the first call date is exactly three years away, the formula for calculating this bond's yield-to-first-call is

$$PV = \frac{PMT}{(1+r)^1} + \frac{PMT}{(1+r)^2} + \frac{PMT}{(1+r)^3} + \cdots + \frac{PMT}{(1+r)^5} + \frac{PMT+FV}{(1+r)^6}$$

where

PV = present value, or the price of the bond
PMT = coupon payment per period
FV = call price paid at call date
r = market discount rate, or required rate of return per period

$$101 = \frac{3}{(1+r)^1} + \frac{3}{(1+r)^2} + \frac{3}{(1+r)^3} + \cdots + \frac{3}{(1+r)^5} + \frac{3+102}{(1+r)^6}$$

$r = 0.03123$

To arrive at the annualized yield-to-first-call, the semiannual rate of 3.123% must be multiplied by two. Therefore, the yield-to-first-call is equal to 3.123% × 2 = 6.25% (rounded).

29. C is correct. The yield-to-second-call is 5.94%. Given the second call date is exactly four years away, the formula for calculating this bond's yield-to-second-call is

$$PV = \frac{PMT}{(1+r)^1} + \frac{PMT}{(1+r)^2} + \frac{PMT}{(1+r)^3} + \cdots + \frac{PMT}{(1+r)^7} + \frac{PMT+FV}{(1+r)^8}$$

where

PV = present value, or the price of the bond
PMT = coupon payment per period
FV = call price paid at call date
r = market discount rate, or required rate of return per period

$$101 = \frac{3}{(1+r)^1} + \frac{3}{(1+r)^2} + \frac{3}{(1+r)^3} + \cdots \frac{3}{(1+r)^7} + \frac{3+101}{(1+r)^8}$$

$r = 0.0297$

To arrive at the annualized yield-to-second-call, the semiannual rate of 2.97% must be multiplied by two. Therefore, the yield-to-second-call is equal to 2.97% × 2 = 5.94%.

30. B is correct. The yield-to-worst is 5.77%. The bond's yield-to-worst is the lowest of the sequence of yields-to-call and the yield-to-maturity. From Questions 27–29, we have the following yield measures for this bond:

Yield-to-first-call: 6.25%
Yield-to-second-call: 5.94%
Yield-to-maturity: 5.77%
Thus, the yield-to-worst is 5.77%.

31. B is correct. The discount or required margin is 236 bps. Given the floater has a maturity of two years and is linked to six-month MRR, the formula for calculating the discount margin is

$$PV = \frac{\frac{(\text{Index} + QM) \times FV}{m}}{\left(1 + \frac{\text{Index} + DM}{m}\right)^1} + \frac{\frac{(\text{Index} + QM) \times FV}{m}}{\left(1 + \frac{\text{Index} + DM}{m}\right)^2} + \cdots + \frac{\frac{(\text{Index} + QM) \times FV}{m} + FV}{\left(1 + \frac{\text{Index} + DM}{m}\right)^4}$$

where

PV = present value, or the price of the floating-rate note = 97

Index = reference rate, stated as an annual percentage rate = 0.01

QM = quoted margin, stated as an annual percentage rate = 0.0080

FV = future value paid at maturity, or the par value of the bond = 100

m = periodicity of the floating-rate note, the number of payment periods per year = 2

DM = discount margin, the required margin stated as an annual percentage rate

Substituting the given values:

$$97 = \frac{\frac{(0.01 + 0.0080) \times 100}{2}}{\left(1 + \frac{0.01 + DM}{2}\right)^1} + \frac{\frac{(0.01 + 0.0080) \times 100}{2}}{\left(1 + \frac{0.01 + DM}{2}\right)^2} + \cdots +$$

$$\frac{\frac{(0.01 + 0.0080) \times 100}{2} + 100}{\left(1 + \frac{0.01 + DM}{2}\right)^4}$$

$$97 = \frac{0.90}{\left(1 + \frac{0.01 + DM}{2}\right)^1} + \frac{0.90}{\left(1 + \frac{0.01 + DM}{2}\right)^2} + \frac{0.90}{\left(1 + \frac{0.01 + DM}{2}\right)^3}$$

$$+ \frac{0.90 + 100}{\left(1 + \frac{0.01 + DM}{2}\right)^4}$$

To calculate DM, begin by solving for the discount rate per period:

$$97 = \frac{0.90}{(1 + r)^1} + \frac{0.90}{(1 + r)^2} + \frac{0.90}{(1 + r)^3} + \frac{0.90 + 100}{(1 + r)^4}$$

$$r = 0.0168$$

Now, solve for DM:

$$\frac{0.01 + DM}{2} = 0.0168$$

$$DM = 0.0236$$

The discount margin for the floater is equal to 236 bps.

32. A is correct. FRN X will be priced at a premium on the next reset date because the quoted margin of 0.40% is greater than the discount, or required, margin of 0.32%. The premium amount is the present value of the extra, or "excess," interest payments of 0.08% each quarter (0.40% − 0.32%). FRN Y will be priced at par value on the next reset date since there is no difference between the quoted and discount margins. FRN Z will be priced at a discount since the quoted margin is less than the required margin.

33. C is correct. The bond equivalent yield is closest to 3.78%. It is calculated as

$$AOR = \left(\frac{\text{Year}}{\text{Days}}\right) \times \left(\frac{FV - PV}{PV}\right)$$

where

> PV = present value, principal amount, or the price of the money market instrument
> FV = future value, or the redemption amount paid at maturity including interest
> Days = number of days between settlement and maturity
> Year = number of days in the year
> AOR = add-on rate, stated as an annual percentage rate (also called bond equivalent yield)

$$AOR = \left(\frac{365}{350}\right) \times \left(\frac{100 - 96.5}{96.5}\right)$$

$$AOR = 1.04286 \times 0.03627$$

$$AOR = 0.03783, \text{ or approximately } 3.78\%$$

34. C is correct. The bond equivalent yield is closest to 4.40%. The present value of the banker's acceptance is calculated as

$$PV = FV \times \left(1 - \frac{\text{Days}}{\text{Year}} \times DR\right)$$

where

> PV = present value, or price of the money market instrument
> FV = future value paid at maturity, or face value of the money market instrument
> Days = number of days between settlement and maturity
> Year = number of days in the year
> DR = discount rate, stated as an annual percentage rate

$$PV = 100 \times \left(1 - \frac{\text{Days}}{\text{Year}} \times DR\right)$$

$$PV = 100 \times \left(1 - \frac{180}{360} \times 0.0425\right)$$

$$PV = 100 \times (1 - 0.02125)$$

$$PV = 100 \times 0.97875$$

$$PV = 97.875$$

The bond equivalent yield (AOR) is calculated as

$$AOR = \left(\frac{\text{Year}}{\text{Days}}\right) \times \left(\frac{FV - PV}{PV}\right)$$

where

> PV = present value, principal amount, or the price of the money market instrument
> FV = future value, or the redemption amount paid at maturity including interest
> Days = number of days between settlement and maturity
> Year = number of days in the year
> AOR = add-on rate (bond equivalent yield), stated as an annual percentage rate

$$AOR = \left(\frac{365}{180}\right) \times \left(\frac{100 - PV}{PV}\right)$$

$$AOR = \left(\frac{365}{180}\right) \times \left(\frac{100 - 97.875}{97.875}\right)$$

$$AOR = 2.02778 \times 0.02171$$

$$AOR = 0.04402, \text{ or approximately } 4.40\%$$

Note that PV is calculated using an assumed 360-day year and AOR (bond equivalent yield) is calculated using a 365-day year.

35. B is correct. All bonds on a par curve are assumed to have similar, not different, credit risk. Par curves are obtained from spot curves, and all bonds used to derive the par curve are assumed to have the same credit risk, as well as the same periodicity, currency, liquidity, tax status, and annual yields. A par curve is a sequence of yields-to-maturity such that each bond is priced at par value.

36. B is correct. The spot curve, also known as the strip, or zero, curve, is the yield curve constructed from a sequence of yields-to-maturity on zero-coupon bonds. The par curve is a sequence of yields-to-maturity such that each bond is priced at par value. The forward curve is constructed using a series of forward rates, each having the same time frame.

37. B is correct. The forward rate can be interpreted to be the incremental or marginal return for extending the time-to-maturity of an investment for an additional time period. The add-on rate (bond equivalent yield) is a rate quoted for money market instruments, such as bank certificates of deposit, and indexes, such as MRR, Libor and Euribor. Yield-to-maturity is the internal rate of return on the bond's cash flows—the uniform interest rate such that when the bond's future cash flows are discounted at that rate, the sum of the present values equals the price of the bond. It is the implied market discount rate.

38. B is correct. The three-year implied spot rate is closest to 1.94%. It is calculated as the geometric average of the one-year forward rates:

$$(1.0080 \times 1.0112 \times 1.0394) = (1 + z_3)^3$$
$$1.05945 = (1 + z_3)^3$$
$$(1.05945)^{1/3} = [(1 + z_3)^3]^{1/3}$$
$$1.01944 = 1 + z_3$$
$$1.01944 - 1 = z_3$$
$$0.01944 = z_3$$
$$z_3 = 1.944\%, \text{ or approximately } 1.94\%$$

39. B is correct. The value per 100 of par value is closest to 105.01. Using the forward curve, the bond price is calculated as follows:

$$\frac{3.5}{1.0080} + \frac{103.5}{(1.0080 \times 1.0112)} = 3.47 + 101.54 = 105.01$$

40. C is correct. The spread component of a specific bond's yield-to-maturity is least likely impacted by changes in inflation in its currency of denomination. The effect of changes in macroeconomic factors, such as the expected rate of inflation in the currency of denomination, is seen mostly in changes in the benchmark yield. The spread or risk premium component is impacted by microeconomic factors specific to the bond and bond issuer, including tax status and quality rating.

41. A is correct. The I-spread, or interpolated spread, is the yield spread of a specific bond over the standard swap rate in that currency of the same tenor. The yield spread in basis points over an actual or interpolated government bond is known as the G-spread. The Z-spread (zero-volatility spread) is the constant spread that is added to each spot rate such that the present value of the cash flows matches the price of the bond.

42. B is correct. The G-spread is closest to 285 bps. The benchmark rate for UK fixed-rate bonds is the UK government benchmark bond. The euro interest rate spread benchmark is used to calculate the G-spread for euro-denominated corporate bonds, not UK bonds. The G-spread is calculated as follows:

Yield-to-maturity on the UK corporate bond:

$$100.65 = \frac{5}{(1 + r)^1} + \frac{5}{(1 + r)^2} + \frac{105}{(1 + r)^3}; \, r = 0.04762, \text{ or } 476 \text{ bps}$$

Yield-to-maturity on the UK government benchmark bond:

$$100.25 = \frac{2}{(1 + r)^1} + \frac{2}{(1 + r)^2} + \frac{102}{(1 + r)^3}; \, r = 0.01913, \text{ or } 191 \text{ bps}$$

The G-spread is $476 - 191 = 285$ bps.

43. A is correct. The value of the bond is closest to 92.38. The calculation is

$$PV = \frac{PMT}{(1 + z_1 + Z)^1} + \frac{PMT}{(1 + z_2 + Z)^2} + \frac{PMT + FV}{(1 + z_3 + Z)^3}$$

$$= \frac{5}{(1 + 0.0486 + 0.0234)^1} + \frac{5}{(1 + 0.0495 + 0.0234)^2} + \frac{105}{(1 + 0.0565 + 0.0234)^3}$$

$$= \frac{5}{1.0720} + \frac{5}{1.15111} + \frac{105}{1.25936} = 4.66 + 4.34 + 83.38 = 92.38$$

44. C is correct. The option value in basis points per year is subtracted from the Z-spread to calculate the OAS. The Z-spread is the constant yield spread over the benchmark spot curve. The I-spread is the yield spread of a specific bond over the standard swap rate in that currency of the same tenor.

CHAPTER 4

INTRODUCTION TO ASSET-BACKED SECURITIES

SOLUTIONS

1. B is correct. Securitization increases the funds available for banks to lend because it allows banks to remove loans from their balance sheets and issue bonds that are backed by those loans. Securitization repackages relatively simple debt obligations, such as bank loans, into more complex, not simpler, structures. Securitization involves transferring ownership of assets from the original owner—in this case, the banks—into a special legal entity. As a result, banks do not maintain ownership of the securitized assets.

2. C is correct. By removing the wall between ultimate investors and originating borrowers, investors can achieve better legal claims on the underlying mortgages and portfolios of receivables. This transparency allows investors to tailor interest rate risk and credit risk to their specific needs.

3. C is correct. Securitization allows for the creation of tradable securities with greater liquidity than the original loans on a bank's balance sheet. Securitization results in lessening the roles of intermediaries, which increases disintermediation. Securitization is a process in which relatively simple debt obligations, such as loans, are repackaged into more complex structures.

4. A is correct. Securitization allows investors to achieve more direct legal claims on loans and portfolios of receivables. As a result, investors can add to their portfolio's exposure to the risk–return characteristics provided by a wider range of assets.

    B is incorrect because securitization does not reduce credit risk but, rather, provides a structure to mitigate and redistribute the inherent credit risks of pools of loans and receivables.

    C is incorrect because securitization does not eliminate the timing risks associated with ABS cash flows but, rather, provides a structure to mitigate and redistribute those risks, such as contraction risk and extension risk.

5. A is correct. In a securitization, the special purpose entity is the special legal entity responsible for the issuance of the asset-backed securities. The servicer, not the SPE, is

responsible for both the collection of payments from the borrowers and the recovery of underlying assets if the borrowers default on their loans.

6. B is correct. In a securitization, the loans or receivables are initially sold by the depositor to the special purpose entity that uses them as collateral to issue the ABS.

A is incorrect because the SPE, often referred to as the issuer, is the purchaser of the collateral rather than the seller of the collateral.

C is incorrect because the underwriter neither sells nor purchases the collateral in a securitization. The underwriter performs the same functions in a securitization as it does in a standard bond offering.

7. C is correct. The first €25 (€5 + €20) million in default are absorbed by the subordinated classes (C and B). The senior Class A bonds will experience a loss only when defaults exceed €25 million.

8. A is correct. Time tranching is the process in which a set of bond classes or tranches is created that allow investors a choice in the type of prepayment risk—extension or contraction—that they prefer to bear. Senior and subordinated bond classes are used in credit tranching. Credit tranching structures allow investors to choose the amount of credit risk that they prefer to bear. Fully and partially amortizing loans are two types of amortizing loans.

9. B is correct. Credit tranching is a form of credit enhancement called subordination in which bond classes or tranches differ as to how they will share losses resulting from defaults of the borrowers whose loans are part of the collateral. This type of protection is commonly referred to as a waterfall structure because of the cascading flow of payments between bond classes in the event of default.

A is incorrect because time tranching involves the creation of bond classes that possess different expected maturities rather than bond classes that differ as to how credit losses will be shared. Time tranching involves the redistribution of prepayment risk, whereas credit tranching involves the redistribution of credit risk.

C is incorrect because although overcollateralization is a form of internal credit enhancement similar to subordination, it is the amount by which the principal amount of the pool of collateral exceeds the principal balance of the securities issued and backed by the collateral pool. Losses are absorbed first by the amount of overcollateralization and then according to the credit tranching structure.

10. A is correct. Time tranching is the creation of bond classes that possess different expected maturities so that prepayment risk can be redistributed among bond classes. When loan agreements provide borrowers the ability to alter payments, in the case of declining interest rates, this prepayment risk increases because borrowers tend to pay off part or all of their loans and refinance at lower interest rates.

B is incorrect because it is possible and quite common for a securitization to have structures with both credit tranching and time tranching.

C is incorrect because the subordinated structures of junior and senior bond classes differ as to how they will share any losses relative to defaults of the borrowers whose loans are in the collateral pool. Junior classes offer protection for senior classes, with losses first realized by the former. The classes are distinguished not by scheduled repayment terms but, rather, by a loss sharing hierarchy in the event of borrower default.

11. A is correct. The legal implication of a special purpose entity, a prerequisite for securitization, is that investors contemplating the purchase of bond classes backed by the assets of the SPE will evaluate the credit risk of those assets independently from the credit rating of the entity that sold the assets to the SPE. This separation of the seller's collateral from

its credit rating provides the opportunity for the SPE to access a lower aggregate funding cost than what the seller might otherwise obtain.

B is incorrect because the absolute priority rule, under which senior creditors are paid in full before subordinated creditors, has not always been upheld in bankruptcy reorganizations. There is no assurance that if a corporate bond has collateral, the rights of the bondholders will be respected. It is this uncertainty that creates the dominant influence of credit ratings over collateral in credit spreads.

C is incorrect because corporate bond credit spreads will reflect the seller's credit rating primarily and the collateral only slightly. Securitization separates the seller's collateral from its credit rating, effectively altering the influence of collateral on the credit spread.

12. C is correct. In a partially amortizing loan, the sum of all the scheduled principal repayments is less than the amount borrowed. The last payment is for the remaining unpaid mortgage balance and is called the "balloon payment."

13. B is correct. Contraction risk is the risk that when interest rates decline, actual prepayments will be higher than forecasted. Extension risk is the risk that when interest rates rise, prepayments will be lower than forecasted. Yield maintenance results from prepayment penalties; the lender is protected from loss in yield by the imposition of prepayment penalties.

14. A is correct. In a recourse loan, the lender has a claim against the borrower for the shortfall between the amount of the mortgage balance outstanding and the proceeds received from the sale of the property. A prepayment option is a benefit to the borrower and would thus not offer protection to the lender. An interest-only mortgage requires no principal repayment for a number of years and will not protect the lender from strategic default by the borrower.

15. B is correct. Bank Nederlandse has a claim against Marolf for EUR1.5 million, the shortfall between the amount of the mortgage balance outstanding and the proceeds received from the sale of the property. This indicates that the mortgage loan is a recourse loan. The recourse/non-recourse feature indicates the rights of a lender in foreclosure. If Marolf had a non-recourse loan, the bank would have been entitled to only the proceeds from the sale of the underlying property, or EUR2.5 million. A bullet loan is a special type of interest-only mortgage for which there are no scheduled principal payments over the entire term of the loan. Since the unpaid balance is less than the original mortgage loan, it is unlikely that Marolf has an interest-only mortgage.

16. A is correct. Because the loan has a non-recourse feature, the lender can look to only the underlying property to recover the outstanding mortgage balance and has no further claim against the borrower. The lender is simply entitled to foreclose on the home and sell it.

17. A is correct. A bullet mortgage is a special type of interest-only mortgage in which there are no scheduled principal repayments over the entire life of the loan. At maturity, a balloon payment is required equal to the original loan amount.

B is incorrect because with a fully amortizing mortgage, the sum of all the scheduled principal repayments during the mortgage's life is such that when the last mortgage payment is made, the loan is fully repaid, with no balloon payment required.

C is incorrect because with a partially amortizing mortgage, the sum of all the scheduled principal repayments is less than the amount borrowed, resulting in a balloon payment equal to the unpaid mortgage balance (rather than the original loan amount).

18. A is correct. In non-recourse loan jurisdictions, the borrower may have an incentive to default on an underwater mortgage and allow the lender to foreclose on the property because the lender has no claim against the borrower for the shortfall. For this reason, such defaults, known as strategic defaults, are more likely in non-recourse jurisdictions and less

likely in recourse jurisdictions, where the lender does have a claim against the borrower for the shortfall.

B is incorrect because strategic defaults in non-recourse jurisdictions do have negative consequences for the defaulting borrowers in the form of a lower credit score and a reduced ability to borrow in the future. These negative consequences can be a deterrent in the incidence of underwater mortgage defaults.

C is incorrect because when a recourse loan defaults, the lender can look to both the property and the borrower to recover the outstanding mortgage balance. In a recourse loan, the lender has a claim against the borrower for the shortfall between the amount of the outstanding mortgage balance and the proceeds received from the sale of the property.

19. A is correct. Non-agency RMBS are credit enhanced, either internally or externally, to make the securities more attractive to investors. The most common forms of internal credit enhancement are senior/subordinated structures, reserve accounts, and over-collateralization. Conforming mortgages are used as collateral for agency (not non-agency) mortgage pass-through securities. An agency RMBS, rather than a non-agency RMBS, issued by a GSE (government sponsored enterprise), is guaranteed by the respective GSE.

20. B is correct. Extension risk is the risk that when interest rates rise, fewer prepayments will occur. Homeowners will be reluctant to give up the benefit of a contractual interest rate that is lower. As a result, the mortgage pass-through security becomes longer in maturity than anticipated at the time of purchase.

21. C is correct. Using CMOs, securities can be created to closely satisfy the asset/liability needs of institutional investors. The creation of a CMO cannot eliminate prepayment risk; it can only distribute the various forms of this risk among various classes of bondholders. The collateral of CMOs is mortgage-related products, not the mortgages themselves.

22. C is correct. For a CMO with multiple sequential-pay tranches, the longest-term tranche will have the lowest contraction (prepayments greater than forecasted) risk because of the protection against this risk offered by the other tranches. The longest-term tranche is likely to have the highest average life and extension risk because it is the last tranche repaid in a sequential-pay tranche.

23. A is correct. PAC tranches have limited (but not complete) protection against both extension risk and contraction risk. This protection is provided by the support tranches. A sequential-pay tranche can protect against either extension risk or contraction risk but not both of these risks. The CMO structure with sequential-pay tranches allows investors concerned about extension risk to invest in shorter-term tranches and those concerned about contraction risk to invest in longer-term tranches.

24. C is correct. The greater predictability of cash flows provided in the planned amortization class (PAC) tranches comes at the expense of support tranches. As a result, investors in support tranches are exposed to higher extension risk and contraction risk than investors in PAC tranches. Investors will be compensated for bearing this risk because support tranches have a higher expected return than PAC tranches.

25. B is correct. CPR is an annualized rate that indicates the percentage of the outstanding mortgage pool balance at the beginning of the year that is expected to be prepaid by the end of the year.

26. C is correct. When interest rates decline, a mortgage pass-through security is subject to contraction risk. Contraction risk is the risk that when interest rates decline, actual prepayments will be higher than forecasted because borrowers will refinance at now-available

lower interest rates. Thus, a security backed by mortgages will have a shorter maturity than was anticipated when the security was purchased.

27. A is correct. The coupon rate of a mortgage pass-through security is called the pass-through rate, whereas the mortgage rate on the underlying pool of mortgages is calculated as a weighted average coupon rate (WAC). The pass-through rate is lower than the WAC by an amount equal to the servicing fee and other administrative fees.

28. B is correct. The SMM is a monthly measure of the prepayment rate or prepayment speed. Contraction risk is the risk that when interest rates decline, actual prepayments will be higher than forecast. So if contraction risk falls, prepayments are likely to be lower than forecast, which would imply a decrease in the SMM.

    A is incorrect because the SMM is a monthly measure of the prepayment rate or pre-payment speed. Extension risk is the risk that when interest rates rise, actual prepayments will be lower than forecast. So if extension risk rises, prepayments are likely to be lower than forecast, which would imply a decrease, not an increase, in the SMM.

    C is incorrect because at 100 PSA, investors can expect prepayments to follow the PSA prepayment benchmark. Based on historical patterns, the PSA standard model assumes that prepayment rates are low for newly initiated mortgages and then speed up as mortgages season. Thus, 100 PSA does not imply that the SMM remains the same but, rather, implies that it will vary over the life of the mortgage.

29. A is correct. If commercial mortgage loans are non-recourse loans, the lender can look to only the income-producing property backing the loan for interest and principal repayment. If there is a default, the lender looks to the proceeds from the sale of the property for repayment and has no recourse against the borrower for any unpaid mortgage loan balance. Call protection and prepayment penalty points protect against prepayment risk.

30. A is correct. With CMBS, investors have considerable call protection. An investor in an RMBS is exposed to considerable prepayment risk, but with CMBS, call protection is available to the investor at the structure and loan level. The call protection results in CMBS trading in the market more like a corporate bond than an RMBS. Both internal credit enhancement and the debt-service-coverage (DSC) ratio address credit risk, not prepayment risk.

31. A is correct. If specific ratios of debt to service coverage are needed and those ratios cannot be met at the loan level, subordination is used to achieve the desired credit rating. Call protection protects investors against prepayment risk. Balloon payments increase the risk of the underlying loans.

32. B is correct. In a non-recourse CMBS, the lender can look only to the income-producing property backing the loan for interest and principal repayment. If a default occurs, the lender can use only the proceeds from the sale of the property for repayment and has no recourse to the borrower for any unpaid balance.

33. B is correct. A critical feature that differentiates CMBS from RMBS is the call protection provided to investors. An investor in an RMBS is exposed to considerable prepayment risk because the borrower has the right to prepay the loan before maturity. CMBS provide investors with considerable call protection that comes either at the structure level or at the loan level.

34. A is correct. An excess spread account, sometimes called excess interest cash flow, is a form of internal credit enhancement that limits credit risk. It is an amount that can be retained and deposited into a reserve account and that can serve as a first line of protection against losses. An excess spread account does not limit prepayment risk—be it extension risk or contraction risk.

35. C is correct. During the lockout period, the cash flow that is paid out to owners of credit card receivable asset-backed securities is based only on finance charges collected and fees.

36. C is correct. Because credit card receivable ABS are backed by non-amortizing loans that do not involve scheduled principal repayments, they are not affected by prepayment risk.

    A is incorrect because auto loan ABS are affected by prepayment risk since they are backed by amortizing loans involving scheduled principal repayments.

    B is incorrect because residential MBS are affected by prepayment risk since they are backed by amortizing loans involving scheduled principal repayments.

37. A is correct. In addition to a senior/subordinated (sequential-pay) structure, many auto loan ABS are structured with additional credit enhancement in the form of overcollateralization and a reserve account, often an excess spread account. The excess spread is an amount that can be retained and deposited into a reserve account that can serve as a first line of protection against losses.

    B is incorrect because in an auto loan ABS, losses are typically applied against the excess spread account and the amount of overcollateralization before the waterfall loss absorption of the sequential-pay structure.

    C is incorrect because in auto loan ABS, proceeds from the repossession and resale of autos are prepayment cash flows rather than a form of credit enhancement for loss protection.

38. C is correct. In credit card receivable ABS, the only way the principal cash flows can be altered is by triggering the early amortization provision. Such provisions are included in the ABS structure to safeguard the credit quality of the issue.

    A is incorrect because expiration of the lockout period does not result in the alteration of principal cash flows but instead defines when principal repayments are distributed to the ABS investors. During the lockout period, principal repayments by cardholders are reinvested. When the lockout period expires, principal repayments by cardholders are distributed to investors.

    B is incorrect because the excess spread account is a credit enhancement for loss absorption. When the excess spread account is depleted, losses are applied against the overcollateralization amount followed by the senior/subordinated structure. The only way principal cash flows can be altered is by triggering the early amortization provision.

39. C is correct. The mezzanine tranche consists of bond classes with credit ratings between senior and subordinated bond classes.

    A is incorrect because the equity tranche falls within and carries the credit rating applicable to the subordinated bond classes.

    B is incorrect because the residual tranche falls within and carries the credit ratings applicable to the subordinated bond classes.

40. C is correct. The key to whether a CDO is viable is whether a structure can be created that offers a competitive return for the subordinated tranche (often referred to as the residual or equity tranche). Investors in a subordinated tranche typically use borrowed funds (the bond classes issued) to generate a return above the funding cost.

    A is incorrect because the viability of a CDO depends on a structure that offers a competitive return for the subordinated tranche rather than the senior tranche.

    B is incorrect because the viability of a CDO depends on a structure that offers a competitive return for the subordinated tranche rather than the mezzanine tranche.

41. A is correct. When the collateral manager fails pre-specified tests, a provision is triggered that requires the payoff of the principal to the senior class until the tests are satisfied. This

reduction of the senior class effectively deleverages the CDO because the CDO's cheapest funding source is reduced.

42. B is correct. CMOs are designed to redistribute cash flows of mortgage-related products to different bond classes or tranches through securitization. Although CMOs do not eliminate prepayment risk, they distribute prepayment risk among various classes of bondholders.

43. B is correct. Covered bonds usually carry lower credit risks and offer lower yields than otherwise similar ABS. The reason is, among other factors, covered bonds provide investors with dual recourse, to the cover pool and also to the issuer. Moreover, covered bonds have a dynamic cover pool, meaning sponsors must replace any prepaid or non-performing assets.

CHAPTER 5

UNDERSTANDING FIXED-INCOME RISK AND RETURN

SOLUTIONS

1. A is correct. A capital gain is least likely to contribute to the investor's total return. There is no capital gain (or loss) because the bond is held to maturity. The carrying value of the bond at maturity is par value, the same as the redemption amount. When a fixed-rate bond is held to its maturity, the investor receives the principal payment at maturity. This principal payment is a source of return for the investor. A fixed-rate bond pays periodic coupon payments, and the reinvestment of these coupon payments is a source of return for the investor. The investor's total return is the redemption of principal at maturity and the sum of the reinvested coupons.

2. C is correct. Because the fixed-rate bond is held to maturity (a "buy-and-hold" investor), interest rate risk arises entirely from changes in coupon reinvestment rates. Higher interest rates increase income from reinvestment of coupon payments, and lower rates decrease income from coupon reinvestment. There will not be a capital gain or loss because the bond is held until maturity. The carrying value at the maturity date is par value, the same as the redemption amount. The redemption of principal does not expose the investor to interest rate risk. The risk to a bond's principal is credit risk.

3. A is correct. Capital gains (losses) arise if a bond is sold at a price above (below) its constant-yield price trajectory. A point on the trajectory represents the carrying value of the bond at that time. That is, the capital gain/loss is measured from the bond's carrying value, the point on the constant-yield price trajectory, and not from the original purchase price. The carrying value is the original purchase price plus the amortized amount of the discount if the bond is purchased at a price below par value. If the bond is purchased at a price above par value, the carrying value is the original purchase price minus (not plus) the amortized amount of the premium. The amortized amount for each year is the change in the price between two points on the trajectory.

4. C is correct. The future value of reinvested cash flows at 8% after five years is closest to 41.07 per 100 of par value.

$$[7 \times (1.08)^4] + [7 \times (1.08)^3] + [7 \times (1.08)^2] + [7 \times (1.08)^1] + 7 = 41.0662$$

The 6.07 difference between the sum of the coupon payments over the five-year holding period (35) and the future value of the reinvested coupons (41.07) represents the "interest-on-interest" gain from compounding.

5. B is correct. The capital loss is closest to 3.31 per 100 of par value. After five years, the bond has four years remaining until maturity and the sale price of the bond is 96.69, calculated as

$$\frac{7}{(1.08)^1} + \frac{7}{(1.08)^2} + \frac{7}{(1.08)^3} + \frac{107}{(1.08)^4} = 96.69$$

The investor purchased the bond at a price equal to par value (100). Because the bond was purchased at a price equal to its par value, the carrying value is par value. Therefore, the investor experienced a capital loss of $96.69 - 100 = -3.31$.

6. B is correct. The investor's five-year horizon yield is closest to 6.62%. After five years, the sale price of the bond is 96.69 (from problem 5) and the future value of reinvested cash flows at 8% is 41.0662 (from problem 4) per 100 of par value. The total return is 137.76 ($= 41.07 + 96.69$), resulting in a realized five-year horizon yield of 6.62%:

$$100.00 = \frac{137.76}{(1 + r)^5}, \quad r = 0.0662$$

7. A is correct. The bond's approximate modified duration is closest to 2.78. Approximate modified duration is calculated as

$$\text{ApproxModDur} = \frac{(PV_-) - (PV_+)}{2 \times (\Delta \text{Yield}) \times (PV_0)}$$

Lower yield-to-maturity by 5 bps to 2.95%:

$$PV_- = \frac{5}{(1 + 0.0295)^1} + \frac{5}{(1 + 0.0295)^2} + \frac{5 + 100}{(1 + 0.0295)^3} = 105.804232$$

Increase yield-to-maturity by 5 bps to 3.05%:

$$PV_+ = \frac{5}{(1 + 0.0305)^1} + \frac{5}{(1 + 0.0305)^2} + \frac{5 + 100}{(1 + 0.0305)^3} = 105.510494$$

$PV_0 = 105.657223$, $\Delta \text{Yield} = 0.0005$

$$\text{ApproxModDur} = \frac{105.804232 - 105.510494}{2 \times 0.0005 \times 105.657223} = 2.78$$

8. C is correct. A bond's modified duration cannot be larger than its Macaulay duration assuming a positive yield-to-maturity. The formula for modified duration is

$$\text{ModDur} = \frac{\text{MacDur}}{1 + r}$$

where r is the bond's yield-to-maturity per period. Therefore, ModDur will typically be less than MacDur.

Effective duration is a measure of curve duration. Modified duration is a measure of yield duration.

9. C is correct. The bond's Macaulay duration is closest to 2.83. Macaulay duration (MacDur) is a weighted average of the times to the receipt of cash flow. The weights are the shares of the full price corresponding to each coupon and principal payment.

Period	Cash Flow	Present Value	Weight	Period × Weight
1	6	5.555556	0.058575	0.058575
2	6	5.144033	0.054236	0.108472
3	106	84.146218	0.887190	2.661570
		94.845806	1.000000	2.828617

Thus, the bond's Macaulay duration (MacDur) is 2.83.

Alternatively, Macaulay duration can be calculated using the following closed-form formula:

$$MacDur = \left\{ \frac{1+r}{r} - \frac{1+r+[N \times (c-r)]}{c \times [(1+r)^N - 1] + r} \right\} - (t/T)$$

$$MacDur = \left\{ \frac{1.08}{0.08} - \frac{1.08 + [3 \times (0.06 - 0.08)]}{0.06 \times [(1.08)^3 - 1] + 0.08} \right\} - 0$$

$$MacDur = 13.50 - 10.67 = 2.83$$

10. A is correct. The interest rate risk of a fixed-rate bond with an embedded call option is best measured by effective duration. A callable bond's future cash flows are uncertain because they are contingent on future interest rates. The issuer's decision to call the bond depends on future interest rates. Therefore, the yield-to-maturity on a callable bond is not well defined. Only effective duration, which takes into consideration the value of the call option, is the appropriate interest rate risk measure. Yield durations like Macaulay and modified durations are not relevant for a callable bond because they assume no changes in cash flows when interest rates change.

11. A is correct. Key rate duration is used to measure a bond's sensitivity to a shift at one or more maturity segments of the yield curve, which result in a change to yield curve shape. Modified and effective duration measure a bond's sensitivity to parallel shifts in the entire curve.

12. B is correct. The effective duration of the pension fund's liabilities is closest to 14.99. The effective duration is calculated as follows:

$$EffDur = \frac{(PV_-) - (PV_+)}{2 \times (\Delta Curve) \times (PV_0)}$$

$$PV_0 = 455.4, \ PV_+ = 373.6, \ PV_- = 510.1, \text{ and } \Delta Curve = 0.0100$$

$$EffDur = \frac{510.1 - 373.6}{2 \times 0.0100 \times 455.4} = 14.99$$

13. B is correct. A bond's yield-to-maturity is inversely related to its Macaulay duration: The higher the yield-to-maturity, the lower its Macaulay duration and the lower the interest

rate risk. A higher yield-to-maturity decreases the weighted average of the times to the receipt of cash flow, and thus decreases the Macaulay duration.

A bond's coupon rate is inversely related to its Macaulay duration: The lower the coupon, the greater the weight of the payment of principal at maturity. This results in a higher Macaulay duration. Zero-coupon bonds do not pay periodic coupon payments; therefore, the Macaulay duration of a zero-coupon bond is its time-to-maturity.

14. A is correct. The presence of an embedded put option reduces the effective duration of the bond, especially when rates are rising. If interest rates are low compared with the coupon rate, the value of the put option is low and the impact of the change in the benchmark yield on the bond's price is very similar to the impact on the price of a non-putable bond. But when benchmark interest rates rise, the put option becomes more valuable to the investor. The ability to sell the bond at par value limits the price depreciation as rates rise. The presence of an embedded put option reduces the sensitivity of the bond price to changes in the benchmark yield, assuming no change in credit risk.

15. A is correct. The portfolio's modified duration is closest to 7.62. Portfolio duration is commonly estimated as the market-value-weighted average of the yield durations of the individual bonds that compose the portfolio.

The total market value of the bond portfolio is 170,000 + 120,000 + 100,000 = 390,000.

The portfolio duration is 5.42 × (170,000/390,000) + 8.44 × (120,000/390,000) + 10.38 × (100,000/390,000) = 7.62.

16. A is correct. A limitation of calculating a bond portfolio's duration as the weighted average of the yield durations of the individual bonds is that this measure implicitly assumes a parallel shift to the yield curve (all rates change by the same amount in the same direction). In reality, interest rate changes frequently result in a steeper or flatter yield curve. This approximation of the "theoretically correct" portfolio duration is *more* accurate when the yield curve is flatter (less steeply sloped). An advantage of this approach is that it can be used with portfolios that include bonds with embedded options. Bonds with embedded options can be included in the weighted average using the effective durations for these securities.

17. B is correct. Bond B has the greatest money duration per 100 of par value. Money duration (MoneyDur) is calculated as the annual modified duration (AnnModDur) times the full price (PV^{Full}) of the bond including accrued interest. Bond B has the highest money duration per 100 of par value.

$$MoneyDur = AnnModDur \times PV^{Full}$$
$$MoneyDur \text{ of Bond A} = 5.42 \times 85.00 = 460.70$$
$$MoneyDur \text{ of Bond B} = 8.44 \times 80.00 = 675.20$$
$$MoneyDur \text{ of Bond C} = 7.54 \times 85.78 = 646.78$$

18. B is correct. The PVBP is closest to 0.0648. The formula for the price value of a basis point is

$$PVBP = \frac{(PV_-) - (PV_+)}{2}$$

where

PVBP = price value of a basis point

PV_- = full price calculated by lowering the yield-to-maturity by 1 bp

PV_+ = full price calculated by raising the yield-to-maturity by 1 bp

Lowering the yield-to-maturity by 1 bp to 4.99% results in a bond price of 85.849134:

$$PV_- = \frac{3}{(1 + 0.0499)^1} + \cdots + \frac{3 + 100}{(1 + 0.0499)^9} = 85.849134$$

Increasing the yield-to-maturity by 1 bp to 5.01% results in a bond price of 85.719638:

$$PV_+ = \frac{3}{(1 + 0.0501)^1} + \cdots + \frac{3 + 100}{(1 + 0.0501)^9} = 85.719638$$

$$PVBP = \frac{85.849134 - 85.719638}{2} = 0.06475$$

Alternatively, the PVBP can be derived using modified duration:

$$ApproxModDur = \frac{(PV_-) - (PV_+)}{2 \times (\Delta Yield) \times (PV_0)}$$

$$ApproxModDur = \frac{85.849134 - 85.719638}{2 \times 0.0001 \times 85.784357} = 7.548$$

$$PVBP = 7.548 \times 85.784357 \times 0.0001 = 0.06475$$

19. B is correct. Convexity measures the "second order" effect on a bond's percentage price change given a change in yield-to-maturity. Convexity adjusts the percentage price change estimate provided by modified duration to better approximate the true relationship between a bond's price and its yield-to-maturity which is a curved line (convex).

   Duration estimates the change in the bond's price along the straight line that is tangent to this curved line ("first order" effect). Yield volatility measures the magnitude of changes in the yields along the yield curve.

20. B is correct. The bond's approximate convexity is closest to 70.906. Approximate convexity (ApproxCon) is calculated using the following formula:

$$ApproxCon = [PV_- + PV_+ - (2 \times PV_0)]/(\Delta Yield^2 \times PV_0)$$

where

PV_- = new price when the yield-to-maturity is decreased
PV_+ = new price when the yield-to-maturity is increased
PV_0 = original price
$\Delta Yield$ = change in yield-to-maturity

$$ApproxCon = [98.782 + 98.669 - (2 \times 98.722)]/(0.001^2 \times 98.722) = 70.906$$

21. C is correct. The expected percentage price change is closest to 1.78%. The convexity-adjusted percentage price change for a bond given a change in the yield-to-maturity is estimated by

$$\%\Delta PV^{Full} \approx [-AnnModDur \times \Delta Yield] + [0.5 \times AnnConvexity \times (\Delta Yield)^2]$$
$$\%\Delta PV^{Full} \approx [-7.020 \times (-0.0025)] + [0.5 \times 65.180 \times (-0.0025)^2] = 0.017754, \text{ or } 1.78\%$$

22. B is correct. The expected percentage price change is closest to −3.49%. The convexity-adjusted percentage price change for a bond given a change in the yield-to-maturity is estimated by

$$\%\Delta PV^{\text{Full}} \approx [-\text{AnnModDur} \times \Delta \text{Yield}] + [0.5 \times \text{AnnConvexity} \times (\Delta \text{Yield})^2]$$
$$\%\Delta PV^{\text{Full}} \approx [-7.140 \times 0.005] + [0.5 \times 66.200 \times (0.005)^2] = -0.034873, \text{ or } -3.49\%$$

23. B is correct. If the term structure of yield volatility is downward-sloping, then short-term bond yields-to-maturity have greater volatility than for long-term bonds. Therefore, long-term yields are more stable than short-term yields. Higher volatility in short-term rates does not necessarily mean that the level of short-term rates is higher than long-term rates. With a downward-sloping term structure of yield volatility, short-term bonds will not always experience greater price fluctuation than long-term bonds. The estimated percentage change in a bond price depends on the modified duration and convexity as well as on the yield-to-maturity change.

24. C is correct. When the holder of a bond experiences a one-time parallel shift in the yield curve, the Macaulay duration statistic identifies the number of years necessary to hold the bond so that the losses (or gains) from coupon reinvestment offset the gains (or losses) from market price changes. The duration gap is the difference between the Macaulay duration and the investment horizon. Modified duration approximates the percentage price change of a bond given a change in its yield-to-maturity.

25. C is correct. The duration gap is equal to the bond's Macaulay duration minus the investment horizon. In this case, the duration gap is positive, and price risk dominates coupon reinvestment risk. The investor risk is to higher rates.

    The investor is hedged against interest rate risk if the duration gap is zero; that is, the investor's investment horizon is equal to the bond's Macaulay duration. The investor is at risk of lower rates only if the duration gap is negative; that is, the investor's investment horizon is greater than the bond's Macaulay duration. In this case, coupon reinvestment risk dominates market price risk.

26. C is correct. The duration gap is closest to 4.158. The duration gap is a bond's Macaulay duration minus the investment horizon. The approximate Macaulay duration is the approximate modified duration times one plus the yield-to-maturity. It is 12.158 (= 11.470 × 1.06).

    Given an investment horizon of eight years, the duration gap for this bond at purchase is positive: 12.158 − 8 = 4.158. When the investment horizon is less than the Macaulay duration of the bond, the duration gap is positive, and price risk dominates coupon reinvestment risk.

27. A is correct. The price increase was most likely caused by a decrease in the bond's credit spread. The ratings upgrade most likely reflects a lower expected probability of default and/or a greater level of recovery of assets if default occurs. The decrease in credit risk results in a smaller credit spread. The increase in the bond price reflects a decrease in the yield-to-maturity due to a smaller credit spread. The change in the bond price was not due to a change in liquidity risk or an increase in the benchmark rate.

28. C is correct. Empirical duration is the best measure—better than analytical duration—of the impact of yield changes on portfolio value, especially under stressed market conditions, for a portfolio consisting of a variety of different bonds from different issuers, such as the portfolio described in Answer C. In this portfolio, credit spread changes on the high-yield bonds may partly or fully offset yield changes on the AAA rated sovereign

bonds and spread changes on the AAA rated corporate bonds; this interaction is best captured using empirical duration. The portfolios described in Answers A and B consist of the same types of bonds from similar issuers—sovereign bonds from similar-rated sovereign issuers (A) and covered bonds from similar-rated corporate issuers (B)—so empirical and analytical durations should be roughly similar in each of these portfolios.

CHAPTER 6

FUNDAMENTALS OF CREDIT ANALYSIS

SOLUTIONS

1. A is correct. Credit migration risk or downgrade risk refers to the risk that a bond issuer's creditworthiness may deteriorate or migrate lower. The result is that investors view the risk of default to be higher, causing the spread on the issuer's bonds to widen.

2. C is correct. Market liquidity risk refers to the risk that the price at which investors transact may be different from the price indicated in the market. Market liquidity risk is increased by (1) less debt outstanding and/or (2) a lower issue credit rating. Because Stedsmart Ltd is comparable to Fignermo Ltd except for less publicly traded debt outstanding, it should have higher market liquidity risk.

3. A is correct. First mortgage debt is senior secured debt and has the highest priority of claims. First mortgage debt also has the highest expected recovery rate. First mortgage debt refers to the pledge of specific property. Neither senior unsecured nor junior subordinate debt has any claims on specific assets.

4. B is correct. Whether or not secured assets are sufficient for the claims against them does not influence priority of claims. Any deficiency between pledged assets and the claims against them becomes senior unsecured debt and still adheres to the guidelines of priority of claims.

5. C is correct. Both analysts and rating agencies have difficulty foreseeing future debt-financed acquisitions.

6. C is correct. Goodwill is viewed as a lower quality asset compared with tangible assets that can be sold and more easily converted into cash.

7. C is correct. The value of assets in relation to the level of debt is important to assess the collateral of the company—that is, the quality and value of the assets that support the debt levels of the company.

8. B is correct. The growth prospects of the industry provide the analyst insight regarding the capacity of the company.

9. A is correct. The construction company is both highly leveraged, which increases credit risk, and in a highly cyclical industry, which results in more volatile earnings.

10. B is correct. The interest expense is €166 million and EBITDA = Operating profit + Depreciation and amortization = €2,660 + 1,214 million = €3,874 million. EBITDA interest coverage = EBITDA/Interest expense = 3,874/166 = 23.34 times.

11. B is correct. Total debt is €4,364 million with Total capital = Total debt + Shareholders' equity = €4,364 + 7,058 = €11,422 million. The Debt/Capital = 4,364/11,422 = 38.21%.

12. A is correct. If the debt of the company remained unchanged but FFO increased, more cash was available to service debt compared to the previous year. Additionally, debt/capital improved, which implies that the ability of Pay Handle Ltd to service their debt also improved.

13. A is correct. Based on four of the five credit ratios, GZ Group's credit quality is superior to that of the industry.

14. A is correct. DCM Group has more financial leverage and less interest coverage than AB plc, which implies greater credit risk.

15. A is correct. Low demand implies wider yield spreads, and heavy supply widens spreads even further.

16. C is correct. Credit risk is the risk of loss resulting from the borrower failing to make full and timely payments of interest and/or principal.

17. C is correct. Market liquidity risk is the risk that the price at which investors can actually transact—buying or selling—may differ from the price indicated in the market.

18. C is correct. Loss severity is the portion of a bond's value (including unpaid interest) an investor loses in the event of default.

19. B is correct. The two components of credit risk are default probability and loss severity. In the event of default, loss severity is the portion of a bond's value (including unpaid interest) an investor loses. A and C are incorrect because spread and market liquidity risk are credit-related risks, not components of credit risk.

20. A is correct. Credit risk has two components: default risk and loss severity. Because default risk is quite low for most high-quality debt issuers, bond investors tend to focus more on this likelihood and less on the potential loss severity.

21. B is correct. The expected loss for a given debt instrument is the default probability multiplied by the loss severity given default. The loss severity is often expressed as (1 − Recovery rate).

22. A is correct. Senior subordinated debt is ranked lower than senior unsecured debt and thus has a lower priority of payment.

23. C is correct. The highest-ranked unsecured debt is senior unsecured debt. Lower-ranked debt includes senior subordinated debt. A and B are incorrect because mortgage debt and second lien loans are secured and higher ranked.

24. C is correct. According to the absolute priority of claims, in the event of bankruptcy, creditors with a secured claim have the right to the value of that specific property before any other claim.

25. A is correct. A second lien has a secured interest in the pledged assets. Second lien debt ranks higher in priority of payment than senior unsecured and senior subordinated debt and thus would most likely have a higher recovery rate.

26. A is correct. Notching is the process for moving ratings up or down relative to the issuer rating when rating agencies consider secondary factors, such as priority of claims in the event of a default and the potential loss severity.

27. C is correct. Structural subordination can arise when a corporation with a holding company structure has debt at both its parent holding company and operating subsidiaries. Debt at the operating subsidiaries is serviced by the cash flow and assets of the subsidiaries before funds are passed to the parent holding company.

28. C is correct. The issuer credit rating usually applies to its senior unsecured debt.

29. A is correct. Second lien debt is secured debt, which is senior to unsecured debt and to subordinated debt.

30. C is correct. An issuer credit rating usually applies to its senior unsecured debt.

31. A is correct. Recognizing different payment priorities, and thus the potential for higher (or lower) loss severity in the event of default, the rating agencies have adopted a notching process whereby their credit ratings on issues can be moved up or down from the issuer rating (senior unsecured).

32. C is correct. As a general rule, the higher the senior unsecured rating, the smaller the notching adjustment. Thus, for corporate bonds rated Aa2/AA, the rating agencies will typically apply smaller rating adjustments, or notches, to the related issue.

33. A is correct. Credit migration is the risk that a bond issuer's creditworthiness deteriorates, or migrates lower. Over time, credit ratings can migrate significantly from what they were at the time a bond was issued. An investor should not assume that an issuer's credit rating will remain the same from the time of purchase through the entire holding period.

34. B is correct. An industry with a high number of suppliers reduces the suppliers' negotiating power, thus helping companies control expenses and aiding in the servicing of debt.

35. A is correct. Credit analysis starts with industry structure—for example, by looking at the major forces of competition, followed by an analysis of industry fundamentals—and then turns to examination of the specific issuer.

36. C is correct. Credit analysts can make judgments about management's character by evaluating the use of aggressive accounting policies, such as timing revenue recognition. This activity is a potential warning flag for other behaviors or actions that may adversely affect an issuer's creditworthiness.

37. B is correct. Capacity refers to the ability of a borrower to service its debt. Capacity is determined through credit analysis of an issuer's industry and of the specific issuer.

38. A is correct. Credit analysts can make judgments about management's character in a number of ways, including by observing its use of aggressive accounting policies and/or tax strategies. An example of this aggressiveness is recognizing revenue prematurely.

39. C is correct. Debt/capital and debt/EBITDA are used to assess a company's leverage. Higher leverage ratios indicate more leverage and thus higher credit risk. Company C's debt/capital (46.3%) and debt/EBITDA (2.5×) are higher than those for Companies A and B.

40. B is correct. The EBITDA/interest expense and EBIT/interest expense are coverage ratios. Coverage ratios measure an issuer's ability to meet its interest payments. A higher ratio indicates better credit quality. Company B's EBITDA/interest expense (62.4×) and EBIT/interest expense (58.2×) are higher than those for Companies A and C.

41. C is correct because Company Y has a higher ratio of free cash flow after dividends to debt than Company X, not lower, as shown in the following table.

$$\text{Free cash flow after dividends as a \% of debt} = \frac{\text{FCF after dividends}}{\text{Debt}}$$

	Company X	Company Y
Cash flow from operations	£3.3	£14.0
Less		
Net capital expenditures	−0.8	−1.1
Dividends	−0.3	−6.1
Free cash flow after dividends	£2.2	£6.8
Debt	£12.2	£29.8
Free cash flow after dividends as a % of debt	(2.2/12.2) × 100	(6.8/29.8) × 100
Free cash flow after dividends as a % of debt	18.0%	22.8%

A is incorrect. Company Y has a lower debt/capital than Company X, as shown in the following table.

$$\text{Debt divided by Capital (\%)} = \frac{\text{Debt}}{(\text{Debt} + \text{Equity})}$$

	Company X	Company Y
Debt	£12.2	£29.8
Capital		
Debt	12.2	29.8
+ Equity	1.3	64.0
Capital	£13.5	£93.8
Debt/Capital (%)	(12.2/13.5) × 100	(29.8/93.8) × 100
Debt/Capital (%)	90.4%	31.8%

B is incorrect because Company Y has a lower debt/EBITDA than Company Y, not higher, as shown in the following table.

	Company X	Company Y
Operating income	£1.1	£13.3
EBIT	£1.1	£13.3
plus		
Depreciation	1.0	3.8
Amortization	0.0	0.0
EBITDA	£2.1	£17.1

Debt	£12.2	£29.8
Debt/EBITDA	12.2/2.1	29.8/17.1
Debt/EBITDA	5.81	1.74

42. A is correct. Compared with Company Y, based on both their debt/capital and their ratios of free cash flow after dividends to debt, which are measures of leverage commonly used in credit analysis, Company X is more highly leveraged, as shown in the following table.

$$\text{Debt divided by Capital (\%)} = \frac{\text{Debt}}{(\text{Debt} + \text{Equity})}$$

	Company X	Company Y
Debt	£2.2	£29.8
Capital		
Debt	2.2	29.8
+ Equity	4.3	64.0
Capital	£6.5	£93.8
Debt/Capital (%)	(12.2/13.5) × 100	(29.8/93.8) × 100
Debt/Capital (%)	90.4%	31.8%

$$\text{Free cash flow after dividends as a \% of debt} = \frac{\text{FCF after dividends}}{\text{Debt}}$$

	Company X	Company Y
Cash flow from operations	£3.3	£14.0
Less		
Net capital expenditures	−0.8	−1.1
Dividends	−0.3	−6.1
Free cash flow after dividends	£2.2	£6.8
Debt	£12.2	£29.8
Free cash flow after dividends as a % of debt	(2.2/12.2) × 100	(6.8/29.8) × 100
Free cash flow after dividends as a % of debt	18.0%	22.8%

43. B is correct. In weak financial markets, including weak markets for equities, credit spreads will widen.

44. B is correct. Weakening economic conditions will push investors to desire a greater risk premium and drive overall credit spreads wider.

45. C is correct. In periods of heavy new issue supply, credit spreads will widen if demand is insufficient.

46. C is correct. Non-sovereign governments typically must balance their operating budgets and lack the discretion to use monetary policy as many sovereigns can.

47. A is correct. Most investors in investment-grade debt focus on spread risk—that is, the effect of changes in spreads on prices and returns—while in high-yield analysis, the focus on default risk is relatively greater.

48. B is correct. Among the most important considerations in sovereign credit analysis is growth and age distribution of population. A relatively young and growing population contributes to growth in GDP and an expanding tax base and relies less on social services, pensions, and health care relative to an older population.

CHAPTER 7

THE TERM STRUCTURE AND INTEREST RATE DYNAMICS

SOLUTIONS

1. Three forward rates can be calculated from the one-, two- and three-year spot rates. The rate on a one-year loan that begins at the end of Year 1 can be calculated using the one- and two-year spot rates; in the following equation, one would solve for $f_{1,1}$:

$$[1 + z_2]^2 = [1 + z_1]^1[1 + f_{1,1}]^1$$

The rate on a one-year loan that starts at the end of Year 2 can be calculated from the two- and three-year spot rates. In the following equation, one would solve for $f_{2,1}$:

$$[1 + z_3]^3 = [1 + z_2]^2[1 + f_{2,1}]^1$$

Additionally, the rate on a two-year loan that begins at the end of Year 1 can be computed from the one- and three-year spot rates. In the following equation, one would solve for $f_{1,2}$:

$$[1 + z_3]^3 = [1 + z_1]^1[1 + f_{1,2}]^2$$

2. For the two-year forward rate one year from now of 2%, the two interpretations are as follows:

- 2% is the rate that will make an investor indifferent between buying a three-year zero-coupon bond or investing in a one-year zero-coupon bond and, when it matures, reinvesting in a zero-coupon bond that matures in two years.
- 2% is the rate that can be locked in today by buying a three-year zero-coupon bond rather than investing in a one-year zero-coupon bond and, when it matures, reinvesting in a zero-coupon bond that matures in two years.

3. A flat yield curve implies that all spot interest rates are the same. When the spot rate is the same for every maturity, successive applications of the forward rate model will show that all the forward rates will also be the same and equal to the spot rate.

4. A. The yield-to-maturity of a coupon bond is the expected rate of return on a bond if the bond is held to maturity, there is no default, and the bond and all coupons are reinvested at the original yield-to-maturity.

   B. Yes, it is possible. For example, if reinvestment rates for the future coupons are lower than the initial yield-to-maturity, a bondholder may experience lower realized returns.

5. If forward rates are higher than expected future spot rates, the market price of the bond will be lower than the intrinsic value. This dynamic occurs because, everything else held constant, the market is currently discounting the bond's cash flows at a higher rate than the investor's expected future spot rates. The investor can capitalize on this scenario by purchasing the undervalued bond. If expected future spot rates are realized, then bond prices should rise, thus generating gains for the investor.

6. The strategy of rolling down the yield curve is one in which a bond trader attempts to generate a total return over a given investment horizon that exceeds the return to bond with maturity matched to the horizon. The strategy involves buying a bond with maturity more distant than the investment horizon. Assuming an upward-sloping yield curve, if the yield curve does not change level or shape, as the bond approaches maturity (or rolls down the yield curve) it will be priced at successively lower yields. So as long as the bond is held for a period less than maturity, it should generate higher returns because of price gains.

7. Some countries do not have active government bond markets with trading at all maturities. For those countries without a liquid government bond market but with an active swap market, there are typically more points available to construct a swap curve than a government bond yield curve. For those markets, the swap curve may be a superior benchmark.

8. The TED spread is the difference between Libor and the US T-bill rate of matching maturity. It is an indicator of perceived credit and liquidity risk. In particular, because sovereign debt instruments are typically the benchmark for the lowest default risk instruments in a given market, and loans between banks (often at Libor) have some counterparty risk, the TED spread is considered to at least in part reflect default (or counterparty) risk in the banking sector.

9. The secured overnight financing rate (SOFR), or overnight cash borrowing rate collateralized by US Treasuries, is a barometer of the US Treasury repurchase (or repo) market. SOFR is a volume-weighted index of all qualified repo market transactions on a given day and is influenced by supply and demand conditions in secured funding markets.

10. The local expectations theory asserts that the total return over a one-month horizon for a five-year zero-coupon bond would be the same as for a two-year zero-coupon bond.

11. Both theories attempt to explain the shape of any yield curve in terms of supply and demand for bonds. In segmented market theory, bond market participants are limited to purchase of maturities that match the timing of their liabilities. In the preferred habitat theory, participants have a preferred maturity for asset purchases, but they may deviate from it if they feel returns in other maturities offer sufficient compensation for leaving their preferred maturity segment.

12. A. Studies have shown that three factors affect Treasury returns: (1) changes in the level of the yield curve, (2) changes in the slope of the yield curve, and (3) changes in the curvature of the yield curve. Changes in the level refer to upward or downward shifts in the yield curve. For example, an upward shift in the yield curve is likely to result

in lower returns across all maturities. Changes in the slope of the yield curve relate to the steepness of the yield curve. Thus, if the yield curve steepens, higher returns for short-maturity bonds and lower returns for long-maturity bonds will likely occur. An example of a change in the curvature of the yield curve is a situation where rates fall at the short and long end of the yield curve while rising for intermediate maturities. In this situation, returns on short and long maturities are likely to rise while declining for intermediate-maturity bonds.

B. Empirically, the most important factor is the change in the level of interest rates.

C. Key rate durations and a measure based on sensitivities to level, slope, and curvature movements can address shaping risk, but effective duration cannot.

13. C is correct. There is no spot rate information to provide rates for a loan that terminates in five years. That is, $f_{2,3}$ is calculated as follows:

$$f_{2,3} = \sqrt[3]{\frac{[1+z_5]^5}{[1+z_2]^2}} - 1$$

This equation indicates that in order to calculate the rate for a three-year loan beginning at the end of two years, one needs the five-year spot rate, z_5, and the two-year spot rate, z_2. However, z_5 is not provided.

14. A is correct. The forward rate for a one-year loan beginning in one year, $f_{1,1}$, is $1.04^2/1.03 - 1 = 5\%$. The rate for a one-year loan beginning in two years, $f_{2,1}$, is $1.05^3/1.04^2 - 1 = 7\%$. This confirms that an upward-sloping yield curve is consistent with an upward-sloping forward curve.

15. C is correct. If one-period forward rates are decreasing with maturity, then the forward curve is downward sloping. This turn implies a downward-sloping yield curve where longer-term spot rates z_{B-A} are less than shorter-term spot rates z_A.

16. C is correct. From the forward rate model, we have

$$[1+z_2]^2 = [1+z_1]^1[1+f_{1,1}]^1$$

Using the one- and two-year spot rates, we have

$$(1+0.05)^2 = (1+0.04)^1[1+f_{1,1}]^1, \text{ so } \frac{(1+0.05)^2}{(1+0.04)^1} - 1 = f_{1,1} = 6.010\%$$

17. C is correct. From the forward rate model,

$$[1+z_3]^3 = [1+z_1]^1[1+f_{1,2}]^2$$

Using the one- and three-year spot rates, we find

$$(1+0.06)^3 = (1+0.04)^1[1+f_{1,2}]^2, \text{ so } \sqrt{\frac{(1+0.06)^3}{(1+0.04)^1}} - 1 = f_{1,2} = 7.014\%$$

18. C is correct. From the forward rate model,

$$[1+z_3]^3 = [1+z_2]^2[1+f_{2,1}]^1$$

Using the two- and three-year spot rates, we find

$$(1+0.06)^3 = (1+0.05)^2[1+f_{2,1}]^1, \text{ so } \frac{(1+0.06)^3}{(1+0.05)^2} - 1 = f_{2,1} = 8.029\%$$

19. A is correct. We can convert spot rates to spot prices to find $DF_3 = \dfrac{1}{(1.06)^3} = 0.8396$. The forward pricing model can be used to find the price of the five-year zero as $DF_B = DF_A \times F_{A,B-A}$, so $DF_5 = DF_3 F_{3,2} = 0.8396 \times 0.8479 = 0.7119$.

20. B is correct. Applying the forward rate model, we find

$$[1 + z_3]^3 = [1 + z_1]^1 [1 + f_{1,1}]^1 [1 + f_{2,1}]^1$$

So $[1 + z_3]^3 = (1 + 0.04)^1 (1 + 0.06)^1 (1 + 0.08)^1$, $\sqrt[3]{1.1906} - 1 = z_3 = 5.987\%$.

21. B is correct. We can convert spot rates to spot prices and use the forward pricing model, so we have $DF_1 = \dfrac{1}{(1.05)^1} = 0.9524$. The forward pricing model is $DF_B = DF_A \times F_{A,B-A}$, so $DF_2 = DF_1 F_{1,1} = 0.9524 \times 0.9346 = 0.8901$.

22. A is correct. The swap rate is the interest rate for the fixed-rate leg of an interest rate swap.

23. A is correct. The swap spread = $1.00\% - 0.63\% = 0.37\%$, or 37 bps.

24. C is correct. The fixed leg of the five-year fixed-for-floating swap will be equal to the five-year Treasury rate plus the swap spread: $2.0\% + 0.5\% = 2.5\%$.

25. A is correct. The TED spread is the difference between the three-month Libor and the three-month Treasury bill rate. If the T-bill rate falls and Libor does not change, the TED spread will increase.

26. A is correct. The Z spread is the single rate that, when added to the rates of the spot yield curve, will provide the correct discount rates to price a particular risky bond.

27. B is correct. The five-year spot rate is determined by using forward substitution and using the known values of the one-year, two-year, three-year, and four-year spot rates, as follows:

$$1 = \frac{0.0437}{1.025} + \frac{0.0437}{(1.03)^2} + \frac{0.0437}{(1.035)^3} + \frac{0.0437}{(1.04)^4} + \frac{1 + 0.0437}{(1 + z_5)^5}$$

$$z_5 = \sqrt[5]{\frac{1.0437}{0.8394}} - 1 = 4.453\%$$

28. B is correct. The spot rates imply an upward-sloping yield curve, $z_3 > z_2 > z_1$. Because nominal yields incorporate a premium for expected inflation, an upward-sloping yield curve is generally interpreted as reflecting a market expectation of increasing, or at least level, future inflation (associated with relatively strong economic growth).

29. C is correct. A one-year loan beginning in three years, or $f_{3,1}$, is calculated as follows:

$$[1 + z_{3+1}]^{3+1} = [1 + z_3]^3 [1 + f_{3,1}]^1$$
$$[1.04]^4 = [1.035]^3 [1 + f_{3,1}]$$

$$f_{3,1} = \frac{(1.04)^4}{(1.035)^3} - 1 = 5.514\%$$

30. C is correct. Exhibit 1 provides five years of par rates, from which the spot rates for z_1, z_2, z_3, z_4, and z_5 can be derived. Thus the forward rate $f_{1,4}$ can be calculated as follows:

$$f_{1,4} = \sqrt[4]{\frac{[1 + z_5]^5}{[1 + z_1]^1}} - 1$$

31. C is correct. The yield-to-maturity, y_3, of Bond Z should be a weighted average of the spot rates used in the valuation of the bond. Because the bond's largest cash flow occurs in Year 3, z_3 will have a greater weight than z_1 and z_2 in determining y_3.
    Using the spot rates:

$$\text{Price} = \frac{\$60}{(1.025)^1} + \frac{\$60}{(1.030)^2} + \frac{\$1,060}{(1.035)^3} = \$1,071.16$$

Using the yield-to-maturity:

$$\text{Price} = \frac{\$60}{[1 + y(3)]^1} + \frac{\$60}{[1 + y(3)]^2} + \frac{\$1,060}{[1 + y(3)]^3} = \$1,071.16$$

The computed result is $y_3 = 3.46\%$, which is closest to the three-year spot rate of 3.50%.

32. A is correct. Alexander projects that the spot curve two years from today will be below the current forward curve, which implies that her expected future spot rates beyond two years will be lower than the quoted forward rates. Alexander would perceive Bond Z to be undervalued in the sense that the market is effectively discounting the bond's payments at a higher rate than she would, and the bond's market price is below her estimate of intrinsic value.

33. B is correct. Nguyen's strategy is to ride the yield curve, which is appropriate when the yield curve is upward sloping. The yield curve implied by Exhibit 1 is upward sloping, which implies that the three-year forward curve is above the current spot curve. When the yield curve slopes upward, as a bond approaches maturity or "rolls down the yield curve," the bond is valued at successively lower yields and higher prices.

34. B is correct. The forward pricing model is based on the no-arbitrage principle and is used to calculate a bond's forward price based on the spot yield curve. The spot curve is constructed by using annualized rates from option-free and default-risk-free zero-coupon bonds.

Equation 2: $DF_B = DF_A \times F_{A,B-A}$; we need to solve for $F_{1,1}$.

$DF_1 = 1/(1 + 0.0225)^1$ and $DF_2 = 1/(1 + 0.0270)^2$,

$F_{1,1} = DF_2/DF_1 = 0.9481/0.9780 = 0.9694.$

35. C is correct. When the spot curve is upward sloping and its level and shape are expected to remain constant over an investment horizon (Shire Gate Advisers' view), buying bonds with a maturity longer than the investment horizon (i.e., riding the yield curve) will provide a total return greater than the return on a maturity-matching strategy.

36. C is correct. The swap spread is a common way to indicate credit spreads in a market. The four-year swap rate (fixed leg of an interest rate swap) can be used as an indication of the four-year corporate yield. Riding the yield curve by purchasing a four-year zero-coupon bond with a yield of 4.75% {i.e., 4.05% + 0.70%, $[P_4 = 100/(1 + 0.0475)^4 = 83.058]$} and then selling it when it becomes a two-year zero-coupon bond with a yield of 3.00% {i.e., 2.70% + 0.30%, $[P_2 = 100/(1 + 0.0300)^2 = 94.260]$} produces an annual return of 6.53%: $(94.260/83.058)^{0.5} - 1.0 = 0.0653$.

37. B is correct. The Z-spread is the constant basis point spread that is added to the default-free spot curve to price a risky bond. A Z-spread of 65 bps for a particular bond would

imply adding a fixed spread of 65 bps to maturities along the spot curve to correctly price the bond. Therefore, for the two-year bond, $z_1 = 2.90\%$ (i.e., $2.25\% + 0.65\%$), $z_2 = 3.35\%$ (i.e., $2.70\% + 0.65\%$), and the price of the bond with an annual coupon of 4.15% is as follows:

$$P = 4.15/(1 + 0.029)^1 + 4.15/(1 + 0.0335)^2 + 100/(1 + 0.0335)^2$$

$$P = 101.54$$

38. C is correct. The Libor–OIS spread is considered an indicator of the risk and liquidity of money market securities. This spread measures the difference between Libor and the OIS rate.

39. C is correct. Liquidity preference theory asserts that investors demand a risk premium, in the form of a liquidity premium, to compensate them for the added interest rate risk they face when buying long-maturity bonds. The theory also states that the liquidity premium increases with maturity.

40. A is correct. Madison's response is correct; research indicates that short-term rate volatility is mostly linked to uncertainty regarding monetary policy, whereas long-term rate volatility is mostly linked to uncertainty regarding the real economy and inflation.

41. B is correct. Because the factors in Exhibit 1 have been standardized to have unit standard deviations, a two-standard-deviation increase in the steepness factor will lead to the yield on the 20-year bond decreasing by 0.6030%, calculated as follows:

Change in 20-year bond yield = –0.3015% × 2 = –0.6030%

42. C is correct. Because the factors in Exhibit 1 have been standardized to have unit standard deviations, a one-standard-deviation decrease in both the level factor and the curvature factor will lead to the yield on the five-year bond increasing by 0.0389%, calculated as follows:

Change in five-year bond yield = 0.4352% – 0.3963% = 0.0389%

43. C is correct. The assistant states that bootstrapping entails *backward* substitution using par yields to solve for zero-coupon rates one by one, in order from latest to earliest maturities. Bootstrapping entails *forward* substitution, however, using par yields to solve for zero-coupon rates one by one, in order from earliest to latest maturities.

44. C is correct. Country C's private sector is much bigger than the public sector, and the government bond market in Country C currently lacks liquidity. Under such circumstances, the swap curve is a more relevant benchmark for interest rates.

45. B is correct. The historical three-year swap spread for Country B was the lowest six months ago. Swap spread is defined as the spread paid by the fixed-rate payer of an interest rate swap over the rate of the "on the run" (most recently issued) government bond security with the same maturity as the swap. The lower (higher) the swap spread, the lower (higher) the return that investors require for credit and/or liquidity risks.

The fixed rate of the three-year fixed-for-floating Libor swap was 0.01% six months ago, and the three-year government bond yield was –0.08% six months ago. Thus the swap spread six months ago was 0.01% – (–0.08%) = 0.09%.

One month ago, the fixed rate of the three-year fixed-for-floating Libor swap was 0.16%, and the three-year government bond yield was –0.10%. Thus the swap spread one month ago was 0.16% – (–0.10%) = 0.26%.

Twelve months ago, the fixed rate of the three-year fixed-for-floating Libor swap was 0.71%, and the three-year government bond yield was –0.07%. Thus, the swap spread 12 months ago was 0.71% – (–0.07%) = 0.78%.

46. A is correct. Country A's yield curve is upward sloping—a condition for the strategy—and more so than Country B's.

47. B is correct. The yield curve for Country B is currently upward sloping, but Tyo expects a reversal in the slope of the current yield curve. This means she expects the resulting yield curve for Country B to slope downward, which implies that the resulting forward curve would lie below the spot yield curve. The forward curve lies below the spot curve in scenarios in which the spot curve is downward sloping; the forward curve lies above the spot curve in scenarios in which the spot curve is upward sloping.

    A is incorrect because the yield curve for Country A is currently upward sloping and Tyo expects that the yield curve will maintain its shape and level. That expectation implies that the resulting forward curve would be above the spot yield curve.

    C is incorrect because the yield curve for Country C is currently downward sloping and Tyo expects a reversal in the slope of the current yield curve. She thus expects the resulting yield curve for Country C to slope upward, which implies that the resulting forward curve would be above the spot yield curve.

48. A is correct. Tyo's projected spot curve assumes that future spot rates reflect, or will be equal to, the current forward rates for all respective maturities. This assumption implies that the bonds for Country A are fairly valued because the market is effectively discounting the bond's payments at spot rates that match those projected by Tyo.

    B and C are incorrect because Tyo's projected spot curves for the two countries do not match the current forward rates for all respective maturities. In the case of Country B, she expects future spot rates to be higher (than the current forward rates that the market is using to discount the bond's payments). For Country C, she expects future spot rates to be lower (than the current forward rates). Hence, she perceives the Country B bond to be currently overvalued and the Country C bond to be undervalued.

49. C is correct. Liquidity preference theory suggests that liquidity premiums exist to compensate investors for the added interest rate risk that they face when lending long term and that these premiums increase with maturity. Tyo and her assistant are assuming that liquidity premiums exist.

50. A is correct. From the forward rate model, $f_{3,2}$, is found as follows:

$$[1 + z_5]^5 = [1 + z_3]^3[1 + f_{3,2}]^2$$

Using the three-year and five-year spot rates, we find

$$(1 + 0.107)^5 = (1 + 0.118)^3[1 + f_{3,2}]^2, \text{ so}$$

$$\sqrt{\frac{(1 + 0.107)^5}{(1 + 0.118)^3}} - 1 = f_{3,2} = 9.07\%$$

51. A is correct. This action is most often consistent with bearish flattening, or short-term bond yields rising more than long-term bond yields resulting in a flatter yield curve.

52. C is correct. When government budget deficits fall, fiscal supply-side effects are most likely to result in lower bond yields.

53. B is correct. A flight to quality is most often associated with bullish flattening, in which the yield curve flattens as long term rates fall by more than short-term rates.

CHAPTER 8

THE ARBITRAGE-FREE VALUATION FRAMEWORK

SOLUTIONS

1. A is correct. This is the same bond being sold at three different prices, so an arbitrage opportunity exists by buying the bond from the exchange where it is priced lowest and immediately selling it on the exchange that has the highest price. Accordingly, an investor would maximize profit from the arbitrage opportunity by buying the bond on the Frankfurt exchange (which has the lowest price, €103.7565) and selling it on the Eurex exchange (which has the highest price, €103.7956) to generate a risk-free profit of €0.0391 (as mentioned, ignoring transaction costs) per €100 par.

   B is incorrect because buying on NYSE Euronext and selling on Eurex would result in a €0.0141 profit per €100 par (€103.7956 − €103.7815 = €0.0141), which is not the maximum arbitrage profit available. A greater profit would be realized if the bond were purchased in Frankfurt and sold on Eurex.

   C is incorrect because buying on Frankfurt and selling on NYSE Euronext would result in an €0.0250 profit per €100 par (€103.7815 − €103.7565 = €0.0250). A greater profit would be realized if the bond were purchased in Frankfurt and sold on Eurex.

2. C is correct. The bond from Exhibit 1 is selling for its calculated value on the NYSE Euronext exchange. The arbitrage-free value of a bond is the present value of its cash flows discounted by the spot rate for zero-coupon bonds maturing on the same date as each cash flow. The value of this bond, 103.7815, is calculated as follows:

	Year 1	Year 2	Year 3	Total PV
Yield-to-maturity	1.2500%	1.500%	1.700%	
Spot rate[1]	1.2500%	1.5019%	1.7049%	
Cash flow	3.00	3.00	103.00	
Present value of payment[2]	2.9630	2.9119	97.9066	103.7815
				(*continued*)

197

	Eurex	NYSE Euronext	Frankfurt
Price	€103.7956	€103.7815	€103.7565
Mispricing (per 100 par value)	0.141	0	–0.025

Notes:

[1]Spot rates are calculated using bootstrapping. For example, Year 2 spot rate (z_2): $100 = 1.5/1.0125 + 101.5/(1 + z_2)^2$; $z_2 = 0.015019$.

[2]Present value calculated using the formula $PV = FV/(1 + r)^n$, where n = number of years until cash flow, FV = cash flow amount, and r = spot rate.

A is incorrect because the price on the Eurex exchange, €103.7956, was calculated using the yield-to-maturity rate to discount the cash flows when the spot rates should have been used. C is incorrect because the price on the Frankfurt exchange, €103.7565, uses the Year 3 spot rate to discount all the cash flows.

3. C is correct. Because Node 2–2 is the middle node rate in Year 2, it will be close to the implied one-year forward rate two years from now (as derived from the spot curve). Node 4–1 should be equal to the product of Node 4–5 and $e^{0.8}$. Lastly, Node 3–2 cannot be derived from Node 2–2; it can be derived from any other Year 3 node; for example, Node 3–2 can be derived from Node 3–4 (equal to the product of Node 3–4 and $e^{4\sigma}$).

4. A is correct. The value of a bond at a particular node, in this case Node 1–2, can be derived by determining the present value of the coupon payment and expected future bond values to the right of that node on the tree. In this case, those two nodes are the middle node in Year 2, equal to 101.5168, and the lower node in Year 2, equal to 102.1350. The coupon payment is 2.5. The bond value at Node 1–2 is calculated as follows:

$$\text{Value} = \frac{2.5 + (0.5 \times 101.5168 + 0.5 \times 102.1350)}{1.014925}$$

$$= 102.7917$$

5. A is correct. Calibrating a binomial interest rate tree to match a specific term structure is important because we can use the known valuation of a benchmark bond from the spot rate pricing to verify the accuracy of the rates shown in the binomial interest rate tree. Once its accuracy is confirmed, the interest rate tree can then be used to value bonds with embedded options. While discounting with spot rates will produce arbitrage-free valuations for option-free bonds, this spot rate method will not work for bonds with embedded options where expected future cash flows are interest-rate dependent (because rate changes impact the likelihood of options being exercised). The interest rate tree allows for the alternative paths that a bond with embedded options might take.

B is incorrect because calibration does not identify mispriced benchmark bonds. In fact, benchmark bonds are employed to prove the accuracy of the binomial interest rate tree, because they are assumed to be correctly priced by the market.

C is incorrect because the calibration of the binomial interest rate tree is designed to produce an arbitrage-free valuation approach and such an approach does not allow a market participant to realize arbitrage profits through stripping and reconstitution.

6. A is correct. Volatility is one of the two key assumptions required to estimate rates for the binomial interest rate tree. Increasing the volatility from 10% to 15% would cause the possible forward rates to spread out on the tree because it increases the exponent in the relationship multiple between nodes ($e^{x\sigma}$, where x = 2 times the number of nodes above the lowest node in a given year in the interest rate tree). Conversely, using a lower

estimate of volatility would cause the forward rates to narrow or converge to the implied forward rates from the prevailing yield curve.

B is incorrect because volatility is a key assumption in the binomial interest rate tree model. Any change in volatility will cause a change in the implied forward rates.

C is incorrect because increasing the volatility from 10% to 15% causes the possible forward rates to spread out on the tree, not converge to the implied forward rates from the current yield curve. Rates will converge to the implied forward rates when lower estimates of volatility are assumed.

7. B is correct. Bond B's arbitrage-free price is calculated as follows:

$$\frac{3}{1.02} + \frac{103}{1.02^2} = 101.9416$$

which is higher than the bond's market price of 100.9641. Therefore, an arbitrage opportunity exists. Since the bond's value (100.9641) is less than the sum of the values of its discounted cash flows individually (101.9416), a trader would perceive an arbitrage opportunity and could buy the bond while selling claims to the individual cash flows (zeros), capturing the excess value. The arbitrage-free prices of Bond A and Bond C are equal to the market prices of the respective bonds, so there is no arbitrage opportunity for these two bonds:

Bond A: $\frac{1}{1.02} + \frac{101}{1.02^2} = 98.0584$

Bond C: $\frac{5}{1.02} + \frac{105}{1.02^2} = 105.8247$

8. C is correct. The first step in the solution is to find the correct spot rate (zero-coupon rates) for each year's cash flow. The benchmark bonds in Exhibit 2 are conveniently priced at par so the yields-to-maturity and the coupon rates on the bonds are the same. Because the one-year issue has only one cash flow remaining, the YTM equals the spot rate of 3% (or $z_1 = 3\%$). The spot rates for Year 2 (z_2) and Year 3 (z_3) are calculated as follows:

$$100 = \frac{4}{1.0300} + \frac{104}{(1 + z_2)^2}; \ z_2 = 4.02\%$$

$$100 = \frac{5}{1.0300} + \frac{5}{(1.0402)^2} + \frac{105}{(1 + z_3)^3}; \ z_3 = 5.07\%$$

The correct arbitrage-free price for the Hutto-Barkley Inc. bond is

$$P_0 = \frac{3}{(1.0300)} + \frac{3}{(1.0402)^2} + \frac{103}{(1.0507)^3} = 94.4828$$

Therefore, the bond is mispriced by $94.9984 - 94.4828 = 0.5156$ per 100 of par value.

A is incorrect because the correct spot rates are not calculated and instead the Hutto-Barkley Inc. bond is discounted using the respective YTM for each maturity. Therefore, this leads to an incorrect mispricing of $94.6616 - 94.9984 = -0.3368$ per 100 of par value.

B is incorrect because the spot rates are derived using the coupon rate for Year 3 (maturity) instead of using each year's respective coupon rate to employ the bootstrap methodology. This leads to an incorrect mispricing of $94.5302 - 94.9984 = -0.4682$ per 100 of par value.

9. B is correct. The Luna y Estrellas Intl. bond contains an embedded option. Method 1 will produce an arbitrage-free valuation for option-free bonds; however, for bonds with embedded options, changes in future interest rates impact the likelihood the option will be exercised and so impact future cash flows. Therefore, to develop a framework that values bonds with embedded options, interest rates must be allowed to take on different potential values in the future based on some assumed level of volatility (Method 2).

   A and C are incorrect because the Hutto-Barkley Inc. bond and the Peaton Scorpio Motors bond are both option-free bonds and can be valued using either Method 1 or Method 2 to produce an arbitrage-free valuation.

10. B is correct. This is the binomial tree that obtains a bond value of 109.0085.

Valuing a 6%, Three-Year Bond

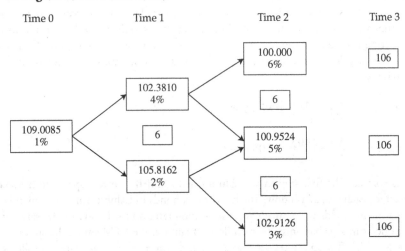

These are the calculations:

$$106/1.06 = 100.0000$$

$$106/1.05 = 100.9524$$

$$106/1.03 = 102.9126$$

$$\frac{6 + (0.5 \times 100.0000 + 0.5 \times 100.9524)}{1.04} = 102.3810$$

$$\frac{6 + (0.5 \times 100.9524 + 0.5 \times 102.9126)}{1.02} = 105.8162$$

$$\frac{6 + (0.5 \times 102.3810 + 0.5 \times 105.8162)}{1.01} = 109.0085$$

A is incorrect because the Time T coupon payment is subtracted from the value in each node calculation for Time T. C is incorrect because it assumes that a coupon is paid at Time 0.

11. B is correct. Based on the dominance principle, an arbitrage opportunity exists. The dominance principle asserts that a financial asset with a risk-free payoff in the future must have a positive price today. Because Asset A and Asset B are both risk-free assets, they should have the same discount rate. Relative to its payoff, Asset A is priced at $500/525, or 0.95238, and Asset B is priced at $1,000/1,100, or 0.90909. Given its higher implied discount rate (10%) and lower corresponding price, Asset B is cheap relative to Asset A, which has a lower implied discount rate (5%) and a higher corresponding price.

    The arbitrage opportunity based on dominance is to sell two units of Asset A for $1,000 and buy one unit of Asset B. There is no cash outlay today, and in one year, the portfolio delivers a net cash inflow of $50 [= $1,100 − (2 × $525)].

12. B is correct. Of the three markets, the New York bond has the lowest yield-to-maturity and, correspondingly, the highest bond price. Similarly, the Hong Kong bond has the highest yield-to-maturity and the lowest bond price of the three markets. Therefore, the most profitable arbitrage trade would be to buy the bond in Hong Kong and sell it in New York.

13. B is correct. The bond value at the upper node at Time 1 is closest to 99.6255. The cash flow at Time 2 is 102.5, the redemption of par value (100) plus the final coupon payment (2.5). Using backward induction, we calculate the present value of the bond at the upper node of Time 1 as 102.5/1.028853 = 99.6255.

14. B is correct. The price of Bond D is closest to 103.3230 and can be calculated using backward induction.

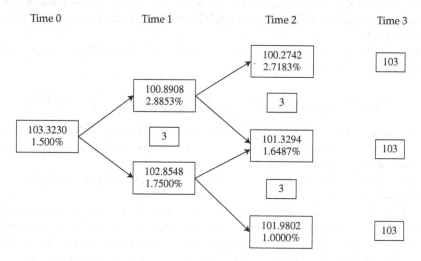

$$\text{Bond value at a node} = \frac{C + (0.5 \times VH + 0.5 \times VL)}{1 + i}$$

Calculations:

The cash flow at Time 3 is 103, the redemption of par value (100) plus the final coupon payment (3).

Time 2 node values:

$$\text{Upper node: } 103/1.027183 = 100.2742$$
$$\text{Middle node: } 103/1.016487 = 101.3294$$
$$\text{Lower node: } 103/1.010000 = 101.9802$$

Working back to Time 1 requires the use of the general expression above.

Time 1 node values:

$$\text{Upper node:} \frac{3 + (0.5 \times 100.2742 + 0.5 \times 101.3294)}{1.028853} = 100.8908$$

$$\text{Lower node:} \frac{3 + (0.5 \times 101.3294 + 0.5 \times 101.9802)}{1.0175} = 102.8548$$

$$\text{Time 0 node value:} \frac{3 + (0.5 \times 100.8908 + 0.5 \times 102.8548)}{1.015} = 103.3230$$

Therefore, the price of the bond is 103.3230.

15. B is correct. Two methods are commonly used to estimate potential interest rate volatility in a binomial interest rate tree. The first method bases estimates on historical interest rate volatility. The second method uses observed market prices of interest rate derivatives.

    Statement 1 is incorrect because there are three requirements to create a binomial interest rate tree, not two. The third requirement is an assumption regarding the interest rate model. Statement 3 is incorrect because the valuation of a bond using spot rates and the valuation of a bond from an interest rate tree will be the same regardless of the volatility assumption used in the model.

16. B is correct. The value of the lower one-period forward rate is closest to 3.5400%. Since the higher one-period forward rate is 5.8365% and interest rate volatility is 25%, the lower rate equals the higher rate multiplied by $e^{-2\sigma}$. This is calculated as $0.058365 \times e^{-0.50} = 0.035400$.

17. B is correct. The present value of Bond D's cash flows following Path 2 is 102.8607 and can be calculated as follows:

$$\frac{3}{1.015} + \frac{3}{(1.015)(1.028853)} + \frac{103}{(1.015)(1.028853)(1.016487)} = 102.8607$$

18. A is correct. Increasing the number of paths using the Monte Carlo method does increase the estimate's statistical accuracy. It does not, however, provide a value that is closer to the bond's true fundamental value.

19. A is correct. The Ho–Lee model is arbitrage free and can be calibrated to closely match the observed term structure.

20. C is correct. Both statements are incorrect because Jones incorrectly describes both types of model. Equilibrium term structure models are factor models that seek to describe the dynamics of the term structure by using fundamental economic variables that are assumed to affect interest rates. Arbitrage-free term structure models use observed market prices of a reference set of financial instruments, assumed to be correctly priced, to model the market yield curve.

21. A is correct. Consistent with Jones's statement, equilibrium term structure models require fewer parameters to be estimated relative to arbitrage-free models, and arbitrage-free models allow for time-varying parameters. Consequently, arbitrage-free models can model the market yield curve more precisely than equilibrium models.

22. C is correct. The Kalotay–Williams–Fabozzi equilibrium term structure model is similar to the Ho–Lee model in that it assumes constant drift, no mean reversion, and constant volatility, but the KWF model describes the log of the dynamics of the short rate, while the Ho–Lee model does not.

VALUATION AND ANALYSIS OF BONDS WITH EMBEDDED OPTIONS

SOLUTIONS

1. C is correct. The call option embedded in Bond #2 can be exercised only at two predetermined dates: 1 October 20X1 and 1 October 20X2. Thus, the call feature is Bermudan style.

2. C is correct. The bond that would most likely protect investors against a significant increase in interest rates is the putable bond (i.e., Bond #3). When interest rates have risen and higher-yield bonds are available, a put option allows the bondholders to put back the bonds to the issuer prior to maturity and to reinvest the proceeds of the retired bonds in higher-yielding bonds.

3. B is correct. A fall in interest rates results in a rise in bond values. For a callable bond, such as Bond #2, the upside potential is capped because the issuer is more likely to call the bond. In contrast, the upside potential for a putable bond, such as Bond #3, is uncapped. Thus, a fall in interest rates would result in a putable bond having more upside potential than an otherwise identical callable bond. Note that A is incorrect because the effective duration of a putable bond increases, not decreases, with a fall in interest rates; the bond is less likely to be put and thus behaves more like an option-free bond. C is also incorrect because the effective convexity of a putable bond is always positive. It is the effective convexity of a callable bond that will change from positive to negative if interest rates fall and the call option is near the money.

4. A is correct:

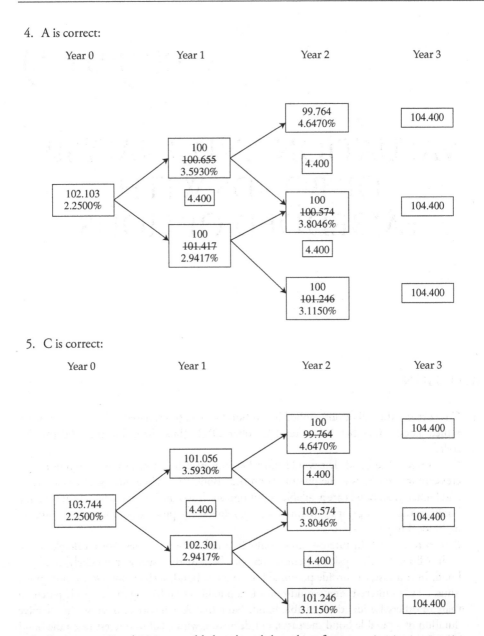

Year 0   Year 1   Year 2   Year 3

```
                                        99.764        104.400
                                        4.6470%
                        100
                        100.655
                        3.5930%         4.400
102.103
2.2500%                 4.400           100           104.400
                                        100.574
                        100             3.8046%
                        101.417
                        2.9417%         4.400
                                        100           104.400
                                        101.246
                                        3.1150%
```

5. C is correct:

Year 0   Year 1   Year 2   Year 3

```
                                        100           104.400
                                        99.764
                        101.056         4.6470%
                        3.5930%
                                        4.400
103.744                 4.400           100.574       104.400
2.2500%                                 3.8046%
                        102.301
                        2.9417%         4.400
                                        101.246       104.400
                                        3.1150%
```

6. C is correct. Bond #3 is a putable bond, and the value of a put option increases as interest rates rise. At higher interest rates, the value of the underlying option-free bond (straight bond) declines, but the decline is offset partially by the increase in the value of the embedded put option, which is more likely to be exercised.

7. C is correct. Regardless of the type of option, an increase in interest rate volatility results in an increase in option value. Because the value of a putable bond is equal to the value of the straight bond *plus* the value of the embedded put option, Bond #3 will increase in value if interest rate volatility increases. Put another way, an increase in interest rate volatility will most likely result in more scenarios where the put option is exercised, which increases the values calculated in the interest rate tree and, thus, the value of the putable bond.

8. C is correct. Bond #2 is a callable bond, and the value of the embedded call option increases as the yield curve flattens. When the yield curve is upward sloping, the one-period forward rates on the interest rate tree are high and opportunities for the issuer to call the bond are fewer. When the yield curve flattens or inverts, many nodes on the tree have lower forward rates, which increase the opportunities to call and, thus, the value of the embedded call option.

9. B is correct. The conversion price of a convertible bond is equal to the par value divided by the conversion ratio—that is, $1,000/31 = $32.26 per share.

10. B is correct. The conversion value of the bond is 31 × $37.50 or $1,162.50, which represents its minimum value. Thus, the convertible bond exhibits mostly stock risk–return characteristics; a fall in the stock price will result in a fall in the convertible bond price. However, the change in the convertible bond price is less than the change in the stock price because the convertible bond has a floor. That floor is the value of the straight (option-free) bond.

11. C is correct. The option-adjusted spread (OAS) is the constant spread added to all the one-period forward rates that makes the arbitrage-free value of a risky bond equal to its market price. The OAS approach is often used to assess bond relative values. If two bonds have the same characteristics and credit quality, they should have the same OAS. If this is not the case, the bond with the largest OAS (i.e., Bond #2) is likely to be underpriced (cheap) relative to the bond with the smallest OAS (i.e., Bond #1).

12. A is correct. The effective duration of a floating-rate bond is close to the time to next reset. As the reset for Bond #6 is annual, the effective duration of this bond is close to 1.

13. B is correct. Effective duration indicates the sensitivity of a bond's price to a 100 bps parallel shift of the benchmark yield curve assuming no change in the bond's credit spread. The effective duration of an option-free bond, such as Bond #3, goes down as interest rates rise. As interest rates rise, a call option moves out of the money, which increases the value of the callable bond and lengthens its effective duration. In contrast, as interest rates rise, a put option moves into the money, which limits the price depreciation of the putable bond and shortens its effective duration. Thus, the bond whose effective duration might lengthen if interest rates rise is the callable bond (i.e., Bond #4).

14. B is correct. The effective duration of Bond #4 can be calculated using Equation 3, where ΔCurve is 20 bps, PV_ is 101.238, and PV_+ is 100.478. PV_0, the current full price of the bond (i.e., with no shift), is not given but can be calculated using Exhibit 3 as follows:

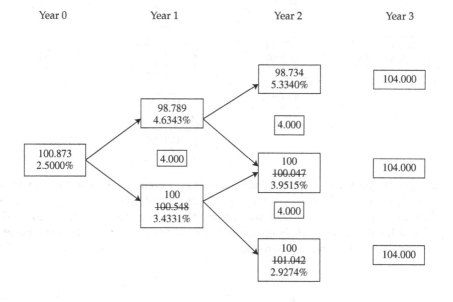

Year 0	Year 1	Year 2	Year 3

Thus, the effective duration of Bond #4 is:

$$\text{EffDur} = \frac{101.238 - 100.478}{2 \times (0.0020) \times (100.873)} = 1.88$$

15. A is correct:

Year 0	Year 1	Year 2	Year 3
		98.714 6.3679%	105.0000 ~~106.3679~~
	99.381 4.5027%	4.5027	
99.697 3.0000%	3.0000	99.991 5.0092%	105.0000 ~~105.0092~~
	99.996 3.5419%	3.5419	
		100.000 3.9404%	103.9404

16. C is correct:

Year 0	Year 1	Year 2	Year 3
		100.000 6.3679%	106.3679
	100.000 4.5057%	4.5027	
100.485 3.0000%	3.5000 ~~3.0000~~	100.000 5.0092%	105.0092
	100.000 3.5419%	3.5419	
		100.000 3.9404%	103.9404

17. B is correct. A convertible bond includes a conversion option, which is a call option on the issuer's common stock. This conversion option gives the bondholders the right to convert their debt into equity. Thus, the value of Bond #9, the convertible bond, is equal to the value of Bond #10, the underlying option-free bond (straight bond), plus the value of a call option on Whorton's common stock.

18. A is correct. The minimum value of a convertible bond is equal to the greater of the conversion value of the convertible bond (i.e., Bond #9) and the current value of the straight bond (i.e., Bond #10).

19. C is correct. The risk–return characteristics of a convertible bond depend on the market price of the issuer's common stock (underlying share price) relative to the bond's conversion price. When the underlying share price is well below the conversion price, the convertible bond exhibits mostly bond risk–return characteristics. In this case, the price of the convertible bond is mainly affected by interest rate movements and the issuer's credit spreads. In contrast, when the underlying share price is above the conversion price, the convertible bond exhibits mostly stock risk–return characteristics. In this case, the price of the convertible bond is mainly affected by the issuer's common stock price movements. The underlying share price ($30) is lower than the conversion price of Bond #9 ($50). Thus, Bond #9 exhibits mostly bond risk–return characteristics and is least affected by Whorton's common stock price movements.

20. C is correct. If the central bank takes actions that lead to lower interest rates, the yields on Alpha's bonds are likely to decrease. If the yield to maturity on Bond 4 (callable) falls below the 1.55% coupon rate, the call option will become valuable and Alpha may call the bond because it is in the money.

     A is incorrect because if the equity market declines, the market value of Alpha stock will also likely decrease. Therefore, Bond 2 (convertible) would have a lower conversion value; hence, the conversion option likely would not be exercised. Because Bond 2 is currently trading out of the money, it will likely trade further out of the money once the price of Alpha stock decreases.

     B is incorrect because Bond 3 (putable) is more likely to be exercised in an increasing rather than a decreasing interest rate environment.

21. C is correct. All four bonds in Exhibit 2 issued by Alpha Corporation offer the same coupon rate and have the same remaining term to maturity. Bond 4 (callable) most likely has a current price that is less than Bond 1 (straight or option free) because investors are short the call option and must be compensated for bearing call risk. Bond 2 (convertible) most likely has a current price that is greater than Bond 1 because investors are paying for the conversion option embedded in Bond 2 and the option has time value associated with it, even though the option is trading out of the money. Similarly, Bond 3 (putable) most likely has a current price that is greater than Bond 1 because investors are paying for the put option.

22. C is correct. The consensus economic forecast is for interest rates to decrease. In an environment of decreasing interest rates, all bond prices should rise, ignoring any price impact resulting from any embedded options. When interest rates fall, the value of the embedded call option in Bond 4 (callable) increases, causing an opposing effect on price. The put option of putable bonds, by contrast, increases in value when interest rates rise rather than decline.

23. C is correct. Bond 4 is a callable bond. Value of an issuer call option = Value of straight bond – Value of callable bond. The value of the straight bond may be calculated using the spot rates or the one-year forward rates.

     Value of an option-free (straight) bond with a 1.55% coupon using spot rates:

$$1.55/(1.0100)^1 + 1.55/(1.012012)^2 + 101.55/(1.012515)^3 = 100.8789$$

The value of a callable bond (at par) with no call protection period cannot exceed 100, as at that price or higher the bond would be called. The value of the call option = 100.8789 – 100 = 0.8789.

24. B is correct. An increase in interest rate volatility will cause the value of the put and call options embedded in Bond 3 and Bond 4 to increase. Bond 3 (putable) would experience an increase in price because the increased value of the put option increases the bond's value. In contrast, Bond 4 (callable) will experience a price decrease because the increased value of the call option reduces the callable bond's value. Bond 2, an out-of-the-money convertible, will resemble the risk–return characteristics of a straight bond and will thus be unaffected by interest rate volatility.

25. A is correct. All else being equal, the value of a put option decreases as the yield curve moves from being upward sloping to flat to downward sloping (inverted). Alternatively, a call option's value increases as the yield curve flattens and increases further if the yield curve inverts. Therefore, if the yield curve became inverted, the value of the embedded option in Bond 3 (putable) would decrease and the value of the embedded option in Bond 4 (callable) would increase.

26. A is correct. The market price of callable Bond 4 with no protection period cannot exceed 100.

27. B is correct. A bond with a larger option-adjusted spread (OAS) than that of a bond with similar characteristics and credit quality means that the bond is likely underpriced (cheap). Bond 7 (OAS 85 bps) is relatively cheaper than Bond 6 (OAS 65 bps).

    C is incorrect because Bond 8 (CCC) has a lower credit rating than Bond 7 (B) and the OAS alone cannot be used for the relative value comparison. The larger OAS (105 bps) incorporates compensation for the difference between the B and CCC bond credit ratings. Therefore, there is not enough information to draw a conclusion about relative value.

28. B is correct. The AI bond's value if interest rates shift down by 30 bps (PV_) is 100.78:

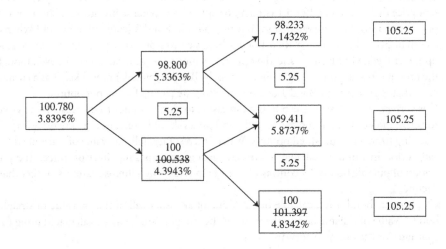

The AI bond's value if interest rates shift up by 30 bps (PV$_+$) is 99.487:

$$\text{EffDur} = \frac{(PV_-) - (PV_+)}{2 \times (\Delta\text{Curve}) \times (PV_0)} = \frac{100.780 - 99.487}{2 \times 0.003 \times 100.200} = 2.15$$

29. A is correct. The AI bond is a callable bond, and the effective duration of a callable bond decreases when interest rates fall. The reason is because a decline in interest rates may result in the call option moving into the money, which limits the price appreciation of the callable bond. Exhibit 1 also shows that the price of the AI bond is 100.200 and that it is callable at par in one year and two years. Thus, the call option is already in the money and would likely be exercised in response to increases in the AI bond's price.

30. C is correct. The BI bond is an option-free bond, and one-sided up-duration and one-sided down-duration will be about equal for option-free bonds.

31. C is correct. The BI bond is an option-free bond. Its longest key rate duration will be in the year of its maturity because the largest cash flow (payment of both coupon and principal) occurs in that year.

32. A is correct. All else being equal, a callable bond will have lower effective convexity than an option-free bond when the call option is in the money. Similarly, when the call option is in the money, a callable bond will also have lower effective convexity than a putable bond if the put option is out of the money. Exhibit 1 shows that the callable AI bond is currently priced slightly higher than its call price of par value, which means the embedded call option is in the money. The put option embedded in the CE bond is not in the money; the bond is currently priced 2.1% above par value. Thus, at the current price, the putable CE bond is more likely to behave like the option-free BI bond. Consequently, the effective convexity of the AI bond will likely be lower than the option-free BI bond and the putable CE bond.

33. A is correct. The conversion price would be adjusted downward because Gillette's expected dividend payment of €0.70 is greater than the threshold dividend of €0.50.

34. B is correct. The market conversion premium per share is equal to the market conversion price minus the underlying share price. The market conversion price is calculated as follows:

$$\text{Market conversion price} = \frac{\text{Convertible bond price}}{\text{Conversion ratio}}$$

$$= \frac{€1,123}{€1,000€10 \text{ per share}} = €11.23 \text{ per share}$$

The market conversion premium per share is then calculated as follows:
Market conversion premium per share = Market conversion price − Underlying share price.

$$= €11.23 - €9.10 = €2.13$$

35. C is correct. The value of a convertible bond with both an embedded call option and a put option can be determined using the following formula:
Value of callable putable convertible bond = Value of straight bond + Value of call option on the issuer's stock − Value of issuer call option + Value of investor put option.

$$\text{Value of callable putable bond} = €978 + €147 - €43 + €26 = €1,108$$

36. A is correct. Over the next year, Gillette believes that Raffarin's share price will continue to increase toward the conversion price but not exceed it. If Gillette's forecast becomes true, the return on the RI bond will increase but at a lower rate than the increase in Raffarin's share price because the conversion price is not expected to be reached.

CHAPTER 10

CREDIT ANALYSIS MODELS

SOLUTIONS

1. B is correct. The following table shows that the credit valuation adjustment (CVA) for the bond is €36.49, the sum of the present values of expected loss. The steps taken to complete the table are as follows.

   Step 1: Exposure at date T is $\dfrac{€1,000}{(1+r)^{4-T}}$, where r is 3%. That is, exposure is computed by discounting the face value of the bond using the risk-free rate and the number of years until maturity.

   Step 2: Recovery = Exposure × Recovery rate.

   Step 3: Loss given default (LGD) = Exposure − Recovery.

   Step 4: Probability of default (POD) on Date 1 is 1.50%. The probability of survival (POS) on Date 1 is 98.50%.

   For subsequent dates, POD is calculated as the annual default probability multiplied by the previous date's POS.

   For example, to determine the Date 2 POD (1.4775%), the annual default probability (1.50%) is multiplied by the Date 1 POS (98.50%).

   Step 5: POS in Dates 2–4 = POS in the previous year − POD.

   That is, POS in year T = POS in year $(T-1)$ − POD in year T.

   POS can also be determined by subtracting the annual default probability from 100% and raising it to the power of the number of years:

   $(100\% - 1.5000\%)^1 = 98.5000\%$

   $(100\% - 1.5000\%)^2 = 97.0225\%$

   $(100\% - 1.5000\%)^3 = 95.5672\%$

   $(100\% - 1.5000\%)^4 = 94.1337\%$

   Step 6: Expected loss = LGD × POD.

   Step 7: Discount factor (DF) for date T is $\dfrac{1}{(1+r)^T}$, where r is 3%.

   Step 8: PV of expected loss = Expected loss × DF.

Date	Exposure	Recovery	LGD	POD	POS	Expected Loss	DF	PV of Expected Loss
0								
1	€915.14	€274.54	€640.60	1.5000%	98.5000%	€9.61	0.970874	€9.33
2	€942.60	€282.78	€659.82	1.4775%	97.0225%	€9.75	0.942596	€9.19
3	€970.87	€291.26	€679.61	1.4553%	95.5672%	€9.89	0.915142	€9.05
4	€1,000.00	€300.00	€700.00	1.4335%	94.1337%	€10.03	0.888487	€8.92
							CVA =	€36.49

The value of the bond if it were default free would be $1{,}000 \times$ DF for Date 4 = €888.49.

Fair value of the bond considering CVA = €888.49 – CVA = €888.49 – €36.49 = €852.00.

Because the market price of the bond (€875) is greater than the fair value of €852, B is correct.

A is incorrect because the market price of the bond differs from its fair value. C is incorrect because although the bond's value if the bond were default free is greater than the market price, the bond has a risk of default, and CVA lowers its fair value to below the market price.

2. B is correct. The recovery rate to be used now in the computation of fair value is $30\% \times 1.25 = 37.5\%$, whereas the default probability to be used is $1.50\% \times 1.25 = 1.875\%$.

Using the steps outlined in the solution to Question 1, the following table is prepared, which shows that the bond's CVA increases to 40.49. Thus, Koning concludes that a change in the probability of default has a greater effect on fair value than a similar change in the recovery rate. The steps taken to complete the table are the same as those in the previous problem. There are no changes in exposures and discount factors in this table.

Date	Exposure	Recovery	LGD	POD	POS	Expected Loss	DF	PV of Expected Loss
0								
1	€ 915.14	€343.18	€571.96	1.8750%	98.1250%	€10.72	0.970874	€10.41
2	€ 942.60	€353.47	€589.12	1.8398%	96.2852%	€10.84	0.942596	€10.22
3	€ 970.87	€364.08	€606.80	1.8053%	94.4798%	€10.95	0.915142	€10.03
4	€1,000.00	€375.00	€625.00	1.7715%	92.7083%	€11.07	0.888487	€9.84
							CVA =	€40.49

Changes in the default probability and recovery rates do not affect the value of the default-free bond. So, it is the same as in the previous question: €888.49.

Fair value of the bond considering CVA = €888.49 – CVA = €888.49 – €40.49 = €848.00

3. A is correct. The following table shows that the CVA for the bond is €42.17, the sum of the present values of expected loss. The steps taken to complete the table are as follows.

Step 1: Exposure at Date 4 is €1,000 + Coupon amount = €1,000 + €60 = €1,060. Exposure at a date T prior to that is the coupon on date T + PV at date T of subsequent coupons + PV of €1,000 to be received at Date 4. For example, exposure at Date 2 is

$$\epsilon 60 + \frac{\epsilon 60}{1 + 0.03} + \frac{\epsilon 60}{(1 + 0.03)^2} + \frac{\epsilon 1,000}{(1 + 0.03)^2} = \epsilon 60 + \frac{\epsilon 60}{1 + 0.03} + \frac{\epsilon 1,060}{(1 + 0.03)^2}$$

$$= \epsilon 1,117.40$$

Steps 2 through 8 are the same as those in the solution to Question 1.

Date	Exposure	Recovery	LGD	POD	POS	Expected Loss	DF	PV of Expected Loss
0								
1	€1,144.86	€343.46	€801.40	1.5000%	98.5000%	€12.02	0.970874	€11.67
2	€1,117.40	€335.22	€782.18	1.4775%	97.0225%	€11.56	0.942596	€10.89
3	€1,089.13	€326.74	€762.39	1.4553%	95.5672%	€11.10	0.915142	€10.15
4	€1,060.00	€318.00	€742.00	1.4335%	94.1337%	€10.64	0.888487	€9.45
							CVA =	€42.17

The value of the bond if it were default free would be €60 × DF$_1$ + €60 × DF$_2$ + €60 × DF$_3$ + €1,060 × DF$_4$ = €1,111.51.

Fair value of the bond considering CVA = €1,111.51 − €42.17 = €1,069.34.

4. A is correct. If default occurs on Date 3, the rate of return can be obtained by solving the following equation for internal rate of return (IRR):

$$\epsilon 1,090 = \frac{\epsilon 60}{1 + \text{IRR}} + \frac{\epsilon 60}{(1 + \text{IRR})^2} + \frac{\epsilon 326.74}{(1 + \text{IRR})^3}$$

In this equation, €60 is the amount of coupon received at Dates 1 and 2 prior to default at Date 3. The amount €326.74 is the recovery at Time 3 (from the CVA table in the solution to the previous question). The solution to the foregoing equation can be obtained using the cash flow IRR function on your calculator.

5. B is correct. For each possible transition, the expected percentage price change, computed as the product of the modified duration and the change in the spread as shown in Exhibit 3 (relating to question 5), is calculated as follows:

> From AA to AAA: −2.75 × (0.60% − 0.90%) = +0.83%
> From AA to A: −2.75 × (1.10% − 0.90%) = −0.55%
> From AA to BBB: −2.75 × (1.50% − 0.90%) = −1.65%
> From AA to BB: −2.75 × (3.40% − 0.90%) = −6.88%
> From AA to B: −2.75 × (6.50% − 0.90%) = −15.40%
> From AA to C: −2.75 × (9.50% − 0.90%) = −23.65%

The expected percentage change in the value of the AA rated bond is computed by multiplying each expected percentage price change for a possible credit transition by its respective transition probability given in Exhibit 3 and summing the products:

(0.0150 × 0.83%) + (0.8800 × 0%) + (0.0950 × −0.55%) + (0.0075 × −1.65%) + (0.0015 × −6.88%) + (0.0005 × −15.40%) + (0.0003 × −23.65%) = −0.0774%

Therefore, the expected return on the bond over the next year is its YTM minus 0.0774%, assuming no default.

6. B is correct. Statement B is correct because a reduced-form credit model involves regression analysis using information generally available in the financial markets, such as the measures mentioned in the statement.

   Statement A is incorrect because it is consistent with the use of a structural model and not a reduced-form model. It is a structural model that is based on the premise that a firm defaults on its debt if the value of its assets falls below its liabilities and that the probability of that event has the characteristics of an option.

   Statement C is incorrect because it is consistent with the use of a structural model and not a reduced-form model. A structural model involves the estimation of a default barrier, and default occurs if the value of firm's assets falls below the default barrier.

7. C is correct. Structural models require information best known to the managers of the company. Reduced-form models require information only generally available in financial markets.

   A is incorrect because although it is literally true, when the models were developed is immaterial. Structural models are currently used in practice by commercial banks and credit rating agencies.

   B is incorrect because computer technology facilitates valuation using option pricing models as well as regression analysis.

8. A is correct. The following tree shows the valuation assuming no default of Bond B2, which pays a 6% annual coupon.

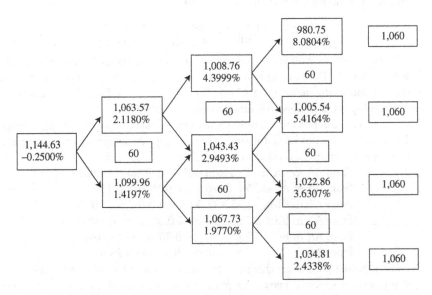

The scheduled year-end coupon and principal payments are placed to the right of each forward rate in the tree. For example, the Date 4 values are the principal plus the coupon of 60. The following are the four Date 3 values for the bond, shown above the interest rate at each node:

$$€1,060/1.080804 = €980.75$$
$$€1,060/1.054164 = €1,005.54$$
$$€1,060/1.036307 = €1,022.86$$
$$€1,060/1.024338 = €1,034.81$$

These are the three Date 2 values:

$$\frac{(0.5 \times €980.75) + (0.5 \times €1,005.54) + €60}{1.043999} = €1,008.76$$

$$\frac{(0.5 \times €1,005.54) + (0.5 \times €1,022.86) + €60}{1.029493} = €1,043.43$$

$$\frac{(0.5 \times €1,022.86) + (0.5 \times €1,034.81) + €60}{1.019770} = €1,067.73$$

These are the two Date 1 values:

$$\frac{(0.5 \times €1,008.76) + (0.5 \times €1,043.43) + €60}{1.021180} = €1,063.57$$

$$\frac{(0.5 \times €1,043.43) + (0.5 \times €1,067.73) + €60}{1.014197} = €1,099.96$$

This is the Date 0 value:

$$\frac{(0.5 \times €1,063.57) + (0.5 \times €1,099.96) + €60}{0.997500} = €1,144.63$$

So, the value of the bond assuming no default is 1,144.63. This value could also have been obtained more directly using the benchmark discount factors from Exhibit 2:

$$€60 \times 1.002506 + €60 \times 0.985093 + €60 \times 0.955848 + €1,060 \times 0.913225$$
$$= €1,144.63$$

The benefit of using the binomial interest rate tree to obtain the VND is that the same tree is used to calculate the expected exposure to default loss.

The credit valuation adjustment table is now prepared following these steps:

Step 1: Compute the expected exposures as described in the following, using the binomial interest rate tree prepared earlier.

The expected exposure for Date 4 is €1,060.
The expected exposure for Date 3 is

$$(0.1250 \times €980.75) + (0.3750 \times €1,005.54) + (0.3750 \times €1,022.86) + (0.1250 \times €1,034.81) + 60 = €1,072.60$$

The expected exposure for Date 2 is

$$(0.25 \times €1,008.76) + (0.50 \times €1,043.43) + (0.25 \times €1,067.73) + €60 = €1,100.84$$

The expected exposure for Date 1 is

$$(0.50 \times €1,063.57) + (0.50 \times €1,099.96) + 60 = €1,141.76$$

Step 2: LGD = Exposure × (1 − Recovery rate).

Step 3: The initial default probability is 1.50%. For subsequent dates, POD is calculated as the default probability multiplied by the previous date's POS.

For example, to determine the Date 2 POD (1.4775%), the default probability (1.5000%) is multiplied by the Date 1 POS (98.5000%).

Step 4: POS is determined by subtracting the default probability from 100% and raising it to the power of the number of years:

$$(100\% - 1.5000\%)^1 = 98.5000\%$$
$$(100\% - 1.5000\%)^2 = 97.0225\%$$
$$(100\% - 1.5000\%)^3 = 95.5672\%$$
$$(100\% - 1.5000\%)^4 = 94.1337\%$$

Step 5: Expected loss = LGD × POD.

Step 6: Discount factors in year T are obtained from Exhibit 2.

Step 7: PV of expected loss = Expected loss × DF.

Date	Exposure	LGD	POD	POS	Expected Loss	DF	PV of Expected Loss
0							
1	€1,141.76	€799.23	1.5000%	98.5000%	€11.99	1.002506	€12.02
2	€1,100.84	€770.58	1.4775%	97.0225%	€11.39	0.985093	€11.22
3	€1,072.60	€750.82	1.4553%	95.5672%	€10.93	0.955848	€10.44
4	€1,060.00	€742.00	1.4335%	94.1337%	€10.64	0.913225	€9.71
						CVA =	€43.39

Fair value of the bond considering CVA = €1,144.63 − CVA = €1,144.63 − €43.39 = €1,101.24.

9. A is correct. The corporate bond's fair value is computed in the solution to Question 8 as €1,101.24. The YTM can be obtained by solving the following equation for IRR:

$$€1,101.24 = \frac{€60}{1 + IRR} + \frac{€60}{(1 + IRR)^2} + \frac{€60}{(1 + IRR)^3} + \frac{€1,060}{(1 + IRR)^4}$$

The solution to this equation is 3.26%.

Valuation of a four-year, 6% coupon bond under no default is computed in the solution to Question 8 as 1,144.63. So, the YTM of a theoretical comparable-maturity government bond with the same coupon rate as the corporate bond, B2, can be obtained by solving the following equation for IRR:

$$€1,144.63 = \frac{€60}{1 + IRR} + \frac{€60}{(1 + IRR)^2} + \frac{€60}{(1 + IRR)^3} + \frac{€1,060}{(1 + IRR)^4}$$

The solution to this equation is 2.18%. So, the credit spread that the analyst wants to compute is 3.26% − 2.18% = 1.08%, or 108 bps.

B is incorrect because it is the spread over the four-year government par bond that has a YTM of 2.25% in Exhibit 2: 3.26% − 2.25% = 1.01%, or 101 bps. Although this spread is commonly used in practice, the analyst is interested in finding the spread over a theoretical 6% coupon government bond.

C is incorrect because it is the YTM of the coupon four-year government bond in Exhibit 2.

10. B is correct. The recovery rate to be used now in the computation of fair value is 30% × 0.75 = 22.500%, whereas the default probability to be used is 1.50% × 0.75 = 1.125%.

The tree that shows the valuation assuming no default of Bond B2 in the solution to Question 8 will not be affected by the foregoing changes. Accordingly, VND remains €1,144.63.

Following the steps outlined in the solution to Question 8, the following table is prepared, which shows that the CVA for the bond decreases to €36.23. Thus, Ibarra concludes that a decrease in the probability of default has a greater effect on fair value than a similar decrease in the recovery rate. The steps taken to complete the table are the same as those in Question 8. There are no changes in exposures or discount factors in this table.

Date	Exposure	LGD	POD	POS	Expected Loss	DF	PV of Expected Loss
0							
1	€1,141.76	€884.87	1.1250%	98.8750%	€9.95	1.002506	€9.98
2	€1,100.84	€853.15	1.1123%	97.7627%	€9.49	0.985093	€9.35
3	€1,072.60	€831.26	1.0998%	96.6628%	€9.14	0.955848	€8.74
4	€1,060.00	€821.50	1.0875%	95.5754%	€8.93	0.913225	€8.16
						CVA =	€36.23

Fair value of the bond considering CVA = €1,144.63 − CVA = €1,144.63 − €36.23 = €1,108.40.

11. A is correct. The following tree shows the valuation assuming no default of the floating-rate note (FRN), B4, which has a quoted margin of 4%.

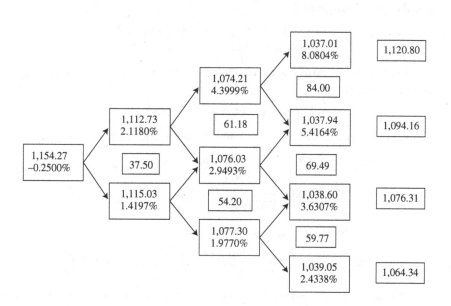

| Date 0 | Date 1 | Date 2 | Date 3 | Date 4 |

The scheduled year-end coupon and principal payments are placed to the right of each forward rate in the tree. For example, the four Date 4 values are the principal plus the coupon.

$$€1,000 × (1 + 0.080804 + 0.04) = €1,120.80$$
$$€1,000 × (1 + 0.054164 + 0.04) = €1,094.16$$
$$€1,000 × (1 + 0.036307 + 0.04) = €1,076.31$$
$$€1,000 × (1 + 0.024338 + 0.04) = €1,064.34$$

The following are the four Date 3 bond values for the note, shown above the interest rate at each node:

$$€1,120.80/1.080804 = €1,037.01$$
$$€1,094.16/1.054164 = €1,037.94$$
$$€1,076.31/1.036307 = €1,038.60$$
$$€1,064.34/1.024338 = €1,039.05$$

The three Date 3 coupon amounts are computed based on the interest rate at Date 2 plus the quoted margin of 4%:

$$€1,000 × (0.043999 + 0.04) = €84.00$$
$$€1,000 × (0.029493 + 0.04) = €69.49$$
$$€1,000 × (0.019770 + 0.04) = €59.77$$

There are three Date 2 bond values:

$$\frac{(0.5 × €1,037.01) + (0.5 × €1,037.94) + €84.00}{1.043999} = €1,074.21$$
$$\frac{(0.5 × €1,037.94) + (0.5 × €1,038.60) + €69.49}{1.029493} = €1,076.03$$
$$\frac{(0.5 × €1,038.60) + (0.5 × €1,039.05) + €59.77}{1.019770} = €1,077.30$$

The two Date 2 coupon amounts are computed based on the interest rate at Date 1 plus the quoted margin of 4%:

$$€1,000 × (0.021180 + 0.04) = €61.18$$
$$€1,000 × (0.014197 + 0.04) = €54.20$$

The Date 1 coupon amount is computed based on the interest rate at date 0 plus the quoted margin of 4%:

$$€1,000 × (-0.0025 + 0.04) = €37.50$$

These are the calculations for the bond values for Date 1 and Date 0:

$$\frac{(0.5 × €1,074.21) + (0.5 × €1,076.03) + €61.18}{1.021180} = €1,112.73$$
$$\frac{(0.5 × €1,076.06) + (0.5 × €1,077.30) + €54.20}{1.014197} = €1,115.0$$

Then, the VND is calculated as follows:

$$\frac{(0.5 × €1,112.73) + (0.5 × €1,115.03) + €37.50}{0.9975} = €1,154.27$$

The expected exposures are then computed using the binomial interest rate tree prepared earlier. For example, the expected exposure for Date 4 is computed as follows:

(0.125 × €1,120.80) + (0.375 × €1,094.16) + (0.375 × €1,076.31) + (0.125 × €1,064.34) = €1,087.07

Similarly, the expected exposure for Date 3 is computed as follows:

(0.125 × €1,037.01) + (0.375 × €1,037.94) + (0.375 × €1,038.60) + (0.125 × €1,039.05) + (0.250 × €84) + (0.500 × €69.49) + (0.250 × €59.77) = €1,108.90

The expected exposures for Dates 2 and 1 are computed similarly, and the credit valuation adjustment table is completed following Steps 2–7 outlined in the solution to Question 8.

Date	Exposure	LGD	POD	POS	Expected Loss	DF	PV of Expected Loss
0							
1	€1,151.38	€805.97	1.5000%	98.5000%	€12.09	1.002506	€12.12
2	€1,133.58	€793.51	1.4775%	97.0225%	€11.72	0.985093	€11.55
3	€1,108.90	€776.23	1.4553%	95.5672%	€11.30	0.955848	€10.80
4	€1,087.07	€760.95	1.4335%	94.1337%	€10.91	0.913225	€9.96
						CVA =	€44.43

Fair value of the FRN considering CVA = €1,154.27 – CVA = €1,154.27 – €44.43 = €1,109.84.

Because the market price of €1,070 is less than the estimated fair value, the analyst should recommend adding to existing positions in the FRN.

B and C are incorrect because the FRN is perceived to be undervalued in the market.

12. A is correct. The changing probability of default will not affect the binomial tree prepared in the solution to Question 11. The Date 1 value remains €1,154.27, which is also the VND. The expected exposures, loss given default, and discount factors are also unaffected by the changing probability of default. The following is the completed credit valuation adjustment table.

Date	Exposure	LGD	POD	POS	Expected Loss	DF	PV of Expected Loss
0							
1	€1,151.38	€805.97	1.5000%	98.5000%	€12.09	1.002506	€12.12
2	€1,133.58	€793.51	0.4925%	98.0075%	€3.91	0.985093	€3.85
3	€1,108.90	€776.23	0.4900%	97.5175%	€3.80	0.955848	€3.64
4	€1,087.07	€760.95	0.4876%	97.0299%	€3.71	0.913225	€3.39
						CVA =	€22.99

Thus, CVA decreases to €22.99.

13. C is correct. The credit rating agencies typically make incremental changes, as seen in a transition matrix provided in Exhibit 3. Ibarra believes the bond is undervalued, because her assessment of the probability of default and the recovery rate is more optimistic than that of the agencies. Therefore, she most likely expects the credit rating agencies to put the issuer on a positive watch.

A is incorrect because the bond is perceived to be undervalued, not overvalued. Ibarra is not expecting a credit downgrade.

B is incorrect because it is not the *most likely* expectation. The rating agencies rarely change an issuer's rating from BBB all the way to AAA. In Exhibit 3 (relating to question 5) the probability of a BBB rated issuer going from BBB to AAA is 0.02%, whereas to go from BBB to A it is 4.80%.

14. A is correct.

B is incorrect because, although generally true for investment-grade bonds, the statement neglects the fact that high-yield issuers sometimes face a downward-sloping credit term structure. Credit term structures are not *always* upward sloping.

C is incorrect because there is a consistent pattern for the term structure of credit spreads: Typically, it is upwardly sloped because greater time to maturity is associated with higher projected probabilities of default and lower recovery rates.

15. C is correct. A covered bond is a senior debt obligation of a financial institution that gives recourse to the originator/issuer as well as a predetermined underlying collateral pool. Each country or jurisdiction specifies the eligible collateral types as well as the specific structures permissible in the covered bond market. Covered bonds usually have either commercial or residential mortgages meeting specific criteria or public sector exposures as underlying collateral.

A is incorrect. The term "covered" is used in foreign exchange analysis, for instance, "covered interest rate parity." In the context of securitized debt, a covered bond is secured by specific assets in addition to the overall balance sheet of the issuer.

B is incorrect because a covered bond does not involve a credit default swap. In addition, an issuer is not likely to sell a credit default swap on its own liability.

16. A is correct. Credit spread migration typically reduces the expected return for two reasons. First, the probabilities for rating changes are not symmetrically distributed around the current rating; they are skewed toward a downgrade rather than an upgrade. Second, the increase in the credit spread is much larger for downgrades than is the decrease in the spread for upgrades.

17. A is correct. The expected return on the Entre Corp. bond over the next year is its yield to maturity plus the expected percentage price change in the bond over the next year. In the following table, for each possible transition, the expected percentage price change is the product of the bond's modified duration of 7.54, multiplied by –1, and the change in the spread, weighted by the given probability:

Expected percentage price change = $(0.0002 \times 6.786\%) + (0.0030 \times 4.524\%) + (0.0480 \times 3.016\%) + (0.8573 \times 0.000\%) + (0.0695 \times -14.326\%) + (0.0175 \times -37.700\%) + (0.0045 \times -60.320\%) = -1.76715\%$.

So, the expected return on the Entre Corp. bond is its yield to maturity plus the expected percentage price change due to credit migration:

Expected return = 5.50% – 1.77% = 3.73%.

	Expected % Price Change (1)	Probability (2)	Expected % Price Change × Probability (1 × 2)
From BBB to AAA	–7.54 × (0.60% – 1.50%) = 6.786%	0.0002	0.00136

(continued)

	Expected % Price Change (1)	Probability (2)	Expected % Price Change × Probability (1 × 2)
From BBB to AA	−7.54 × (0.90% − 1.50%) = 4.524%	0.0030	0.01357
From BBB to A	−7.54 × (1.10% − 1.50%) = 3.016%	0.0480	0.14477
From BBB to BB	−7.54 × (3.40% − 1.50%) = −14.326%	0.0695	−0.99566
From BBB to B	−7.54 × (6.50% − 1.50%) = −37.700%	0.0175	−0.65975
From BBB to CCC, CC, or C	−7.54 × (9.50% − 1.50%) = −60.320%	0.0045	−0.27144
		Total:	−1.76715

18. C is correct. The credit spread can be calculated in three steps:

Step 1: Estimate the value of the three-year VraiRive bond assuming no default. Based on Kowalski's assumptions and Exhibits 2 and 3, the value of the three-year VraiRive bond assuming no default is 100.0000.

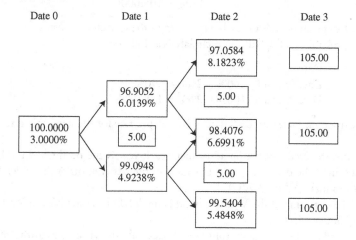

Supporting calculations:

The bond value in each node is the value of next period's cash flows discounted by the forward rate. For the three nodes on Date 2, the bond values are as follows:

$$105/1.081823 = 97.0584$$
$$105/1.066991 = 98.4076$$
$$105/1.054848 = 99.5404$$

For the two nodes on Date 1, the two bond values are as follows:

$$[(0.5 \times 97.0584) + (0.5 \times 98.4076) + 5.00]/1.060139 = 96.9052$$
$$[(0.5 \times 98.4076) + (0.5 \times 99.5404) + 5.00]/1.049238 = 99.0948$$

Finally, for the node on Date 0, the bond value is

$$[(0.5 \times 96.9052) + (0.5 \times 99.0948) + 5.00]/1.030000 = 100.0000$$

Therefore, the VND for the VraiRive bond is 100.0000.

Step 2: Calculate the credit valuation adjustment, and then subtract the CVA from the VND from Step 1 to establish the fair value of the bond. The CVA equals the sum of the present values of each year's expected loss and is calculated as follows:

Date	Expected Exposure	Loss Given Default	Probability of Default	Discount Factor	Present Value of Expected Loss
1	103.0000	68.6667	2.0000%	0.970874	1.3333
2	103.3535	68.9023	1.9600%	0.920560	1.2432
3	105.0000	70.0000	1.9208%	0.862314	1.1594
				CVA =	3.7360

Supporting calculations:

The expected exposures at each date are the bond values at each node, weighted by their risk-neutral probabilities, plus the coupon payment:

$$\text{Date 1: } (0.5 \times 96.9052) + (0.5 \times 99.0948) + 5.00 = 103.0000$$
$$\text{Date 2: } (0.25 \times 97.0584) + (0.5 \times 98.4076) + (0.25 \times 99.5404) + 5.00$$
$$= 103.3535$$
$$\text{Date 3: } 105.0000$$

The loss given default on each date is 2/3 of the expected exposure.

The probability of default on each date is as follows:

Date 1: 2%
Date 2: $2\% \times (100\% - 2\%) = 1.96\%$
Date 3: $2\% \times (100\% - 2\%)^2 = 1.9208\%$

The discount factor on each date is $1/(1 + \text{spot rate for the date})$ raised to the correct power.

Finally, the credit valuation adjustment each year is the product of the LGD times the POD times the discount factor, as shown in the last column of the table. The sum of the three annual CVAs is 3.7360.

So, the fair value of the VraiRive bond is the VND less the CVA, or VND − CVA = 100 − 3.7360 = 96.2640.

Step 3: Based on the fair value from Step 2, calculate the yield to maturity of the bond, and solve for the credit spread by subtracting the yield to maturity on the benchmark bond from the yield to maturity on the VraiRive bond. The credit spread is equal to the yield to maturity on the VraiRive bond minus the yield to maturity on the three-year benchmark bond (which is 5.0000%). Based on its fair value of 96.2640, the VraiRive bond's yield to maturity is

$$96.2640 = \frac{5}{(1 + \text{YTM})} + \frac{5}{(1 + \text{YTM})^2} + \frac{105}{(1 + \text{YTM})^3}$$

Solving for YTM, the yield to maturity is 6.4082%. Therefore, the credit spread on the VraiRive bond is 6.4082% − 5.0000% = 1.4082%.

19. C is correct. A decrease in the risk-neutral probability of default would decrease the credit valuation adjustment and decrease the credit spread. In contrast, increasing the bond's loss-given-default assumption and increasing the probability-of-default assumption would increase the credit valuation adjustment and decrease the fair value of the bond (and increase the yield to maturity and the credit spread over its benchmark).

20. A is correct. For investment-grade bonds with the highest credit ratings, credit spreads are extremely low, and credit migration is possible only in one direction given the implied lower bound of zero on credit spreads. As a result, the credit term structure for the most highly rated securities tends to be either flat or slightly upward sloping. Securities with lower credit quality, however, face greater sensitivity to the credit cycle. Credit spreads would decrease, not increase, with the expectation of economic growth. There is a countercyclical relationship between credit spreads and benchmark rates over the business cycle. A strong economic climate is associated with higher benchmark yields but lower credit spreads because the probability of issuers defaulting declines in such good times.

21. A is correct. Positive-sloped credit spread curves may arise when a high-quality issuer with a strong competitive position in a stable industry has low leverage, strong cash flow, and a high profit margin. This type of issuer tends to exhibit very low short-term credit spreads that rise with increasing maturity given greater uncertainty due to the macroeconomic environment, potential adverse changes in the competitive landscape, technological change, or other factors that drive a higher implied probability of default over time. Empirical academic studies also tend to support the view that the credit spread term structure is upward sloping for investment-grade bond portfolios.

22. B is correct. The auto ABS is granular, with many small loans relative to the size of the total portfolio. The auto loans are also homogeneous. These characteristics support using the portfolio-based approach. A loan-by-loan approach would be inefficient because of the large number of basically similar loans; this approach is best for a portfolio of discrete, large loans that are heterogeneous. A statistics-based approach would work for a static book of loans, whereas the auto loan portfolio would be dynamic and would change over time.

23. B is correct. The expected exposure is the projected amount of money that an investor could lose if an event of default occurs, before factoring in possible recovery. The expected exposure for both Bond I and Bond II is $100 + 5 = 105$.

24. C is correct. The loss given default is a positive function of the expected exposure to default loss and a negative function of the recovery rate. Because Bond II has a lower recovery rate than Bond I and the same expected exposure to default loss ($100 + 5 = 105$), it will have a higher loss given default than Bond I will have. The loss given default for Bond I is $105 \times (1 - 0.40) = 63.00$. The loss given default for Bond II is $105 \times (1 - 0.35) = 68.25$.

25. B is correct. In the event of no default, the investor is expected to receive 105. In the event of a default, the investor is expected to receive $105 - [105 \times (1 - 0.40)] = 42$. The expected future value of the bond is, therefore, the weighted average of the no-default and default amounts, or $(105 \times 0.98) + (42 \times 0.02) = 103.74$.

26. B is correct. The risk-neutral default probability, P^*, is calculated using the current price, the expected receipt at maturity with no default (that is, $100 + 5 = 105$), the expected receipt at maturity in the event of a default (that is, $0.40 \times 105 = 42$), and the risk-free rate of interest (0.03):

$$100 = \frac{[105 \times (1 - P^*)] + (42 \times P^*)}{1.03}$$

Solving for P^* gives 0.031746, or 3.1746%.

27. A is correct. The CVA is the sum of the present value of expected losses on the bond, which from Exhibit 2 is 3.3367.

28. C is correct. The expected percentage price change is the product of the negative of the modified duration and the difference between the credit spread in the new rating and the old rating:

   Expected percentage price change $= -4.2 \times (0.0175 - 0.01) = -0.0315$, or -3.15%

29. B is correct. A reduced-form model in credit risk analysis uses historical variables, such as financial ratios and macroeconomic variables, to estimate the default intensity. A structural model for credit risk analysis, in contrast, uses option pricing and relies on a traded market for the issuer's equity.

30. B is correct. Observation 1 is incorrect, but Observation 2 is correct. The actual default probabilities do not include the default risk premium associated with the uncertainty in the timing of the possible default loss. The observed spread over the yield on a risk-free bond in practice does include liquidity and tax considerations, in addition to credit risk.

CHAPTER 11

CREDIT DEFAULT SWAPS

SOLUTIONS

1. A is correct. Deem Advisors would prefer a cash settlement. Deem Advisors owns Bond 2 (trading at 50% of par), which is worth more than the cheapest-to-deliver obligation (Bond 1, also a senior secured bond, trading at 40% of par). Based on the price of this cheapest-to-deliver security, the estimated recovery rate is 40%. Thus, Deem Advisors can cash settle for $6 million [= (1 − 40%) × $10 million] on its CDS contract and sell the bond it owns, Bond 2, for $5 million, for total proceeds of $11 million. If Deem Advisors were to physically settle the contract, only $10 million would be received, the face amount of the bonds, and it would deliver Bond 2.

   B is incorrect because if Deem Advisors were to physically settle the contract, it would receive only $10 million, which is less than the $11 million that could be obtained from a cash settlement. C is incorrect because Deem Advisors would not be indifferent between settlement protocols as the firm would receive $1 million more with a cash settlement in comparison to a physical settlement.

2. C is correct. A downward-sloping credit curve implies a greater probability of default in the earlier years than in the later years. Downward-sloping curves are less common and often are the result of severe near-term stress in the financial markets.

   A is incorrect because a flat credit curve implies a constant hazard rate (conditional probability of default). B is incorrect because an upward-sloping credit curve implies a greater probability of default in later years.

3. A is correct. UNAB experienced a credit event when it failed to make the scheduled coupon payment on the outstanding subordinated unsecured obligation. Failure to pay, a credit event, occurs when a borrower does not make a scheduled payment of principal or interest on outstanding obligations after a grace period, even without a formal bankruptcy filing.

   B is incorrect because a credit event can occur without filing for bankruptcy. The three most common credit events are bankruptcy, failure to pay, and restructuring.

   C is incorrect because a credit event (failure to pay) occurs when a borrower does not make a scheduled payment of principal or interest on *any* outstanding obligations after a grace period, even without a formal bankruptcy filing.

4. C is correct. An approximation for the upfront premium is (Credit spread − Fixed coupon rate) × Duration of the CDS. To buy 10-year CDS protection, Deem Advisors would have to pay an approximate upfront premium of 1,400 bps [(700 − 500) × 7], or 14% of the notional.

   A is incorrect because 200 bps, or 2%, is derived by taking the simple difference between the credit spread and the fixed coupon rate (700 − 500), ignoring the duration component of the calculation. B is incorrect because 980 bps, or 9.8%, is the result of dividing the credit spread by the fixed coupon rate and multiplying by the duration of the CDS [(700/500) × 7].

5. B is correct. Deem Advisors purchased protection and therefore is economically short and benefits from an increase in the company's spread. Since putting on the protection, the credit spread increased by 200 bps, and Deem Advisors realizes the profit by entering into a new, offsetting contract (sells protection to another party at a higher premium).

   A is incorrect because a decrease (not increase) in the spread would result in a loss for the credit protection buyer. C is incorrect because Deem Advisors, the credit protection buyer, would profit from an increase in the company's credit spread, not break even.

6. A is correct. A difference in credit spreads in the bond market and CDS market is the foundation of the basis trade strategy. If the spread is higher in the bond market than in the CDS market, it is said to be a negative basis. In this case, the bond credit spread is currently 4.50% (bond yield minus Libor) and the comparable CDS contract has a credit spread of 4.25%. The credit risk is cheap in the CDS market relative to the bond market. Since the protection and the bond were both purchased, if convergence occurs, the trade will capture the 0.25% differential in the two markets (4.50% − 4.25%).

   B is incorrect because the bond market implies a 4.50% credit risk premium (bond yield minus the market reference rate) and the CDS market implies a 4.25% credit risk premium. Convergence of the bond market credit risk premium and the CDS credit risk premium would result in capturing the differential, 0.25%. The 1.75% is derived by incorrectly subtracting Libor from the credit spread on the CDS (= 4.25% − 2.50%).

   C is incorrect because convergence of the bond market credit risk premium and the CDS credit risk premium would result in capturing the differential, 0.25%. The 2.75% is derived incorrectly by subtracting the credit spread on the CDS from the current bond yield (= 7.00% − 4.25%).

7. C is correct. Parties to CDS contracts generally agree that their contracts will conform to ISDA specifications. These terms are specified in the ISDA master agreement, which the parties to a CDS sign before any transactions are made. Therefore, to satisfy the compliance requirements referenced by Chan, the sovereign wealth fund must sign an ISDA master agreement with SGS.

8. A is correct. A CDS index (e.g., CDX and iTraxx) would allow the Fund to simultaneously fully hedge multiple fixed-income exposures. A tranche CDS will also hedge multiple exposures, but it would only partially hedge those exposures.

9. A is correct. Based on Exhibit 1, the probability of survival for the first year is 99.78% (100% minus the 0.22% hazard rate). Similarly, the probability of survival for the second and third years is 99.65% (100% minus the 0.35% hazard rate) and 99.50% (100% minus the 0.50% hazard rate), respectively. Therefore, the probability of survival of the Orion bond through the first three years is equal to 0.9978 × 0.9965 × 0.9950 = 0.9893, and the probability of default sometime during the first three years is 1 − 0.9893, or 1.07%.

10. B is correct. The trade assumes that £6 million of five-year CDS protection on Orion is initially sold, so the Fund received the premium. Because the credit spread of the Orion CDS narrowed from 150 bps to 100 bps, the CDS position will realize a financial gain. This financial gain is equal to the difference between the upfront premium received on the original CDS position and the upfront premium to be paid on a new, offsetting CDS position. To close the position and monetize this gain, the Fund should unwind the position by buying protection for a lower premium (relative to the original premium collected).

11. B is correct. The gain on the hypothetical Orion trade is £117,000, calculated as follows.

$$\text{Approximate profit} = \text{Change in credit spread (in bps)} \times \text{Duration} \times \text{Notional amount}$$
$$\text{Approximate profit} = (150 \text{ bps} - 100 \text{ bps}) \times 3.9 \times £6 \text{ million}$$
$$\text{Approximate profit} = 0.005 \times 3.9 \times £6 \text{ million}$$
$$= £117,000$$

The Fund gains because it sold protection at a spread of 150 bps and closed out the position by buying protection at a lower spread of 100 bps.

12. B is correct. Based on Outlook 1, Chan and Smith anticipate that Europe's economy will weaken. In order to profit from this forecast, one would buy protection using a high-yield CDS index (e.g., iTraxx Crossover) and sell protection using an investment-grade CDS index (e.g., iTraxx Main).

13. B is correct. To take advantage of Chan's view of the US credit curve steepening in the short term, a curve trade will entail shorting (buying protection using) a long-term (20-year) CDX and going long (selling protection using) a short-term (2-year) CDX. A steeper curve means that long-term credit risk increases relative to short-term credit risk.

14. B is correct. The shares of Zega can be sold at a higher price as a result of the unsolicited bid in the market. If Delta Corporation issues significantly more debt, there is a higher probability that it may default. If the Fund sells protection on Delta now, the trade will realize a profit as credit spreads widen. An equity-versus-credit trade would be to go long (buy) the Zega shares and buy protection on Delta.

CHAPTER 12

OVERVIEW OF FIXED-INCOME PORTFOLIO MANAGEMENT

SOLUTIONS

1. B is correct. Permot has the highest percentage of floating-coupon bonds and inflation-linked bonds. Bonds with floating coupons protect interest income from inflation because the reference rate should adjust for inflation. Inflation-linked bonds protect against inflation by paying a return that is directly linked to an index of consumer prices and adjusting the principal for inflation. Inflation-linked bonds protect both coupon and principal payments against inflation.

    The level of inflation protection for coupons equals the percentage of the portfolio in floating-coupon bonds plus the percentage of the portfolio in inflation-linked bonds:

    Aschel = 2% + 3% = 5%
    Permot = 34% + 28% = 62%
    Rosaiso = 17% + 21% = 38%

    Thus, Permot has the highest level of inflation protection, with 62% of its portfolio in floating-coupon and inflation-linked bonds.

2. B is correct. The rolling yield is the sum of the coupon income and the rolldown return. Coupon income is the sum of the bond's annual current yield and interest on reinvestment income. Cécile assumes that there is no reinvestment income for any of the three funds, and the yield income for Aschel will be calculated as follows:

    Coupon income = Annual average coupon payment/Current bond price
    = $3.63/$117.00
    = 0.0310, or 3.10%

The rolldown return is equal to the bond's percentage price change assuming an unchanged yield curve over the horizon period. The rolldown return will be calculated as follows:

$$\text{Rolldown return} = \frac{\left(\text{Bond price}_{End\text{-}of\text{-}horizon\ period} - \text{Bond price}_{Beginning\text{-}of\text{-}horizon\ period}\right)}{\text{Bond price}_{Beginning\text{-}of\text{-}horizon\ period}}$$

$$= \frac{(\$114.00 - \$117.00)}{\$117.00}$$

$$= -0.0256, \text{ or } -2.56\%$$

Rolling yield = Coupon income + Rolldown return = 3.10% − 2.56% = 0.54%.

3. B is correct. The return for Aschel is 7.71%, calculated as follows:

$$r_P = \frac{r_I \times (V_E + V_B) - V_B \times r_B}{V_E}$$

$$= r_I + \frac{V_B}{V_E}(r_I - r_B)$$

$$= 6.20\% + \frac{\$42.00 \text{ million}}{\$94.33 \text{ million}}(6.20\% - 2.80\%)$$

$$= 7.71\%$$

4. C is correct. Rosaiso is the only fund that holds bonds with embedded options. Effective duration should be used for bonds with embedded options. For bonds with embedded options, the duration and convexity measures used to calculate the expected change in price based on the investor's views of yields to maturity and yield spreads are effective duration and effective convexity. For bonds without embedded options, convexity and modified duration are used in this calculation.

5. A is correct. Liability-based mandates are investments that take an investor's future obligations into consideration. Liability-based mandates are managed to match expected liability payments with future projected cash inflows. These types of mandates are structured in a way to ensure that a liability or a stream of liabilities can be covered and that any risk of shortfalls or deficient cash inflows for a company is minimized.

6. A is correct. The optimal strategy for Villash is the sale of 100% of Bond 1, which Cécile considers to be overvalued. Because Villash is a tax-exempt foundation, tax considerations are not relevant and Cécile's investment views drive her trading recommendations.

7. B is correct. The domestic bond portfolio's return objective is to modestly outperform the benchmark. Its risk factors, such as duration, are to closely match the benchmark. Small deviations in sector weights are allowed, and tracking error should be less than 50 bps year. These features are typical of enhanced indexing.

8. A is correct. Floating-coupon bonds provide inflation protection for the interest income because the reference rate should adjust for inflation. The purchase of fixed-coupon bonds as outlined in Strategy 1 provides no protection against inflation for either interest or principal. Strategy 1 would instead be superior to Strategy 2 in funding future liabilities (better predictability as to the amount of cash flows) and reducing the correlation between the fund's domestic bond portfolio and equity portfolio (better diversification).

9. C is correct. Since the fund's clients are taxable investors, there is value in harvesting tax losses. These losses can be used to offset capital gains within the fund that will otherwise be distributed to the clients and result in higher tax payments, which decreases the total

value of the investment to clients. The fund has to consider the overall value of the investment to its clients, including taxes, which may result in the sale of bonds that are not viewed as overvalued. Tax-exempt investors' decisions are driven by their investment views without regard to offsetting gains and losses for tax purposes.

10. C is correct. Bond 3 is most likely to be the least liquid of the three bonds presented in Exhibit 1 and will thus most likely require the highest liquidity premium. Low credit ratings, longer time since issuance, smaller issuance size, smaller issuance outstanding, and longer time to maturity typically are associated with lower liquidity (and thus a higher liquidity premium). Bond 3 has the lowest credit quality and the longest time since issuance of the three bonds. Bond 3 also has a smaller issue size and a longer time to maturity than Bond 1. The total issuance outstanding for Bond 3 is smaller than that of Bond 2 and equal to that of Bond 1.

11. B is correct. The total expected return is calculated as follows:

Total expected return =
Rolling yield

+/– E(Change in price based on investor's benchmark yield view)
+/– E(Change in price due to investor's view of credit spread)
+/– E(Currency gains or losses)

where Rolling yield = Coupon income + Rolldown return.

Return Component	Formula	Calculation
Coupon income	Annual coupon payment/Current bond price	€2.25/€98.45 = 2.29%
+ Rolldown return	$\dfrac{\left(\text{Bond price}_{End\text{-}of\text{-}horizon\ period} - \text{Bond price}_{Beginning\text{-}of\text{-}horizon\ period}\right)}{\text{Bond price}_{Beginning\text{-}of\text{-}horizon\ period}}$	(€98.62 – €98.45)/€98.45 = 0.17%
= Rolling yield	Coupon income + Rolldown return	2.29% + 0.17% = 2.46%
+/– E(Change in price based on investor's benchmark yield view)	$(-MD \times \Delta Yield) + [½ \times Convexity \times (\Delta Yield)^2]$	(-5.19×0.0015) $+ [½ \times 22 \times (0.0015)^2]$ = –0.78%
+/– E(Change in price due to investor's view of credit spread)	$(-MD \times \Delta Spread) + [½ \times Convexity \times (\Delta Spread)^2]$	(-5.19×0.0013) $+ [½ \times 22 \times (0.0013)^2]$ = –0.67%
+/– E(Currency gains or losses)	Given	0.65%
= Total expected return		**1.66%**

12. C is correct. The sector weights, risk and return characteristics, and turnover for Manager C differ significantly from those of the index, which is typical of an active management mandate. In particular, Manager C's modified duration of 6.16 represents a much larger deviation from the benchmark index modified duration of 5.22 than that of the other managers, which is a characteristic unique to an active management mandate.

CHAPTER 13

LIABILITY-DRIVEN AND INDEX-BASED STRATEGIES

SOLUTIONS

1. A is correct. Type I liabilities have cash outlays with known amounts and timing. The dates and amounts of Kiest's liabilities are known; therefore, they would be classified as Type I liabilities.

2. C is correct. Structural risk arises from the design of the duration-matching portfolio. It is reduced by minimizing the dispersion of the bond positions, going from a barbell structure to more of a bullet portfolio that concentrates the component bonds' durations around the investment horizon. With bond maturities of 1.5 and 11.5 years, Portfolio C has a definite barbell structure compared with those of Portfolios A and B, and it is thus subject to a greater degree of risk from yield curve twists and non-parallel shifts. In addition, Portfolio C has the highest level of convexity, which increases a portfolio's structural risk.

3. A is correct. The two requirements to achieve immunization for multiple liabilities are for the money duration (or BPV) of the asset and liability to match and for the asset convexity to exceed the convexity of the liability. Although all three portfolios have similar BPVs, Portfolio A is the only portfolio to have a lower convexity than that of the liability portfolio (31.98, versus 33.05 for the $20 million liability portfolio), and thus, it fails to meet one of the two requirements needed for immunization.

4. B is correct. Portfolio B is a laddered portfolio with maturities spread more or less evenly over the yield curve. A desirable aspect of a laddered portfolio is liquidity management. Because there is always a bond close to redemption, the soon-to-mature bond can provide emergency liquidity needs. Barbell portfolios, such as Portfolio C, have maturities only at the short-term and long-term ends and thus are much less desirable for liquidity management.

5. A is correct. Serena believes that any shift in the yield curve will be parallel. Model risk arises whenever assumptions are made about future events and approximations are used to measure key parameters. The risk is that those assumptions turn out to be wrong and the

approximations are inaccurate. A non-parallel yield curve shift could occur, resulting in a mismatch of the duration of the immunizing portfolio versus the liability.

6. B is correct. Kiest has a young workforce and thus a long-term investment horizon. The Global Aggregate and Global Aggregate GDP Weighted Indexes have the highest durations (7.73 and 7.71, respectively) and would be appropriate for this group. Global High Yield is the least appropriate due to its relatively shorter duration.

7. B is correct. Low tracking error requires an indexing approach. A pure indexing approach for a broadly diversified bond index would be extremely costly because it requires purchasing all the constituent securities in the index. A more efficient and cost-effective way to track the index is an enhanced indexing strategy, whereby Serena would purchase fewer securities than the index but would match primary risk factors reflected in the index. Closely matching these risk factors could provide low tracking error.

8. B is correct. Although a significant spread between the market price of the underlying fixed-income securities portfolio and an ETF's NAV should drive an authorized participant to engage in arbitrage, many fixed-income securities are either thinly traded or not traded at all. This situation might allow such a divergence to persist.

9. C is correct. Asset–liability management strategies consider both assets and liabilities in the portfolio decision-making process. Leah notes that DFC's previous fixed-income manager attempted to control for interest rate risk by focusing on both the asset and the liability side of the company's balance sheet. The previous manager thus followed an asset–liability management strategy.

10. C is correct. Enhanced indexing is especially useful for investors who consider environmental, social, or other factors when selecting a fixed-income portfolio. Environmental, social, and corporate governance (ESG) investing, also called socially responsible investing, refers to the explicit inclusion or exclusion of some sectors, which is more appropriate for an enhanced index strategy relative to a full index replication strategy. In particular, Approach 2 may be customized to reflect client preferences.

11. B is correct. Immunization is the process of structuring and managing a fixed-income portfolio to minimize the variance in the realized rate of return and to lock in the cash flow yield (internal rate of return) on the portfolio, which in this case is 9.85%.

12. C is correct. Molly is correct that measurement error can arise even in immunization strategies for Type 1 cash flows, which have set amounts and set dates. Also, a parallel shift in yield curves is a sufficient but not a necessary condition to achieve the desired outcome. Non-parallel shifts as well as twists in the yield curve can change the cash flow yield on the immunizing portfolio; however, minimizing the dispersion of cash flows in the asset portfolio mitigates this risk. As a result, both statements are correct.

13. B is correct. In the case of a single liability, immunization is achieved by matching the bond portfolio's Macaulay duration with the horizon date. DFC has a single liability of $500 million due in nine years. Portfolio 2 has a Macaulay duration of 8.9, which is closer to 9 than that of either Portfolio 1 or 3. Therefore, Portfolio 2 will best immunize the portfolio against the liability.

14. C is correct. Structural risk to immunization arises from twists and non-parallel shifts in the yield curve. Structural risk is reduced by minimizing the dispersion of cash flows in the portfolio, which can be accomplished by minimizing the convexity for a given cash flow duration level. Because Portfolio 4 has the lowest convexity compared with the other two portfolios and also has a Macaulay duration close to the liability maturity of nine years, it minimizes structural risk.

15. B is correct. The use of an index as a widely accepted benchmark requires clear, transparent rules for security inclusion and weighting, investability, daily valuation, availability of past returns, and turnover. Because the custom benchmark is valued weekly rather than daily, this characteristic would be inconsistent with an appropriate benchmark.

16. B is correct. DFC has two types of assets, short term and intermediate term. For the short-term assets, a benchmark with a short duration is appropriate. For the intermediate-term assets, a benchmark with a longer duration is appropriate. In this situation, DFC may wish to combine several well-defined sub-benchmark categories into an overall blended benchmark (Benchmark 2). The Bloomberg Barclays Short-Term Treasury Index is an appropriate benchmark for the short-term assets, and SD&R uses a 50% weight for this component. The longer-duration Bloomberg Barclays US Corporate Bond Index is an appropriate benchmark for the intermediate-term assets, and SD&R uses a 50% weight for this component. As a result, Molly should recommend proposed Benchmark 2.

17. C is correct. It may be impossible to acquire zero-coupon bonds to precisely match liabilities because the city's liabilities have varying maturities and amounts. In many financial markets, zero-coupon bonds are unavailable.

18. C is correct. An investor having an investment horizon equal to the bond's Macaulay duration is effectively protected, or immunized, from the first change in interest rates, because price and coupon reinvestment effects offset for either higher or lower rates.

19. A is correct. An upward shift in the yield curve reduces the bond's value but increases the reinvestment rate, with these two effects offsetting one another. The price effect and the coupon reinvestment effect cancel each other out in the case of an upward shift in the yield curve for an immunized liability.

20. A is correct. Minimizing the convexity of the bond portfolio minimizes the dispersion of the bond portfolio. A non-parallel shift in the yield curve may result in changes in the bond portfolio's cash flow yield. In summary, the characteristics of a bond portfolio structured to immunize a single liability are that it (1) has an initial market value that equals or exceeds the present value of the liability, (2) has a portfolio Macaulay duration that matches the liability's due date, and (3) minimizes the portfolio convexity statistic.

21. C is correct. Under an enhanced indexing strategy, the index is replicated with fewer than the full set of index constituents but still matches the original index's primary risk factors. This strategy replicates the index performance under different market scenarios more efficiently than the full replication of a pure indexing approach.

22. C is correct. The laddered approach provides both diversification over time and liquidity. Diversification over time offers the investor a balanced position between two sources of interest rate risk: cash flow reinvestment and market price volatility. In practice, perhaps the most desirable aspect of a laddered portfolio is liquidity management, because as time passes, the portfolio will always contain a bond close to maturity.

23.

Template for Question 23

Recommend the portfolio in Exhibit 1 that would *best* achieve the immunization. (circle one)

Portfolio A

Portfolio B

Portfolio C

Justification:

Portfolio A is the most appropriate portfolio because it is the only one that satisfies the three criteria for immunizing a single future outflow (liability), given that the cash flow yields are sufficiently close in value:

1. Market Value: Portfolio A's initial market value of $235,727 exceeds the outflow's present value of $234,535. Portfolio B is not appropriate because its market value of $233,428 is less than the present value of the future outflow of $234,535. A bond portfolio structured to immunize a single liability must have an initial market value that equals or exceeds the present value of the liability.
2. Macaulay Duration: Portfolio A's Macaulay duration of 9.998 closely matches the 10-year horizon of the outflow. Portfolio C is not appropriate because its Macaulay duration of 9.503 is furthest away from the investment horizon of 10 years.
3. Convexity: Although Portfolio C has the lowest convexity at 108.091, its Macaulay duration does not closely match the outflow amount. Of the remaining two portfolios, Portfolio A has the lower convexity at 119.055; this lower convexity will minimize structural risk.

Default risk (credit risk) is not considered because the portfolios consist of government bonds that presumably have default probabilities approaching zero.

24.

Template for Question 24

Determine the *most appropriate* immunization portfolio in Exhibit 2. (circle one)

Portfolio 1

Portfolio 2

Portfolio 3

Justification:

Portfolio 2 is the most appropriate immunization portfolio because it is the only one that satisfies the following two criteria for immunizing a portfolio of multiple future outflows:

1. Money Duration: Money durations of all three possible immunizing portfolios match or closely match the money duration of the outflow portfolio. Matching money durations is useful because the market values and cash flow yields of the immunizing portfolio and the outflow portfolio are not necessarily equal.
2. Convexity: Given that the money duration requirement is met by all three possible immunizing portfolios, the portfolio with the lowest convexity that is above the outflow portfolio's convexity of 135.142 should be selected. The dispersion, as measured by convexity, of the immunizing portfolio should be as low as possible subject to being greater than or equal to the dispersion of the outflow portfolio. This will minimize the effect of non-parallel shifts in the yield curve. Portfolio 3's convexity of 132.865 is less than the outflow portfolio's convexity, so Portfolio 3 is not appropriate. Both Portfolio 1 and Portfolio 2 have convexities that exceed the convexity of the outflow portfolio, but Portfolio 2's convexity of 139.851 is lower than Portfolio 1's convexity of 147.640. Therefore, Portfolio 2 is the most appropriate immunizing portfolio.

The immunizing portfolio needs to be greater than the convexity (and dispersion) of the outflow portfolio. But, the convexity of the immunizing portfolio should be minimized in order to minimize dispersion and reduce structural risk.

25. Chaopraya's strategy immunizes well for parallel shifts, with little deviation between the outflow portfolio and the immunizing portfolio in market value and BPV. Because the money durations are closely matched, the differences between the outflow portfolio and the immunizing portfolio in market value are small and the duration gaps (as shown by the difference in Δ Portfolio BPVs) between the outflow portfolio and the immunizing portfolio are small for both the upward and downward parallel shifts.

Chaopraya's strategy does not immunize well for the non-parallel steepening and flattening twists (i.e., structural risks) shown in Exhibit 3. In those cases, the outflow portfolio and the immunizing portfolio market values deviate substantially and the duration gaps between the outflow portfolio and the immunizing portfolio are large.

CHAPTER 14

YIELD CURVE STRATEGIES

SOLUTIONS

1. B is correct. The modified duration of a fixed-income portfolio is approximately equal to the market value-weighted average of the bonds in the portfolio, so the barbell has a modified duration of 5.049, or (1.922 + 8.175)/2), which is larger than that of either the bullet (4.241) or the equally weighted portfolio (4.779, or (1.922 + 4.241 + 8.175)/3.

2. A is correct. The change in portfolio value due to a rise in Australian government rate levels may be calculated using Equation 3:

$$\%\Delta PV^{Full} \approx -(ModDur \times \Delta Yield) + [\tfrac{1}{2} \times Convexity \times (\Delta Yield)^2]$$

where ModDur and Convexity reflect portfolio duration and convexity, respectively. Therefore, the bullet portfolio declines by 2.093%, or −2.093% = (−4.241 × 0.005) + [0.5 × 22.1 × (0.005²)], followed by a drop of 2.343% for the equally weighted portfolio, or −2.343% = (−4.779 × 0.005) + [0.5 × 37.4 × (0.005²)], and a drop of 2.468% for the barbell portfolio, or −2.468% = (−5.049 × 0.005) + [0.5 × 45.05 × (0.005²)].

3. B is correct. A bear flattening scenario is a decrease in the yield spread between long- and short-term maturities driven by higher short-term rates. The manager must therefore position her portfolio to benefit from rising short-term yields. Under A, the receive-fixed 2-year swap is a synthetic long position, increasing portfolio duration that will result in an MTM loss under bear flattening. The receive-fixed swap in answer C will increase duration in long-term maturities. In the case of B, the pay-fixed swap with twice the money duration of the barbell will more than offset the existing long position, resulting in net short 2-year and long 9-year bond positions in the overall portfolio and a gain under bear flattening.

4. C is correct. A bull flattening is a decrease in the yield spread between long- and short-term maturities driven by lower long-term yields-to-maturity. Both A and B involve changes in portfolio exposure to short-term rates, while C increases the portfolio exposure to long-term rates to benefit from a fall in long-term yields-to-maturity.

5. B is correct. The portfolio value change due to lower Australian government rate levels may be calculated using Equation 3:

$$\%\Delta PV^{Full} \approx -(ModDur \times \Delta Yield) + [\tfrac{1}{2} \times Convexity \times (\Delta Yield)^2]$$

where ModDur and Convexity reflect portfolio duration and convexity, respectively. Therefore, the barbell portfolio rises by 1.276%, or $(-5.049 \times -0.0025) + [0.5 \times 45.05 \times (-0.0025^2)]$, followed by the equally weighted portfolio at 1.207%, or $(-4.779 \times -0.0025) + [0.5 \times 37.4 \times (-0.0025^2)]$, and the bullet portfolio at 1.067%, or $(-4.241 \times -0.0025) + [0.5 \times 22.1 \times (-0.0025^2)]$.

6. A is correct. The bullet portfolio has the same convexity as the 45.5-year bond, or 22.1. The barbell portfolio in B has portfolio convexity of 45.05, $= (4.9 + 85.2)/2$, while the equally weighted portfolio has portfolio convexity of 37.4, $= (4.9 + 22.1 + 85.2)/3$.

7. C is correct. The butterfly spread is equal to twice the medium-term yield minus the short-term and long-term yields, as in Equation 2, or −28 bps, or −0.28% + (2 × 0.55%) − 1.10%.

8. A is correct. A positive butterfly view indicates an expected decrease in the butterfly spread due to an expected rise in short- and long-term yields-to-maturity combined with a lower medium-term yield-to-maturity. The investor therefore benefits from a long medium-term (bullet) position and a short short-term and long-term (barbell) portfolio. The portfolio in answer B represents the opposite exposure and benefits from a negative butterfly view, while in C, combining short barbell and long equally weighted portfolios leaves the investor with bullet portfolio exposure.

9. B is correct. The 30-year pay-fixed swap is a "short" duration position and also results in negative carry (that is, the fixed rate paid would exceed MRR received) in an upward-sloping yield curve environment; therefore, it is the least attractive static curve strategy. In the case of a.), the manager enters a "buy-and-hold" strategy by purchasing the 10-year zero-coupon bond and extends duration, which is equal to 9.80 = 10/1.02 since the Macaulay duration of a zero equals its maturity, and ModDur = MacDur/(1+r) versus 7.25 for the index. Under c.), the manager introduces leverage by purchasing a long-term bond and financing it at a lower short-term repo rate.

10. C is correct. Rolldown return is the difference between the price of the 5-year bond and that of a 4.5-year bond at the *same* yield-to-maturity. A 5-year zero-coupon bond trading at a premium has a negative yield. As the price "pulls to par" over time, the premium amortization will be a loss to the investor. A reflects the full price appreciation since it is calculated using the lower yield-to-maturity, while B equals E (Δ Price due to investor's view of benchmark yield).

11. B is correct. The value of a bond with an embedded option is equal to the sum of the value of an option-free bond plus the value to the embedded option. With a putable bond, the embedded put option is owned by the bond investor, who can exercise the option if yields-to-maturity increase, as in this scenario. Under A, the embedded call option is owned by the bond issuer, who is more likely to exercise if yields-to-maturity decrease (that is, the bond investor is short the call option). As for C, the option-free bond underperforms the putable bond given the rise in value of the embedded put option.

12. A is correct. Effective duration is a yield duration statistic that measures interest rate risk using a parallel shift in the benchmark yield curve (ΔCurve), as in Equation 8. Effective duration measures interest rate risk for complex bonds whose future cash flows are

uncertain because they are contingent on future interest rates. Both Macaulay duration (B) and modified duration (C) are relevant statistics only for option-free bonds.

13. C is correct. A steepening of the yield curve involves an increase in the slope, or the difference between long-term and short-term yields-to-maturity. An optimal portfolio positioning strategy is one that combines a short duration exposure to long-term bonds and a long duration exposure to short-term bonds. Portfolio C involves the right (but not the obligation) to purchase a 2-year bond, which will increase in value as short-term yields fall with the right to pay-fixed on a 30-year swap, which increases in value if long-term yields rise. Portfolio A involves the sale of two options. Although they will expire unexercised in a steeper curve environment, the investor's return is limited to the two option premia. Portfolio B is the opposite of Portfolio C, positioning the investor for a flattening of the yield curve.

14. A is correct. Recall from Equation 11 that the sum of the key rate durations equals the effective portfolio duration. The approximate (first-order) change in portfolio value may be estimated from the first (modified) term of Equation 3, namely (−EffDur × ΔYield). Solving for this using the −1.22 effective duration difference multiplied by 0.005 equals 0.0061%, or 61 bps.

15. B is correct. A positive butterfly indicates a decrease in the butterfly spread due to an expected rise in short- and long-term yields-to-maturity combined with a lower medium-term yield-to-maturity. Since the active portfolio is short duration versus the index in the 2-year, 5-year, and 30-year maturities and long duration in the 10-year, it will generate excess return if the butterfly spread falls.

16. A is correct. A net positive key rate duration difference indicates a long duration position relative to the index, while a net negative duration difference indicates a short position. Relative to the index, the active portfolio is "short" in the 2-year, 5-year, and 30-year maturities and "long" the 10-year maturity versus the index. The pay-fixed 10-year swap and long 2-year, 5-year, and 30-year bond futures positions best offset these differences.

17. C is correct. Forward rate bias is defined as an observed divergence from interest rate parity conditions under which active investors seek to benefit by borrowing in a lower-yield currency and investing in a higher-yield currency. A is incorrect since lower-yielding currencies trade at a forward premium. B is incorrect due to covered interest rate parity; fully hedged foreign currency fixed-income investments will tend to yield the domestic risk-free rate.

18. A is correct. Since both strategies use zero-coupon bonds, the rolldown return is calculated from expected bond price changes from "rolling down" the THB yield curve, which is assumed to be static.
Buy and Hold: 1.00% = (100.00 − 99.009)/99.009
Yield Curve Rolldown: 3.01% = (99.009 − 96.1169)/96.1169

19. A is correct. Under a static yield curve assumption, expected returns are equal to rolldown return plus changes in currency over the investment horizon. Using Equation 12, we solved for R_{FC} for both portfolios in Question 18, and R_{FX} is 1.5%. Expected returns are:
Buy and Hold: $E(R)$ = 2.515%, or $(1.01 \times 1.015) - 1$
Yield Curve Rolldown: $E(R)$ = 4.555%, or $(1.0301 \times 1.015) - 1$

20. C is correct. In a higher THB yield scenario in one year, the Yield Curve Rolldown expected return would fall since a higher THB yield-to-maturity in one year would reduce the price at which the investor could sell the 1-year zero in one year. The Buy-and-Hold portfolio return will be unaffected since the 1-year bond matures at the end of the investment horizon.

21. C is correct. A duration-neutral flattening trade involves a short 2-year bond position and a long 10-year bond position, which have a "matched" duration or portfolio duration of zero. This portfolio will realize a gain if the slope of the yield curve—that is, the difference between short-term and long-term yields—declines. Yield curve inversion is an extreme version of flattening in which the spread between long-term and short-term yields-to-maturity falls below zero. The bear steepening in A involves an unchanged 2-year yield-to-maturity with a rise in the 10-year yield-to-maturity, causing a portfolio *loss*. The bull flattening in B combines a constant 2-year yield-to-maturity with lower 10-year rates, resulting in a gain on the 10-year bond position and an unchanged 2-year bond position.

CHAPTER 15

FIXED-INCOME ACTIVE MANAGEMENT: CREDIT STRATEGIES

SOLUTIONS

1. A is correct. A bond's empirical duration is often estimated by running a regression of its price returns on changes in a benchmark interest rate.

2. B is correct. An increase in interest rates results in a decrease in the bond price. An increase in the credit spread also results in a decrease in the bond price. For the EKN bond, its modified duration shows the effect of the 20 bp increase in interest rates. The approximate percentage price change resulting from the increase in interest rates is $-8.47 \times 0.0020 = -1.694\%$. The spread duration shows the effect of the 20 bp increase in the credit spread. The approximate percentage price change resulting from the increase in the credit spread is $-8.47 \times 0.0020 = -1.694\%$. The combined effect is a total change of -3.388%, or a price decrease of roughly 3.4%.

3. C is correct. An increase in a bond's recovery rate will lower the loss severity, or LGD, because $LGD = (1 - RR)$. Recall the simple one-period relationship between credit spreads, LGD, and the POD as Spread $\approx$ LGD $\times$ POD. A lower LGD will result in a lower spread.

4. C is correct. A bond's yield spread includes both credit and liquidity risk. Liquidity risk depends on both market conditions and the specific supply-and-demand dynamics of each fixed-income security.

5. A is correct. The G-spread is the difference between the corporate bond YTM and a linear interpolation of the 10-year and 20-year government bond YTMs. To calculate the approximate 12-year government rate, solve for the weights of the 10-year bond as 80% ($= (20 - 12)/(20 - 10)$) and the 20-year bond as 20% (or $(1 - 80\%)$), noting that $(80\% \times 10) + (20\% \times 20) = 12$. The 12-year government rate is 1.94% (or $(80\% \times 1.85\%) +$

(20% × 2.30%)), and the difference between the corporate bond YTM and the 12-year interpolated government rate is 0.860%.

6. B is correct. The I-spread is an estimate of the corporate bond's spread over an interpolated swap benchmark. We can solve for the 10-year and 20-year swap rates as 2.05% (= 0.20% + 1.85%) and 2.55% (= 0.25% + 2.30%), respectively, by adding the swap spread to the respective government bond. The 12-year swap rate is 2.15% (or (80% × 2.05%) + (20% × 2.55%)), and the difference between the corporate bond YTM and the 12-year interpolated government rate is 0.80%.

7. C is correct. The ASW is an estimate of the spread over MRR versus the bond's original coupon rate to maturity, which is equal to the difference between the corporate bond coupon of 3.00% and the 12-year swap rate of 2.15%, or 0.85%.

8. A is correct. The 20 bp increase in the 20-year government YTM causes the 12-year interpolated government YTM to rise 4 bps to 1.98% (or (80% × 1.85%) + (20% × 2.50%)). The corporate bond percentage price change can be estimated based on the YTM change multiplied by modified duration ($-\text{ModDur} \times \Delta\text{Yield}$) familiar from earlier lessons. This percentage price change can be calculated as -0.4% ($= -9.99 \times 0.04\%$).

9. C is correct. The yield spread is the simple difference between a bond's all-in YTM and a current on-the-run government bond of similar maturity, while the G-spread is an interpolation of government benchmark yields. If the government bond yield curve is flat, these two measures will equal one another.

10. A is correct. Recall that $\text{ExcessSpread} \approx (\text{Spread}_0/\text{Periods Per Year}) - (\text{EffSpreadDur} \times \Delta\text{Spread})$, so we combine the 6-month return with the spread duration–based price change estimate to get 3.775% ($= (2.75\% \times 0.5) - (6 \times -0.4\%)$).

11. B is correct. The instantaneous holding period return equals $-\text{EffSpreadDur} \times \Delta\text{Spread} = -5 \times 0.5\%$ or -2.50%.

12. C is correct. The expected excess spread is equal to the change in spread multiplied by effective spread duration ($-(\text{EffSpreadDur} \times \Delta\text{Spread})$) less the product of LGD and POD, which we can solve for to get 2.70% ($= (-6 \times 0.50\%) - (0.75\% \times 40\%)$).

13. A is correct. The coverage ratio measures cash flow available to service debt, with a higher ratio indicating a lower probability of financial distress.

14. C is correct. Structural credit models use market-based variables to estimate an issuer's asset value and asset value volatility, defining the likelihood of default as the probability of the asset value falling below that of liabilities, with zero net assets defined as the default threshold.

15. B is correct. Recall that expected excess spread is defined as follows:

$$\text{E [ExcessSpread]} \approx \text{Spread}_0 - (\text{EffSpreadDur} \times \Delta\text{Spread}) - (\text{POD} \times \text{LGD})$$

Because $\Delta\text{Spread} = 0$, the expected excess spread is the simple difference between current OAS and expected loss, so E[ExcessSpread] is 0.90%, 1.00%, and 0.25% for the A-, BBB-, and B rated categories, respectively.

16. A is correct. E[ExcessSpread] from Question 15 is 0.90%, 1.00%, and 0.25% for the A-, BBB-, and B rated categories, respectively. The excess spread of the 50% A rated and 50% BBB rated portfolio is 0.95% ($= (0.9\% + 1.00\%/2)$) versus the equally weighted portfolio expected excess return of 0.7167% ($= (0.90\% + 1.00\% + 0.25\%)/3$) for a positive active return of 0.233%, while B and C return less than the equally weighted benchmark.

17. A is correct. If spreads rise 10% across all ratings categories, we can use E [ExcessSpread] ≈ $\text{Spread}_0 - (\text{EffSpreadDur} \times \Delta\text{Spread}) - (\text{POD} \times \text{LGD})$ to solve for expected excess spread as follows:

Rating Category	Current OAS	New OAS	Expected Loss (POD × LGD)	EffSpreadDur	E(Excess Spread)
A	1.00%	1.100%	0.10%	7	0.200%
BBB	1.75%	1.925%	0.75%	6	−0.050%
BB	2.75%	3.025%	2.50%	5	−1.125%

18. C is correct. Both A and B represent "long" risk positions that would increase rather than offset the benchmark yield and credit spread risk to the portfolio manager related to the illiquid bond.

19. C is correct. Parametric methods in A are not well suited for non-normally distributed returns or option-based portfolios, while historical simulation assumes no probability distribution and accommodates options.

20. C is correct. The incremental VaR measures how the additional portfolio position would change the overall portfolio's VaR measure.

21. A is correct. The expected change in yield based on a 99% confidence interval for the bond and a 1.50% yield volatility over 21 trading days equals 16 bps = (1.50% × 2.33 standard deviations × √21). We can quantify the bond's market value change by multiplying the familiar (−ModDur × ΔYield) expression by bond price to get $1,234,105 = ($75 million × 1.040175 × (−9.887 × .0016)).

22. B is correct. For example, if the reference entity's credit spread trades at 1.50% versus a standard coupon rate of 1.00%, the CDS contract will be priced at a discount equal to the 0.50% difference multiplied by the effective CDS spread duration times the contract notional. Under A, the contract is priced at a premium to par because the protection buyer is receiving an "above market" periodic premium.

23. C is correct. Because the market premium is 0.75% above the 1.00% standard investment-grade CDS coupon, the protection buyer must pay the protection seller 6.5625% (= $\text{EffSpreadDur}_{CDS} \times \Delta\text{Spread}$, or 8.75 × 0.75%) of the fixed notional amount upon contract initiation; the initial CDS price is therefore 93.4375 per 100 of notional with a CDS spread of 175 bps.

24. A is correct. The CDS spread decline of 0.15% leads to a new CDS contract price of 94.75 per 100 face value (= $1 - (\text{EffSpreadDur}_{CDS} \times \Delta\text{Spread})$ or (8.75 × 0.60%)). The protection buyer (short risk) position therefore realizes an approximate mark-to-market loss of €131,250 (= (94.75 − 93.4375)/100 × €10,000,000) because of the 0.15% decline in CDS spreads.

25. B is correct. Selling protection on the CDX index is a "long" credit spread risk position, while purchasing protection on the CDX Financials subindex is a "short" credit spread risk position, leaving the investor with a long index position without exposure to financial reference entities in the CDX index. Both A and C increase exposure to financial sector issuers.

26. A is correct. The late expansion phase is typically associated with accelerating growth, peak profits, stable leverage, and a decline in defaults.

27. B is correct. Investors should exercise caution in interpreting credit spread curve shape for distressed debt issuers because their bonds tend to trade at a price close to the recovery rate. A is incorrect because the high-yield spread curve tends to invert during a contraction, while C is incorrect because a high-yield curve inversion is related to the relationship between near-term and long-term default as opposed to DTS.

28. C is correct. A credit curve roll-down strategy will generate positive return only under an upward-sloping credit spread curve. As for A, the benchmark yield changes must be separated from changes due to credit spreads, and under B, a synthetic credit roll-down strategy involves selling protection using a single-name CDS contract for a longer maturity.

29. C is correct. The investor benefits from a short risk (as protection buyer) on the 10-year CDX IG index and long risk (as protection seller) on the 5-year CDX IG index, duration matching the notional value by increasing 5-year notional 1.82 times (= 8.9/4.9) versus the 10-year.

30. A is correct. Because an economic contraction is often associated with a sharp rise in shorter-term high-yield spreads and spread curve flattening in investment grade and inversion in high yield, the most appropriate choice is to take a short risk (purchase protection) in five-year high-yield spreads and a long position (sell protection) in five-year investment-grade spreads. Answers B and C position the investor to benefit from a steeper investment-grade and high-yield spread curve, respectively.

31. B is correct. Fixed exchange rate regimes in A usually result in greater instability and a higher probability of financial distress, while higher domestic currency YTMs in emerging economies in C are a sign of expected currency depreciation, not appreciation, over time.

32. A is correct. We solve for the excess spread by subtracting Expected Loss from the respective OAS:

Rating Category	OAS	EffSpreadDur	Expected Loss	E(Excess Spread)
USD IG	1.25%	4.5	0.40%	0.85%
USD HY	3.00%	5.5	2.25%	0.75%
EUR IG	1.15%	4.75	0.50%	0.65%
EUR HY	3.25%	6	2.50%	0.75%

Recall that the United States–based investor must convert the euro return to US dollars using $R_{DC} = (1 + R_{FC})(1 + R_{FX}) - 1$, so the USD IG and USD HY positions comprising half the portfolio return an average 0.80%, while the EUR IG and EUR HY positions return −1.314% in US dollar terms (= $((1 + ((0.65\% + 0.75\%)/2)) \times 0.98) - 1$), so −0.257% = ((0.80% − 1.314%)/2).

33. A is correct. Given that high-yield spreads are expected to fall the most in an economic recovery, the manager should choose the portfolio with the highest percentage of EUR HY credit exposure.

34. A is correct. Covered bonds perform relatively well in a downturn versus other fixed-income bonds with real estate exposure because the investor also has recourse to the issuer.

35. C is correct. Under a "flight to quality" scenario, macroeconomic factors driving government bond YTMs lower cause high-yield bond credit spreads to rise because of an increased likelihood and expected higher severity of financial distress. This relationship is captured in the difference between empirical and analytical duration measures.

CFA Institute

ABOUT THE
CFA PROGRAM

The Chartered Financial Analyst® (CFA®) designation is a globally recognized standard of excellence for measuring the competence and integrity of investment professionals. To earn the CFA charter, candidates must successfully pass through the CFA Program, a global graduate-level self-study program that combines a broad curriculum with professional conduct requirements as preparation for a wide range of investment specialties.

Anchored by a practice-based curriculum, the CFA Program is focused on the knowledge identified by professionals as essential to the investment decision-making process. This body of knowledge maintains current relevance through a regular, extensive survey of practicing CFA charterholders across the globe. The curriculum covers 10 general topic areas, ranging from equity and fixed-income analysis to portfolio management to corporate finance, all with a heavy emphasis on the application of ethics in professional practice. Known for its rigor and breadth, the CFA Program curriculum highlights principles common to every market so that professionals who earn the CFA designation have a thoroughly global investment perspective and a profound understanding of the global marketplace.

www.cfainstitute.org